KU-341-328

That's the
way it
Crumbles

Matthew Engel

That's the way it Crumbles

The American Conquest of English

P

PROFILE BOOKS

First published in Great Britain in 2017 by
PROFILE BOOKS LTD
3 Holford Yard
Bevin Way
London
WC1X 9HD
www.profilebooks.com

Copyright © Matthew Engel, 2017

1 3 5 7 9 10 8 6 4 2

Printed and bound in Great Britain by Clays, St Ives plc

Typeset in Garamond by MacGuru Ltd

The moral right of the author has been asserted.

All rights reserved. Without limiting the rights under copyright reserved above, no part of this publication may be reproduced, stored or introduced into a retrieval system, or transmitted, in any form or by any means (electronic, mechanical, photocopying, recording or otherwise), without the prior written permission of both the copyright owner and the publisher of this book.

A CIP catalogue record for this book is available from the British Library.

ISBN 978 1 78125 668 8
eISBN 978 1 78283 262 1

To HILARY, who for Christmas 2016
bought me a jar marked Cookies,

and to MARILYN, who after forty-four years in Britain
nearly always remembers to say to-*mah*-to.

CONTENTS

A NOTE ON THE TEXT

Beyond living memory and before recording devices, it is not at all certain how people spoke and what words they used. The written language is only a guide. I have tried in this book to work out when, how and why American words might have entered the British vocabulary. This is an art not a science. And there will be honest errors. But I am certain that any words I have mistakenly categorised as American will be more than cancelled out by the Americanisms I have omitted.

I would be delighted to receive politely worded suggestions for amendments and additions at engel.england@gmail.com. Where appropriate, changes will be made in any subsequent editions.

In the text, words and phrases that went into common British use that I believe to have been minted in America are in ***bold italics***. Words that originated in Britain and were then re-imported from the US are marked in ***bold italics*** with a †. OED stands for the Oxford English Dictionary.

'That's the way the cookie crumbles and the ball bounces.'
– Lew Burdette, Milwaukee Braves baseball pitcher, after his team lost the
1958 World Series to the New York Yankees.

Fran (Shirley MacLaine): 'Why can't I ever fall in love with
    somebody nice like you?'
Bud (Jack Lemmon): 'Yeah, well. That's the way it crumbles.
    Cookie-wise.'
                    – *The Apartment*, directed by Billy Wilder, 1960.

INTRODUCTION

THERE'LL BE BLUEBIRDS

In 1942 Vera Lynn, 'the Forces' Sweetheart', recorded a song including the refrain that, perhaps more than anything else, summed up the British attitude to the Second World War:

There'll be bluebirds over
The white cliffs of Dover
Tomorrow
Just you wait and see.

Those fifteen words said it all: this horror would not last for ever; Britain would just have to keep a stiff upper lip and it would soon be over. The air would no longer be filled with Spitfires and Messerschmitts, and the characteristic sights and sounds of the English summer skies would return. That's what we were fighting for.

Lynn's popularity, cemented by other hits like 'We'll Meet Again', was almost universal. As one historian of war songs put it, her lyrics would 'articulate fairly basic emotions for those unused to expressing emotions of any sort'. That was an important service to a nation with a stiff-upper-lip epidemic.

There were some dissenters, however. For a start, there was my father, Flight Lieutenant Max Engel, who couldn't stand the sound of her voice: 'She ruined my war,' he would say. More influentially, but just as unsuccessfully, some of the top brass in both the BBC and the Army thought she was bad for morale. The corporation's controller of programmes called for waltzes, marches and cheerful music with 'more virile lyrics' and the 'elimination of crooning, sentimental numbers, drivelling words, slush, innuendoes and so on'.

And then there were the ornithologists, whose successors wince to this day whenever they hear that opening line. The bluebird is an American bird, a kind of thrush, found in three different forms across the United States. There never were any bluebirds over Dover or anywhere else in Britain, before or after 1942. Not one, ever.

It is a well-loved bird in the US, among the smaller percentage of the population which cares about such matters there: the bluebird kills a lot of pests in gardens, and culturally has a longstanding association with good times ('the Bluebird of Happiness', 'Mr Bluebird's on my shoulder', 'I'm always chasing rainbows, waiting to find a little bluebird in vain').

How then did such a palpably alien symbol become the embodiment of Britain's wartime spirit? John McEwen, *The Oldie*'s ornithological columnist, has tried to argue that Lynn was right: swallows, Britain's bluest bird after the kingfisher, often gather for a pre-migratory party over the Kent coast, and that they constitute blue birds, if not exactly bluebirds. Others have tried to find a connection to the blue uniforms of the RAF.

The most convincing explanation came from the singer herself, in her long and revered old age as Dame Vera. 'It's American,' she said in 2007, just after her 90th birthday. 'You don't get bluebirds over here, do you?' Her tone, according to *The Times*, was apologetic. The composer, Walter Kent, first saw the white cliffs nearly fifty years after he wrote the song; the lyricist, Nat Burton, who died young, almost certainly never saw them at all.

Does any of this actually matter? There is such a thing as artistic licence, after all. And we all make mistakes. On their own, those lyrics would merely be an obscure curiosity. But the bluebirds have to be seen as part of an invading force that proved far more effective than the Luftwaffe. Largely unseen, unending, seemingly unstoppable. The American language.

***

The history of the two major strands of English – British and American – now falls into two equal parts. British settlers arrived on the American continent in the early seventeenth century: the best-known group, the Pilgrim Fathers, reached Massachusetts in 1620. The British prevailed against all comers and ensured that the new-found land would become first a British colony and then an English-speaking independent nation. For the first 200 years these Americans took the language they brought with them and shaped it to their own ends.

And then, round about 1820, they began exporting the words they had themselves created, or retained in stock long after the British had made the words redundant. The Americans did not foist their language on Britain; the British found it useful, attractive or both. This process sped up as America outstripped in population and power what was once the mother country. In 1928 a single technological advance increased the speed of travel exponentially, and the process continued rapidly after peace returned to the white cliffs.

Now, as we approach 2020, the American words the British invited into their homes are in danger of taking over. And it has become possible to imagine a time – 2120 would be a plausible and arithmetically neat guesstimate – when American English absorbs the British version completely. The child will have eaten its mother, but only because the mother insisted. This book is an attempt, feeble though it might be, to try to ensure that prediction does not come true.

Much of what follows is the story of how the cultural relationship between Britain and America has turned upside down over the centuries, how that has affected the British vocabulary and created Britain's current self-imposed verbal enslavement.

It is also a *cri de cœur*, a call to arms, a ***wake-up call***. Forgive that last cliché, but it has all the hallmarks of a classic Americanism. Until about the nineteenth century, it seems the British didn't wake up, they just *woke*. They understood well enough that waking involved getting up. Maybe adding the *up* at all was American influence: adding the likes of *up, down, in, out, to* or *from* to a verb is often but not always an indicator of that.[1]

However, turning a verb into an adjective and then compounding it to create a new phrase is exceedingly American. In any case I think the whole idea of a wake-up call must be American. Until quite recently being woken in a British hotel normally involved the night porter bringing in a pot of tea, fresh milk, a china cup and saucer and a morning paper. There might not have been a phone in the room at all.

But that's not the kind of wake-up call I mean. Somewhere along the line the phrase turned into a metaphor. The earliest such use I have so far found is an ice hockey report in *The New York Times* in 1975. Over in Britain it popped up in a headline in the *Guardian* only two years later, but appeared again only very sporadically until the 1990s. By the first four years of the twenty-first century the *Guardian* was reporting wake-up calls – some real, most metaphorical – at an average of two and a half times a week.

In the chapters that follow there will be references to hundreds of other words and phrases, many of them now totally integrated into the community and accepted as upstanding members of society, their American origins forgotten. There can be no question of deporting them. Who would sign the order? Go far enough back, and everyone in Britain has foreign blood.

What matters here is context. The United States has now become the chief source of new vocabulary because its technological and cultural dominance has become overwhelming. The technology alone would not be enough; it is the cultural sway that really matters. The consequences of this are felt across the world, not just in Britain, and not just in countries where English is the primary language.

It has become entirely imaginable that our descendants will inherit

---

1 Technically I believe this constitutes adding an adverbial particle to create a phrasal verb. Such terms will be used very sparingly in the pages ahead because I don't really understand them myself.

a world that is essentially American. Some of the old languages and customs would undoubtedly persist, though in some cases perhaps just as curiosities. Worse fates may yet await this planet, but this one alone would offer a dull, grey future to humankind.

In the crisis of intellectual climate change, Britain is the equivalent of the coastal plains and islets most likely to be swamped by rising sea levels, because here the American inundation is already well under way. It is not that no one cares; I have evidence that they do. But no one has worked out what to do about it.

***

Let us get two things straight right now: this crisis is not the Americans' fault; and this is not an anti-American book. The United States is the dominant force in the world partly because of its size, wealth, industrial might and military strength. Because it is a magnet for the world's talent. And because the most potent, the most beneficial, the most important idea on the planet is an American invention: 'government of the people, by the people, for the people'.

Each new technological breakthrough has strengthened America's place in the British imagination: steamships, the telegraph, electricity, the telephone, aviation, radio, cinema, television, satellites, the internet. But there are still significant cultural differences. One is that Americans read the Bible more zestfully than the British – and Chapter 11 of Genesis might encourage them to believe that homogenisation was an entirely wholesome development.

'And the whole earth was of one language, and of one speech,' it begins. Noah's descendants decided to build a tower that would reach to the heavens. God, feeling threatened, decided to confound them by muddling up their languages until they could not understand each other. And the Tower of Babel failed as a building project because of a communications breakdown among the workforce.

God's views on the current situation are somewhat opaque. But the Babelisation process is undoubtedly being reversed. At the start of 2017 there were thought to be about 7,000 extant languages in the world, from Aari (Ethiopia) to Zuni (New Mexico). At least 220 have been wiped out in the past fifty years; some researchers suggest that in the next century almost half the survivors will go, which would mean one language vanishing – when its last speaker dies – every ten days. One, just one, of those 7,000 is now assuming the role of global language, the one that would be employed by the workers on the modern Babel. It is English, but a form of English, and that form is primarily American.

This developing linguistic monoculture clearly has many pluses for communication. But it is also a catastrophe for the delicate cultural ecology of our planet. In the disappearing rainforests of New Guinea and the Amazon, tribal languages, built up over millennia, just curl up and die. In France, the rock singers perform in English and the kids all say 'c'est *cool*' to the irritation of their parents, while the elite tries frantically to erect linguistic walls.

In what one might call the minor English-speaking countries, starting with Britain, the advantages of this arrangement are obvious. Who needs a second language? If there is a hotel in the world where the receptionist does not speak English, it probably doesn't have plumbing, never mind room service. We can get by; if all else fails we can just gesticulate or shout. And we can absorb most of the US-inspired neologisms without even noticing.

Older people do notice, especially when an American usage starts to drive out a British one. And there is often a wider form of Americanisation lying behind it. It is hard for *film* to hold on against *movie* because movie is the more common word in America, and most of the films we watch are American-made and focus on American life with American scripts and a made-in-Hollywood world view as the message. *Fries* began to compete with chips in Britain when McDonald's arrived. Now *cookies* are appearing in profusion.

And that's the way the language crumbles.

***

In 1998 Peter Preston, the former editor of the *Guardian*, published a well-received novel, *51st State*. It had a remarkably percipient premise. A chancer of a British prime minister calls a referendum about Britain's continuing membership of the European Union, wanting and expecting the answer Remain to shut up his rebellious backbenchers. He loses, and is obliged to resign to be replaced by a Cabinet minister with no fingerprints on the original decision.

Spot on so far. What happens next is that the economic consequences of the fictional Brexit are so horrendous and intractable that Britain is forced to accept an offer of perpetual hospitality from another country: the United States.

What might be called 51st Stateism is always an underlying theme in British political consciousness. Indeed, it can be dated back long before there were fifty states. The journalist W.T. Stead said Britain should be absorbed by the US in 1900, at which point Britain could have ranked 46th. In 1946 Churchill swatted away a suggestion that Britain might become the 49th state. In 2016 there was even a 51st State Rock Festival in North London.

But it is far from an exclusively British concept. The phrase '51st State' is of course used in the two places that most plausibly aspire to the title: Washington DC and Puerto Rico. In Canada it is a regular part of political discourse, nearly always as a term of disparagement. It crops up in places as improbable as Poland and Albania.

Subject to how things really do play out in post-Brexit Britain, my sense is that Preston overstates the ease with which the British would shrug off the symbols of independence like the monarchy, and understates the way in which Britain has already given away the reality. Quite early in the book the new PM does look back to the days when he wore *short pants* rather than short trousers. It is not clear whether this is an accidental authorial Americanism, a deep-laid clue to what might soon be about to happen, or an editing decision to help American readers.

I think the idea of Britain being formally annexed by the US is a fantasy. The British would come over all patriotic and huffy, and unite against it. The process of subjugation is going well enough without anyone drawing attention to it. In foreign and defence policy the British long ago gave away almost all their independence of action. Now they are losing independence of expression.

***

I first broached this subject in public in 2010. I had gradually become ever more irritated by the constant usage, in conversation and in the media, of words that only a few years before had been confined to America. I was wittering on about this over dinner to my friend Marilyn Warnick, the books editor of the *Mail on Sunday* and a long-established transplanted American. 'Don't talk about it. Write it,' she said.

So I did, initially for her newspaper. And it went, as the Americans said first, *viral*. It appeared under the heading 'Say No to the Get-Go' and received well over a thousand emails, nearly all supportive. Most of the readers added their own unfavourite Americanisms, some of which really were Americanisms and some of which weren't. Gratify-ingly, very few of the emails began '*Hi Matthew*'.

The single column turned into a series until, after two months, I wearily pulled the plug myself. A year later I took the subject on to the BBC Radio 4 programme for such hobby-horses, Fourthought. This time there were over 2,000 responses – again almost all sup-portive. Except that the thesis also reached the ears of the online lexicographical community, some of whom have not quite learned the niceties of civil disagreement and disputed my right to offer an opinion at all. One American said it was none of my business because I was not a 'qualified lexicographer'.

It was true that there were complexities involved that I had not fully comprehended, especially the extent to which words we regard as American had their origins in Britain. But the greater truth is that if my teenage daughter talks to her friends about kicking some-one's *butt*, it's not because she is in touch with the terminology of cooperage or grouse-shooting. If she says *ass* it's not because she's self-consciously reverting to the eighteenth-century pronunciation of *arse*. If she says *gotten* it's not because she's part of an intellectual movement trying to restore the Tudor use of the past participle of *get*. It's because, in common with almost every other member of her generation, she has been watching too much American TV.

The old view among 'qualified lexicographers' is that correct lan-guage was something to be determined by an elite. Anything that failed to meet certain standards – though those standards them-selves were constantly changing – would be characterised as dialect, regional, slang, cant, vulgar or, most damningly, a barbarism. But this kind of prescriptivism is wholly out of fashion. Now lexicographers usually see themselves as descriptivists, there to record the mysterious routes that words take, not to impede their flow (while perhaps in some cases seeking to deter contrary opinions).

In British newspapers these two opposite poles are represented by Simon Heffer of the *Daily Telegraph*, a member of the do-as-I-say school, and Oliver Kamm of *The Times*, a do-as-you-like man. Me, I instinctively lean towards the Kamm school, in a yes-but kind of way. I am all for the latest neologisms, if they are elegant, expressive and useful. ***What's not to like?***[2] This, however, is a situation that demands more than relaxed complacency. It is an existential crisis.

I have spent my adult life writing in English: three to four million published words, mostly in the *Guardian* and the *Financial Times*, which means some of the words were long ones. I have spent even more of my life speaking English. The writer Gyles Brandreth once estimated that an average person would say 860,341,500 words over the course of an average lifespan. Not being the strong, silent type, I am probably already well over the billion mark, nearly all those words being in British English. One way and another, I think that gives me some right to use up yet more words to fret about the future of the language. It has changed around me, as happens in every generation. And that change has primarily involved the absorption of American words into everyday English usage.

This is part of a much broader picture, involving at least five different phenomena.

1. The emergence of English as the unchallenged global language, a role once envisaged for the artificial constructions of Esperanto or Volapük.
2. The infiltration of English words into other, less robust, languages. *C'est cool, n'est-ce pas?* Not necessarily.

---

2 I am myself trying to propagate the phrase *teenile dementia*: the mental illness suffered by humans between puberty and maturity, often transmitted by reverse heredity as they drive their parents mad.

3. The ongoing takeover by the dominant form of English – American English – of all other variants, not just British but also Australian, Canadian, Indian, Singaporean, wherever.

4. The decline and probable extinction of small languages, unless their speakers have the resources and the willpower to protect and preserve their traditions.

5. The collapse of old dialects and accents. This really is unstoppable, if modern civilisation continues. A century ago, there were hundreds of distinctive and identifiable local accents in Britain. There are still a few dozen, and even some new ones, caused by immigration, but the old ones are rapidly merging, sometimes in startling ways. Recent research suggests that even in Scotland people are beginning to acquire a Londonish twang from watching too many episodes of *EastEnders*.

The spread of the American language can be seen as a triumph for the nation's one great unifying belief: capitalism, which proved superior to Soviet Communism in spreading human happiness. But unfettered capitalism led to Victorian children being sent up chimneys. Likewise free trade is a desirable objective; but if it is not sensibly regulated, then powerful entities bully less powerful ones out of the market.

And the same goes for free trade in words. It is healthy and, in the modern world, inevitable. But the terms have to be fair. If America has a near monopoly of the whole business, it is a disaster.

Dame Vera herself was conscious of the problem and tried to overcome it in her work. 'I didn't use Americanisms and my accent stayed English,' she said during her long and happy post-war life.[3] 'I stopped listening to American singers' records so that I wouldn't self-consciously copy them.' I'm just a bit sorry that she didn't dare speak up in 1942 and demand the right to change 'bluebirds' to 'swallows'. Which would have worked just as well. But she kept a *stiff upper lip*. Which is an Americanism.

---

3 She reached 100 in March 2017.

***

At the start of this century I spent two years living in Maryland, on the edge of Washington. We have close family ties there and made wonderful friends. I have been to the US on dozens of other occasions, for work, pleasure and sometimes both: to all fifty states, from Denali, Alaska to Key West, Florida. I adore baseball, *Doonesbury*, *The Simpsons*, *Breaking Bad*, the works of Philip Roth, the Coen Brothers and Leonard Cohen.[4]

As a writer, there are few things I enjoy more than prowling through some small Midwestern town, hearing the lonesome whistle of a freight train – a place where everyone is up for a chat and will compliment me on my accent and then help me explore the ways in which our cousin-countries are different. I once wrote a column headlined 'Fifty ways to love America'. The number was constrained only by the space available.

It is difficult to write a novel without the letter E, but it has been done.[5] It would be totally impossible to write a coherent book in English without words imported from the United States. Just as it would be unthinkable to get by without the benefit of American inventions.

But the joy of America for an Englishman is that it *is* different, often subtly and unexpectedly so: two nations – 'divided,' as the old line attributed to G.B. Shaw has it, 'by a common language'. That division is getting narrower, a direct result of Britain's cultural cringe. I love my own country too and I want to keep loving it for itself, not as a cheap imitation.

When I wrote my *Mail on Sunday* series the editors shared my indignation about the strange conflation *get-go* ('the outset, the very beginning' – Oxford English Dictionary), which had apparently

---

4 Canadian, I know, but he was also an observantly Jewish Buddhist, so let's not over-classify.

5 *Gadsby* by E.V. Wright (US, 1939) and *La Disparition* by Georges Perec (France, 1969), translated E-lessly into English by Gilbert Adair (UK, 1994). In all cases, the author's name on the cover was exempt.

crawled out of an American freighter in an English port and then started breeding, like the beetle that killed Britain's elm trees.

I assumed that *get-go* (or *git-go*) was a graduate of the Midwestern School of Pointless Tautology, like *you betcha*. It turns out to be a Black American word, which appeared in the 1950s, possibly deriving from a 1958 Hank Mobley number called 'Git-Go Blues'. The oppression felt under slavery and in the ghettoes has enriched all forms of English, not least in the usage of that lovely word *cool* that so entrances French teenagers. *Get-go* fits into a different category: it is a word picked up amid the constant cacophony of American influence, one which the British started to assume was part of their own language.

It is inelegant, repetitive, etymologically ludicrous: a parrot-word, its uselessness pointed up by the fact that it is normally used only in the phrase 'from the get-go': it's not portable or adaptable. It actually seems to be an inferior variation of the perfectly reasonable Americanism *from the word go*, first recorded in the ghosted life story of Davy Crockett in 1834 ('I was plaguy well pleased with her from the word go') before making what might have been its English debut in a *Daily Mirror* football report in 1905.

Get-go has travelled a little faster. It first reached *The New York Times* in 1968 in a first-person piece from a gang leader-turned-writer from the New York district of Spanish Harlem. The paper's reporters picked it up and stuck it in the most inappropriate sentences ('From the get-go, the Pope was impressed' – 1990) and it appeared intermittently, mainly in sports reports, thereafter. Later in the 1990s it began creeping into the British media.

In 2010, while I was in the midst of writing my *Mail on Sunday* columns, the politician Michael Gove used *get-go* in an interview on BBC Radio 4. Gove was then Britain's Education Secretary, the most prescriptive in history, a man who, had he not been dismissed, might have got round to ordering all children to speak Latin in the playground. Heroically, the interviewer John Humphrys upbraided him and got a rare apology.

Curiously, I have never ever heard *get-go* in conversation, either in America or Britain, which may be testament to my own sheltered life, not having spent enough time in Spanish Harlem or, far more terrifying, the Gove household. I'm not prescriptive: if a word works, we should buy it, whatever it is and wherever it's from. This one, in my view, does not and it is a symptom of a terrible condition: mindless *copy-catting* of another country's language.[6]

If we are to stop this, it is necessary to understand the process. And it's time to tell the whole story. From the get-go.

---

6 *Copy-cat* looks as though it must be an Americanism: cited as 'a favourite term of my grandmother' by the Maine writer Sarah Orne Jewett in 1896; not spotted in Britain until 1918.

1

FOR SHAME,
MR JEFFERSON!

The first word from the New World to come to England is thought to have arrived in 1533. It was *guaiacum*, the bark of a Haitian tree which was believed to be a cure for syphilis. On the face of it, this might sustain the view of America as 'the last best hope of earth' (Abraham Lincoln).

On the other hand, since syphilis had never been recorded in Europe until Columbus's sailors came back, it might support the opposing view, of America as 'the Great Satan' (Ayatollah Khomeini). Furthermore, *guaiacum* did not work as a cure, though it was said to be considerably less unpleasant than taking the only known alternative, mercury. This might reinforce the image of America as the home of attractively packaged, well-marketed, meretricious innovations designed to fool the unwary. All these descriptions of the New World have enduring validity.

At that stage, the English – about to lose themselves in internal warfare over religion – were not much interested in this New-Found Land. Up to the 1550s, nearly a thousand books had apparently appeared in Europe referring to America, but only a dozen in England, half of them devoted to syphilis. However, various works about the

Americas were then translated by the scholar Richard Eden, who used many previously unrecorded English words including *cacao, cannibal* and *iguana*, all of which have a claim to be regarded as early Americanisms – and also some that Eden evidently coined himself, including *conflagration, despicable, monstrosity* and *plentifulness.*

Eden's book helped stimulate the Elizabethan court's interest in the possibilities of exploration. In 1587 Britain established a colony on Roanoke Island, off North Carolina; within three years the 120 settlers vanished without trace. In 1607 another group landed in Virginia and called their settlement Jamestown, after the new King. They might have gone the same way as Roanoke had they not stumbled into the ideal place for growing the hip new drug known as *tobacco*.[1] During a rare truce with the native Americans after the marriage of John Rolfe to the chief's daughter, Pocahontas, they were offered the pick of the natives' own crop.

Rolfe sent it to London, where the relaxing and allegedly healthy qualities of tobacco, imported from Spanish American outposts, were already being appreciated. Despite James I's stern views about smoking, the London Company, which had funded the Virginia venture, sensed a profit centre rather than a bottomless pit, and sent out reinforcements and various governors.

One of those governors, Sir George Yeardley, who took over in 1619, was sufficiently benign or idle enough to call in assistance from the populace and thus created something that looked vaguely like a democracy. No such help was requested from the twenty-odd Africans who had arrived that same year and became the unwilling founders of another American tradition: slavery.

In 1620 another group of pioneers set out to practise their own stern and unPopish version of Christianity, so they planned, elsewhere inside the vaguely defined borders of Virginia. They got lost and instead arrived several hundred miles north, where they created their own New England. The rest is history.

As the historians Nevins and Commager put it more than three centuries later,

---

1 Via Spanish, from the Haitian Carib word for the pipe used to smoke it.

Here was a great shaggy continent, its Eastern third covered with pathless forests, its mountains, rivers, lakes and rolling plains all upon a grandiose scale; its Northern stretches fiercely cold in winter, its Southern areas burning hot in summer; filled with wild beasts, and peopled by a warlike, cruel and treacherous people still in the Stone Age of culture.

In many respects it was a forbidding land. It could be reached only by a voyage so perilous that some ships buried as many as they landed. But despite all the drawbacks, it was admirably fitted to become the home of an energetic, thriving people.

And so the energetic people set about getting rid of the Stone Age ones and the forests and the wild beasts. In all of this they substantially succeeded, making the place a good deal less shaggy and creating the most powerful and influential country the world has ever known.

***

Even before the Pilgrim Fathers made it to Massachusetts, the Virginians had needed words for the strange fauna they had to confront. Never having seen even a Eurasian elk, they borrowed the word **moose** from the local aboriginals. Similarly, they took the words that mutated into **raccoon** and **opossum**. These were inevitably mentioned in reports to London, and presumably became the first words imported from the settlers themselves.

In 1621 the grammarian Alexander Gill, high master of St Paul's School, noted that both *maize* and *canoe*, which had been passed from native languages through Spanish, were becoming English words. Eden had used both (as *maisium* and *canoas*). The New England colonists, who were quicker than the Virginians to knuckle down to farming, latched on to maize as a crop but avoided the actual word. They gave their new find the homely term used for the staple crop in the old country: *corn*. This decision is still causing confusion in Britain nearly 400 years later.

And so the colonists settled down and sent home the news that there was something to be said for America. The population grew fast from 4,600 in 1630, but it took 120 years for it to reach a million. And in that time contact between the satellite and mother-ship England was very tenuous. The sea was stormy, the ships were primitive and the journey often fatal. To the average Englishman, America must have seemed far more distant than the moon, an important presence in everyone's lives. Perhaps it was regarded as we might think of Mars: somewhere life might just be possible but not a life we are ever likely to experience.

In 1682 the literate portion of England was briefly transfixed by the first American bestseller: the first-person account by Mary Row-landson, the wife of a Massachusetts clergyman, of being captured by Indian raiders. It is indeed searing stuff and must have entrenched other Americans in their beliefs: their love of God; their hatred of the 'brutishness of this barbarous enemy'; their distrust of 'the vast and howling wilderness'. To readers safe in London it may have sounded like an adventure. Even the difference in title seems telling. In New England it was published as *The Sovereignty and Goodness of God*; in old England it was called *A True History*.

Those who did move to America tended to be the persecuted and the prosecuted; the desperate, the misfits and the chancers; but also the practical, the imaginative and the brave. And, with time, their progeny began to talk in a way that made them sound different to the folks back home, in their pronunciation and intonation, as well as their vocabulary.

Their new home was engrossing enough for them not to worry too much about what might be happening anywhere else. Books would have been the main source of possible information but the Virgin-ians were not especially bookish. The New England Puritans certainly were zealous readers, but were focused on just the one book. Harvard, founded in 1636, had only just acquired copies of the works of Shake-speare and Milton for its library by 1723. And there was still no sign of Pope, Dryden or Swift.

The exact linguistic process that occurred is a matter of some dispute. But quite obviously American English needed new words to describe the new environment, and not just the unfamiliar flora and fauna. Early on, the neologisms came primarily from the Indians either directly (like **tomahawk**, noted by John Smith, the founder of Jamestown, in 1612) or by imaginative translation (**big chief, warpath, pipe of peace, bury the hatchet**).

Some were picked up from the other Europeans who were sniffing around for opportunities, initially the Spanish, who donated the words they used to describe a cornucopia of mixed blessings: as well as *tobacco*, *tomato*, *chocolate*, *potato* and *mosquito* went direct to London before the British settlement began. Smith himself gathered *cockroach* from the Spanish (*la cucaracha*). Later, everyone from French explorers to Chinese migrants would start adding their words to the swirling gene pool of the American vocabulary.

And that pool didn't just swirl: it burbled and gurgled and burst its banks. As the land between New England and Virginia was infilled by new arrivals – Quakers to Pennsylvania initially, Catholics to Maryland – a society began to develop that was inevitably less rooted and more mobile than in Europe. And even though the roads were notoriously bad, it was relatively easy to move along the coastal waters.

The settlers brought with them their regional and dialect words. When Professor Higgins announced at the start of Shaw's *Pygmalion* that, merely by listening to an accent, 'I can place any man within six miles. I can place him within two miles in London. Sometimes within two streets,' he was being boastful but not entirely ludicrous. In America this soon became, except within a few urban and rustic enclaves, impossible.

Migrants, especially the less educated, brought with them the words they used naturally back home, and spread them around. Many stuck, even if they had died out in Britain. This might constitute an example of what is known to philologists as colonial lag: the theory that the language changes more slowly in outposts than in the mother country. Hence the continuing myth that somewhere in the Appalachians are tribes of check-shirted, straggly-bearded, Trump-voting hillbillies making their own moonshine and speaking perfect Shakespearean English. Colonial lag might explain the accents on remote New Zealand farms or some of the orotundities of Indian

English. But it would be a gross simplification of the Anglo-American linguistic relationship.

The language back home was certainly changing, quite dramatically as it happened. It is thought that, perhaps as late as 1800, even royalty used the short A, now associated with northern England and the US, in words like *path* and *grass*. 'Parth' and 'grarss' were Cockney. Shortly afterwards the upper classes adopted the Cockney version. By that time the American accent had taken shape and kept its short As, but the American vocabulary was only just starting to flex its muscles.

The night he arrived near Boston in 1663, the Englishman John Josselyn became perhaps the first traveller to record a word that had changed meanings in America, when he noted that an *ordinary*, which in England, among other things, denoted a kind of gastropub, had mutated into a simple boozer. Thousands of less finicky distinctions lay ahead.

Josselyn had been to New England before, in 1638, where he had far less mundane experiences. He experienced 'a fearful form of wind called a *hurricane*', and then another storm with 'two of the greatest and fearfullest thunder-claps that ever were heard, I am confident'.[2] He also killed eighty snakes – some three yards long – within a stone's throw of his house, and concluded that 'there are many stranger things in the world than are to be seen between London and Staines'. All of which would have fed the growing perception that here indeed was a far-from-ordinary land, full of exotic dangers, some of which had to be endured, others resolved by the musket.

And other words were changing that Josselyn did not notice. *Creek*, which in Britain was and is primarily a saltwater inlet, began to be extended to any brook or stream. Many of the gentle English topographical words – *heath* and *hurst, mere* and *marsh*, now mainly surviving in the names of suburbs and housing estates – were forgotten to be replaced by bolder words for a bigger, bolder geography. In came *swamp, ravine* and *bluff.*

---

2 As a word, *hurricane* had arrived in England – slightly bedraggled, as a *furacano* – through Richard Eden. And Sir Walter Raleigh experienced what he called a *hurlecano* in the West Indies.

Bluff is thought to be the first American word ever to be excoriated by an English writer. In 1736 Francis Moore visited Savannah and noted 'the bank of the river (which they call in barbarous English a bluff) is steep'. The word *barbarous* might not have been meant quite as viciously as it now sounds. Nowadays it is used only to describe a terrorist atrocity; Moore just meant a word that was not standard English. But it was not intended as a compliment, and thus might be seen as the start of the ongoing process whereby the snotty-nosed Brits disparaged the American language.

However, the Moore sideswipe may also be seen as the beginning of the next period of Anglo-American linguistic relationship. Firstly, the population of the colonies was about to stop just growing and start exploding: from 1.1 million in 1750 to 2.7 million in 1780, excluding native Americans but including more than half a million blacks, nearly all in the south, the vast majority enslaved.

America still had skill shortages in many areas, and one of them was writing. It was not an acute problem: at that stage the colonies needed blacksmiths more than wordsmiths. But those who did write also tended to be enslaved – to the form and fashion set in London. The eighteenth century marked the apogee of linguistic prescriptiveness.

Britain was becoming a country governed by laws rather than monarchical whim, and the same standards were being applied to the written word. The most successful writers saw themselves self-consciously in the stylised Greek and Roman traditions. Freewheeling Shakespearean spellings and usages were frowned on, and offenders were subject to the withering scorn of literary panjandrums like Lord Chesterfield and Dr Johnson. 'Good order and authority are now necessary,' proclaimed Chesterfield, welcoming Johnson's Dictionary in 1755. In one of his famous letters to his son, Chesterfield warned: 'few things are more disagreeable than to hear a Gentleman talk the barbarisms, the solecisms, and the Vulgarisms of Porters'.

Johnson included a handful of New World words in the dictionary, mostly the obvious ones like *moose* and *maize* and *tobacco*, but also ***barbecue*** – 'a term used in the West Indies for dressing a hog whole'. He also mentions *gotten* as the past participle of *get*, so it had clearly not yet disappeared from English English. He resisted any sideswipes against American words,[3] though he was fond of exclaiming in public: 'I love all mankind. Except the Americans.'

The appearance of the dictionary has to be seen in a wider context. Eleven years later Sir William Blackstone published his *Commentaries on the Laws of England*, which did a similar job to Johnson by making sense of the vagaries of common law. The late eighteenth century was also the heyday of the grammarians, led by Robert Lowth, Bishop of London, who was regarded as the arch-prescriptivist, and his heir Lindley Murray. The upshot was that in the last four decades of the eighteenth century, in David Crystal's words, the English-speaking world 'was more unified in the way it was taught spelling, grammar, and vocabulary than it had ever been before. Or would ever be again.'

At this stage, the only words that had successfully travelled east across the Atlantic were the essential descriptive nouns. And even educated Englishmen were still hazy about America. Henry Hitchings noted an article in the *Gentleman's Magazine* in 1752 which mentioned 'a fair American' and then explained that 'by an American I do not mean an Indian, but one descended of British parents born in America'.

The French were vaguer still about what lay over the ocean, but more imaginative. Le Comte de Buffon, regarded as the pre-eminent natural historian of the era, insisted that America was a place of swamps with a cold, wet climate where all species become enfeebled.[4] What's more, any species imported into America for economic reasons would soon succumb to its new environment and produce lines of puny, feeble offspring. His Dutch-born follower, Cornelius de Pauw, also influential in France, added that the whole wretched place was 'deluged with lizards, snakes, serpents, reptiles and monstrous insects' and the people imbued with 'a moronic spirit'.

The ignorance must have decreased somewhat during the Seven Years War (1756–63), which left the British in apparent control of

---

3 Unlike the ones he served up to *banter* ('barbarous'), *flippant* ('a word of no great authority') and *fun* ('a low cant word').
4 Maybe he was getting it muddled with Britain.

North America, and ensured that the word American became more generally applied to the white man rather than the red. Britain would soon learn a great deal more than it wished to know about the Americans, but for the moment the colonists' cultural deference continued unabated. Indeed, no one was more cowed by the British elite's disapproval than the great father figure of the Revolution, Benjamin Franklin.

In correspondence with the Scottish philosopher David Hume he wrote: 'I hope with you that we shall always in America make the best English of this Island [i.e. Britain] our standard, and I believe it will be so.' Hume, however, reproved him for using the words *pejorate*, *colonize* and *unshakeable*, and Franklin duly apologised. All three had been used by British writers more than a century earlier, by Francis Bacon in the case of *colonize*.

Hume himself wrote optimistically, in 1767, about the future of English in 'our solid and increasing establishments in America'. By then, however, those establishments were already starting to totter. The United States' fundamental mythology suggests that pre-revolutionary America was a land suffering terribly under the imperial yoke. In practice, white (and indeed red) Americans were far freer than the British. The colonists were operating a functioning local democracy: distance saw to that. The hated taxes were primarily to fund the defence of their own territory, and the rates were lower than in Britain. Anyway, the colonists were skilled evaders: the stamp tax raised less than the cost of collection.

There was also a substantial minority of Americans who were appalled by the whole business of rebellion. And among the British elite there were also different opinions. As revolution moved closer, Dr Johnson was implacable: 'Government is necessary to man, and where obedience is not compelled, there is no government. If the subject refuses to obey, it is the duty of authority to use compulsion.' Chesterfield had died by then but, writing to his son in 1765, during the stamp duty dispute, he had put himself on the right side of history: 'I never saw a froward [sic] child mended by whipping; and I would not have the mother country become a stepmother.'

After the split, pro-British sentiment – covered by the word

Toryism – became a negligible factor in American politics: the Revolution worked out well enough to prevent any nostalgia for monarchy and redcoats. But social and linguistic conservatism – in the sense of a lingering attachment to the old country's manners and methods – remained an underlying strain, and one that has never wholly gone away. However, it was soon to be in retreat, like the British soldiery.

As the new order took shape, there was a conscious rejection of Englishness. Thus developed the American disdain for tea, a drink henceforth associated with old ladies and wimps (though George Washington, who did not have to prove his patriotism with pointless gestures, always loved his cuppa). And a Lord of the Flies quality, a defiant playfulness, began to characterise American attitude towards language. Now they could not merely do want they wanted, and say what they wanted, they could say it any way they wanted, and to hell with Chesterfield and Johnson. In the words of Thomas Jefferson, 'the new circumstances under which we are placed call for new words, new phrases and for the transfer of old words to new objects'. They no longer needed just a word to indicate a *moose* or a **moccasin**, they also needed a lexicon for their new politics.

This might seem a strange time to have been worrying about vocabulary, but these issues were at the heart of the infant nation's deliberations. At the Continental Congress in 1776, which led to the Declaration of Independence, it was not even certain that the national language would be English. There were voices in favour of Hebrew, French, Greek and Algonquin. Finally, Roger Sherman of Connecticut summed up: 'It would be more convenient for us to keep the language as it was, and make the English speak Greek'.

But would the English spoken in the new nation be the King's English or something else? That was an altogether more troublesome question. Five months before the British finally surrendered in 1781, a series of articles appeared in a Pennsylvania journal with the byline 'Druid'. The author was the Rev. John Witherspoon, a Scottish-born Presbyterian minister who had emigrated thirteen years earlier to become president of the New Jersey college that was to mutate into Princeton University.

'I have heard in this country, in the senate, at the bar, and from the pulpit, and see daily in dissertations from the press, errors in grammar, improprieties ... and vulgarisms which hardly any person of the same class in point of rank and literature would have fallen into in Great Britain,' Witherspoon wrote. Given that the two countries were then at war, this might have got him deported or locked up.[5] But Witherspoon's patriotism was, like Washington's, beyond reproach: he had been the only clergyman to sign the Declaration of Independence, and his leadership had made Princeton a hotbed of revolutionary fervour.

He divided these errors into eight categories, the first of which he called *Americanisms*, a word never previously recorded. It meant, he said, 'phrases or terms or a construction of sentences, even among persons of rank and education, different from the use ... in Great Britain'. Witherspoon listed a dozen examples of Americanisms, which offers the fullest catalogue yet of the extent to which the languages had begun to diverge. They included:

> *Either* to indicate more than two.
> *Fellow countrymen*: 'an evident tautology'.
> Saying *a certain Thomas Benson* rather than *a certain person called Thomas Benson*.
> †*Mad* meaning angry.
> *Notify* the public, rather than inform: 'In English ... we do not notify the person of the thing, we notify the thing to the person.'

It is a pretty mixed bag. The first three do not appear to be American-born, though they may well have emerged in Britain after Witherspoon emigrated; anyway, *fellow* often helps before *countryman*; otherwise it can mean a rustic rather than a compatriot. *Mad* in this sense does have some British pedigree, but obviously had never reached Witherspoon's ears; it returned into more general British use much, much later. According to the OED, *notify* in the sense Witherspoon disliked was rare in Britain before the twentieth century.

---

5 Or at a British university these days, *no-platformed*.

It was certainly not a full list. When Franklin returned to America in 1785 after nine years as Ambassador to France, he was horrified to find people using to †*advocate*, to *notice*, to *progress* and to *oppose*. So much so that he wrote to Noah Webster, who had already made a name for himself from his reading and spelling books, asking for help in exterminating them. He had gone to the wrong man.

The meaning of words mattered more in the United States than in Britain, because the country now had a written constitution, only slightly easier to alter than the Bible. And the precise meaning of each word in it was to assume a lasting importance, to an extent unthinkable in the pragmatic and protean British Constitution. Had the Second Amendment ('A well regulated militia being necessary to the security of a free state, the right of the people to keep and bear arms shall not be infringed.') been better drafted in 1791, we might know for sure whether the Founding Fathers really wanted their most deranged and embittered successors to go around staging mass murders.

Webster's view was that vocabulary, spelling and grammar were for Americans to decide, not the British, and he set about promulgating that position with a ceaseless, very American, energy. He was an obsessive self-publicist who in almost any other time or place would have been dismissed as a particularly irritating crank. As it was, he became the founding father of the American language.

He had set out his stall in 1789, in his *Dissertation on the English Language*: 'to copy foreign manners implicitly is to reverse the order of things, and begin our political existence with the corruptions and vices which have marked the declining glories of other republics'. Webster predicted that American and English would drift apart to become as different as Dutch and German. This did not quite come true, but they did separate in the short and medium term, and it was largely a self-fulfilling prophecy. Webster made it happen.

In particular, he was responsible for the differences in spelling that have caused low-level irritation between Britain and the US for the last two centuries, and complete orthographical chaos for the poor old Canadians.

In his *Compendious Dictionary of the English Language*, in 1806, which was not as compendious as his later dictionaries, he established the principles by which he

1. Took out final Ks to create words like *music* and *logic*. 'The use of *k* … affords a remarkable proof of the corruption of language by means of heedless writers,' he said in his preface.
2. Transposed the endings of -er words to create *theater*, *center* and *specter*. In this he insisted he was rescuing English from being polluted by French.
3. Removed the -our ending to invent *color*, *honor*, *labor*, *flavor* and *misdemeanor*, for the same reason.
4. Insisted on *defense* and *offense*, not *defence* and *offence*.
5. Removed the final E to produce *determin*, *medicin* and *examin*.[6]

Most of the ideas were carried through until Webster's final and most influential dictionary, that of 1828. On the first, he succeeded in changing all forms of English. On the next three, he achieved his objective by setting the standards for his own country. He failed on the last.

Webster himself was not consistent, since he continued to enjoy a *frolick*. And in later life he began to have some second thoughts. But really! Webster was a pernicious mischief-maker. It is absolutely right that different forms of English should have their own character, traditions and idiom: that's the argument of this book. But on spelling there is an obvious advantage in consistency. Other would-be spelling reformers have failed because there are bound to be anomalies and, frankly, it doesn't matter to a language how words are spelt as long as there is a standard to which everyone adheres. Webster, by creating confusion, was not guilty of a *misdemeanor*; it was a felony.

---

6 It is, however, a myth that Webster or any other American was responsible for the -ize endings to verbs like *organize* and *realize*. According to the Oxford Dictionaries blog the -ize ending is in fact much older than the -ise even in British English; it is just that in Britain you have a choice. Sometimes.

One word that failed to make it to the 1806 Webster, nor indeed the seminal 1828 version, was *belittle*. Yet it was to become one of the first of the battleground words, the territory on which the ceaseless Anglo-American linguistic war would be contested. The first known usage came from Thomas Jefferson in his *Notes on the State of Virginia*, an eloquent, erudite exposition on the delights of the state, first published in 1785 when Jefferson was the American trade representative in Paris: 'So far the Count de Buffon has carried this new theory of the tendency of nature to belittle her productions on this side the Atlantic,' he wrote.

This was picked up in London two years later by an anonymous reviewer in *The European Magazine*: 'Belittle! What an expression! It may be an elegant one in Virginia, and even perfectly intelligible; but for our part, all we can do is, to guess at its meaning. For shame, Mr Jefferson! … Oh spare us, we beseech you, our mother-tongue!'

Self-parodying arrogance was to be characteristic of the English response to American writing and language for many years to come. But actually the effete snob who wrote this did have a point. *Belittle* was to acquire two meanings: one the literal one of making, or appearing to make, something smaller; the other one is the now far more common meaning – to disparage.

Since Buffon had specifically been theorising that American animals were small, it would seem that Jefferson had the first definition in mind. But his next sentence goes on to say of Buffon's theory: 'Its application to the race of whites, transplanted from Europe, remained for the Abbé Raynal: "America has not yet produced one good poet … one able mathematician, one man of genius in a single art or a single science".' This suggests Jefferson meant the other version. So the snotty reviewer was right; the intellectual giant of American statesmanship was being ambiguous.

Still, this new coinage made its way slowly into his country's language, and even more slowly into British English. In 1879 the Irish Nationalist MP F.H. McDonnell wrote to *The Times* accusing his opponents of 'trying to belittle the gravity of Irish discontent'. And Jefferson had won. But belittling American writers was what English *literati* would keep doing for many of the intervening years. And as for Buffon's theories, it was hardly necessary for Jefferson to spend 325 pages refuting them: a single monosyllable might have sufficed.

Belittle did make it into the pioneering dictionary of Americanisms, produced by John Pickering in 1816. Pickering had worked in the American Legation in London circa 1800 and was appalled by the realisation that the English of England differed so much from his own. His purpose in logging the differences was not to celebrate the brave new language, but to get it to conform. Maybe he had been teased about his vocabulary in the London taverns; he certainly took to heart the kind of anti-American strictures ('For shame, Mr Jefferson!') that were now appearing regularly in the English reviews.

So he began collecting words used in America which he had not come across in England; his book contained about 500 of them. Later scholars have belittled Pickering because all but about seventy of those words had indeed come over from Britain, where Pickering would not have heard them either because they had fallen into disuse or were only ever used in provincial dialects.

This argument is still used today as an irrelevant gotcha to denounce anyone in Britain who complains about Americanisms. But it was a legitimate criticism of Pickering, since his professed concern was to try to enable Americans to read the great works of literature. If it were true that US English was more the language of Shakespeare than British English, Americans would actually be better equipped for the task than anyone else.

Right at the start, Pickering picked out †*accomplished*, *advocate* (as a verb), *annulment*, **appreciation**, **arrived** and **awful**. The first two were certainly not original Americanisms: *accomplished* pops up in both *Cymbeline* (c.1611) and *Pride and Prejudice* (1813), a rare double, which suggests it was at least lurking in the language somewhere. *Advocate* was and is a technical Scottish legal term, and its more general meaning has been traced back in England to 1599; nonetheless it was one of the American usages that offended Franklin and its appearances in *The Times* were infrequent before 1816. *Annulment* goes back to Caxton and did not obviously disappear thereafter.

But the next three were palpable hits. **Appreciation**, in the financial sense, was first used by John Adams, later Washington's successor as President, in 1777. The OED can find no British usage until the future Chancellor of the Exchequer George Goschen mentions 'a considerable appreciation in the value of gold' in 1883. Pickering's point about *arrived* was simply that the English said '*we are arrived*' and the Americans '*we have arrived*'. A study of *The Times* vindicates him: '*we have arrived*' starts appearing after 1830 and drives out its former rival around 1870.

The last is something special. One of the early nineteenth-century travellers from Britain to the US was John Lambert. He was not enthusiastic about the place, especially about what he heard in rural New England. 'What an *awful* wind!' they kept telling him. '*Awful* hole!' '*Awful* hill!' '*Awful* mouth!' '*Awful* nose!' He did not like the twang in which they said it either.

Awful in this sense had to decouple itself from its earlier meaning of 'inspiring awe', and indeed in the early days the two are hard to disentangle, especially when the awful moment arrived of a prisoner facing execution, as it often did in that era. Keats, perhaps knowingly, wrote in a letter in 1818: 'It is an awful while since you have heard from me.' In 1834 Charles Lamb was explicit: 'She is indeed, as the Americans would express it, something awful.'

Lambert knew what he thought:

> Colloquial barbarisms ... among the peasantry of a country, are excusable; but when they are used in composition by writers, they become disgusting. I could collect hundreds of others equally absurd, which have been invented by Americans who are desirous of introducing, what they call, an American language; but unless they resort to the Catabaw, Chactaw, or Kickapoo dialects, I am sure they will never accomplish it by murdering the English language.

He might be less sanguine now. *Awful* does seem to have been one of the first words to make the journey east. Now of course it is almost a diagnostic word of middle-class, middle-aged cup-of-tea British conversation ('*Awful* wind!'), whereas Americans are much more associated with *awesome* (or 'ossum'), which in turn has travelled to Britain to become the staple term of approval among the young.

∗∗∗

By 1815 Anglo-American relations had become very complex. Britain's loss of the American colonies had been an abject failure militarily and philosophically. The country no longer led the world as a bastion of liberty; it had been superseded. Against that, Britain had a very different experience of revolution: the American experiment might not have been a disaster – *yet*. But look what happened in France. Britain had been forced to confront an existential threat to its own primitive form of freedom and democracy from an ambitious and ruthless dictator, and where were the Americans during all that? Being damned nuisances, that's what.

The Americans saw their treatment on the high seas at the hands of the Royal Navy as a threat to their hard-won independence. Britain refused to recognise that British-born sailors had any right to be serving the United States, and regularly kidnapped and press-ganged them on to their own ships. This kind of bullying helped bring about the messy and equivocal War of 1812, which has little place in American folk memory and none at all in Britain's.[7]

Some historians use the formulation that it was this little war, even though neither side can be said to have won it, that finally established the reality of American independence. Intellectually, however, true independence was still far away. As Webster complained in 1817: 'There is nothing which, in my opinion, so debases the genius and character of my countrymen, as the implicit confidence they place in English authors, and their unhesitating submission to their opinions, their derision, and their frowns.'

More than that, this great big child of a country could be reduced to collective tears by the comments of the motley collection of Grub

---

7 Except for the song 'Battle of New Orleans', which the skiffle star Lonnie Donegan took to No.2 in the UK charts in 1959. Which is very British, since it was a battle Britain unquestionably lost.

Streeters who contributed to the proliferating British literary reviews. Every time one of these buzzing wasps mentioned America they stung, and the brave New Worlders just howled: 'The style of Mr Adams [John Quincy, the sixth President] is in general very tolerable English which, for an American composition, is no moderate praise' ... 'no aristocratical distinctions – even in their vocabulary' ... 'torrent of barbarous phraseology' ... 'The work now before us ... is completely American, in paper, printing, composition, and spirit; coarse, bombastic and bitter' ... 'The Yankees appear to us a testy and quarrelsome race ... society has rapidly degenerated'.

When they talked amongst themselves, British writers were no more polite about the Americans. 'See what it is to have a nation to take its place among civilised states before it has either gentlemen or scholars!' wrote Robert Southey to W.S. Landor in 1812. In reply, Landor protested mildly before adding 'I detest the American character as much as you do'.

In 1824 Sir Walter Scott, writing to Maria Edgeworth, was mildly complimentary about American energy and patriotism, then continued, 'they are as yet rude in their ideas of social intercourse, and totally ignorant, speaking generally, of all the art of good-breeding which consists primarily of the postponement of one's own petty wishes or comforts to those of others'.

One article cut through intellectual America's fragile self-esteem like no other. More than a century later, H.L. Mencken, no word-mincer himself, was still referring to it, in his great work *The American Language*, as 'the famous sneer of Sydney Smith'. It appeared in 1820, in the *Edinburgh Review*, perhaps the most influential of all the magazines, at the end of what was mostly a precis of an unpromising volume called *Statistical Annals of the United States of America*. Having dutifully listed some of the things the country had achieved, Smith began riffing about what it had not:

In the four quarters of the globe, who reads an American book? or goes to an American play? or looks at an American picture or statue? What does the world yet owe to American physicians or surgeons? What new substances have their chemists discovered?

or what old ones have they analysed? What new constellations have been discovered by the telescopes of Americans? What have they done in the mathematics? Who drinks out of American glasses? or eats from American plates? or wears American coats or gowns? or sleeps in American blankets? Finally, under which of the old tyrannical governments of Europe is every sixth man a slave, whom his fellow-creatures may buy, sell and torture?

This was of course pretty much the point Raynal made in France decades earlier. But the early-twentieth-century American academic William B. Cairns, who masochistically collected the insults from the reviews over the period 1785 to 1833, gives Smith pride of place: 'It was the question "Who reads an American book?" which was a thousand times quoted, answered, railed at, wept over, even down to the time of persons still living. Few other single sentences have aroused so many international heart-burnings and done so much harm.'

Cairns thought it was quite unfair for Smith to mention slavery. Then he grudgingly admitted that 'the most irritating thing about these charges was their approximation to truth'. Almost no one did read an American book before 1820. As it happens, just as Smith's review appeared, Washington Irving's *Sketch Book*, including the story of Rip Van Winkle, was starting to gain attention in Britain, partly because a half-decent American book was such a novelty. James Fenimore Cooper would soon be an even bigger hit. But against that, in Britain this was the era of Austen, Coleridge, Scott, Lamb, Hazlitt, Keats, Shelley, Wordsworth and Byron. As Mencken himself was to say in another context, 'Injustice is relatively easy to bear. What stings is justice.'

Furthermore, Sydney Smith was hardly a candidate for the Axis of Evil. He was a churchman famous for his literary elegance, his wit and his broad humane sympathies. Four years later he would write another article in the *Edinburgh Review*, a remarkably perceptive one foreshadowing America's future greatness; it was much kinder to the country in general but even angrier about slavery. No one in the US quoted that.

These early exchanges were obviously very much of their times. The literary magazines these days are the very epitome of the Anglo-American academic alliance, at least the one that exists between worldly liberal-minded metropolitans. But there is something in the dusty file copies of the old magazines that persists. The New World was anxious for the approbation of the Old, sometimes uncertain of its ground, and petulant when thwarted or misunderstood. The Old World was conscious of the New's growing power, and at once appalled by it, fascinated, condescending and jealous. Then and now in both cases.

The first Smith article can be seen as a turning point because at that moment he could have added: 'Who borrows an American word?' Keats did, but that was a rarity. Indeed, since as Smith said, no one (well, hardly anyone) had read any American books, at least since Mary Rowlandson's time, there was no easy route for a neologism to be transmitted.

Robert Burchfield, the editor of the OED, would later record: 'Until about 1820 the movement of vocabulary was almost all westward to America.' The words that had gone east in the two centuries since the *Mayflower* had been essential to convey a few essential facts about the New World, not to make a more general contribution to humanity. The wind was about to veer round 180 degrees.

Whatever those involved with the literary magazines may have thought, the average Briton probably entertained a less jaundiced opinion of America. The royal family was a bad joke: 1820 was the year mad King George was succeeded by the Prince Regent, his dissolute grandson. Their ministers were reactionary. The franchise was corrupt. Political repression had reached a peak with the Six Acts of 1819. The penal system was outrageous. Religious freedom was incomplete.

Above all, poverty was widespread and being exacerbated by the spread of mechanisation. Emigration had been almost impossible during the decades of war against the French, but by 1820 almost everyone must have known someone who knew someone who had gone to America and come good. Word would have seeped back. From a country where labour was plentiful and land scarce, to a country where land was plentiful and labour scarce ... how could anyone with a spark of ambition not be tempted?

At times of unrest, the government even encouraged the exodus, though they preferred to direct it towards the British possessions, Canada and the Cape. Even so, by the late 1820s the migration had become an exodus. The journey was still harsh and perilous, but it was getting easier: the cause of scurvy had finally been identified; and steamships were just over the horizon. The population of the US began to explode.

And for those back home, an America of the imagination was becoming more accessible. In 1826 came the first great bestseller from the American interior, Cooper's *The Last of the Mohicans*, centred on a bro-mance between the frontiersman hero Natty Bumppo and his two red-skinned companions. And thus began the enduring love affair between the stay-at-homes of the world and the stories of the Wild West.

Cooper's book was set back in the Seven Years War, and Bumppo was reputedly based on the old Appalachian woodsman Daniel Boone. But reality was now about to match fiction: America was on the march west, into a future bounded only by the Pacific. The process was embodied by Andrew Jackson, victor of the Battle of New Orleans, elected in 1829 as the first President unconnected with the Founding Fathers. Mencken painted a vivid picture of him: 'ignorant, pushful, impatient of restraint and precedent, an iconoclast, a Philistine, an Anglophobe in every fibre ... from the extreme backwoods ... amid surroundings but little removed from savagery'.

Cooper's literary style was wordy and ponderous and very much in the English tradition. But imagine how thrilling the stories must have seemed to a reader in damp and repressive England. Fundamentally, America attracted and imported people because it fired their imagination. It was able to start exporting its vocabulary for the same reason.

Less partisan historians than Mencken suggest Jackson's bumpkinism was somewhat feigned for electoral advantage, and he would not have been the last American politician to try that trick.[8] And his image led to him being credited as the originator of what is probably the most famous of all Americanisms: *OK*, which was said to be the

---

8 But then he would not have been the last to be a complete ignoramus either.

way the unlettered old booby signed off documents he wanted to approve – his short form for 'oll korrect'.

That persisted as a theory for the origin of OK for 130 years. It had a lot of competition, though. People claimed OK came from the Choctaw word *okeh*; from an early telegraphic term, Open Key; from Orrin Kendall biscuits, popular in the Civil War; from an Indian chief called Old Keokuk; from an early railway freight-agent, Obadiah Kelly, who initialled bills of lading.

Or it was not American at all. It was German, short for Oberst Kommandant; no, it was Greek, *olla kalla* = all good; or French, from a rum-producing town in Haiti, Aux Cayes. Or Elizabethan English. But the Andrew Jackson version was the best known, particularly in Britain, where it appeared on the label of OK Sauce.[9]

Semi-finally, the etymologist Allen Walker Read announced in 1963 that he had found OK in a Boston newspaper from 1839. Later Read trumped himself, and discovered the word dated back one year earlier when the Boston press was playing around with initials for such phrases as GTDHD (give the devil his due) and OKKBWP (one kind kiss before we part). And indeed it did stand for Oll Korrect, but it was nothing to do with Jackson. Coincidentally or otherwise, OK was also the nickname of Jackson's vice president and successor, Martin Van Buren: Old Kinderhook, his home town. And thus it was adopted by van Buren's supporters and stuck, as has Read's explanation, so far.[10]

Whatever, OK has a simple and enduring power. Wherever it is in the world that English is least spoken – maybe somewhere in Western China or North Korea – OK will be understood, if not always interpreted correctly because it is so very flexible. It can, drawn out to its fullest length, be the expression of delight used by a politician in the first flush of victory. Or it can be the equivalent of the Hindi word *acha*, which experienced travellers understand

9 In my childhood, anyway. OK was a milder version of the British brown-sauce staple, HP. It is said to be still obtainable from Chinese supermarkets.

10 American newspapers are far less playful these days. However, the wordplay still happens on the internet. IMHO and FWIW, it is one of the web's great pluses. LOL.

as 'I know precisely what you want but have no intention of doing anything about it.'

OK?

***

In 1820, the year Sydney Smith found himself ranked with George III on the American Most Wanted list, a less gifted writer in *The New Monthly* wrote a *jeu d'esprit* making fun of American words.

'An author is called a *composuist*; instead of a country being compromised, it is *compromitted*; so we find **Christianization**, *constitutionality*, *consternated*, *customable*, †*governmental*, *deputize*, *gubernatorial*, *happifying*, **lengthy**, and a thousand other similar improvements. At the meaning of these words, however, we can make a tolerable guess, for we hear something like them at home; but when we hear of *reluct*, and *scow*, and *slangwhanger*, and **squiggle**, and **slush**, and **squirm**, it certainly makes us look very *awful*.'

That constitutes an interesting list in that it offers a snapshot of what a literate Englishman conceived to be Americanisms at that time. The unknown author appears to have stolen the words wholesale from Pickering, whose dictionary had been namechecked earlier in his article: every one is in there. But Anon. obviously did not recognise them, so – even if some of the words do have their roots within archaic English or local dialect – they surely cannot have been part of the accepted language at that time.

Governmental may be a doubtful case since it was in regular use in *The Times* in its earliest days, the late 1780s, and the OED has a British citation from 1662. Of the other seventeen words on that list, seven have disappeared even from American conversation, which will happify many readers.[11]

Scow is a nautical term with Scottish and Irish roots, meaning a flat-bottomed boat; British sailors would probably call it a *lighter*. *Gubernatorial* is normally used only in Britain when rarefied political pundits start discussing the election of state governors

---

11 But what a shame we lost *slangwhanger*: a loud-mouthed journalist or politician.

in even-numbered Novembers. *Christianization* is largely obsolete, mainly because the movement is in the other direction: *de-Christianization* might be a different matter. *Constitutionality* is certainly accepted as an English word, though of its nature more used in reports from the US. The other six, including of course *awful*, are used every day wherever English is spoken: even in countries where *slush* is not a feature of the weather, there are plenty of other usages slushing about.

Even if we accept Burchfield's contention that 1820 was the year the wind changed direction, the breeze was still fickle and untrustworthy. There was no oral long-distance connection. American books were only just starting to be read in quantity. Daily newspapers were in their infancy, and reports from American papers haphazard. So it took a while for words to arrive.

But they came. *Constitutionality* had indeed already been mentioned in the House of Commons, in 1810. *Christianization* was used by a speaker at a Scottish church meeting in 1838.

Deputize is complicated: Pickering defined it as what we now call *depute*, i.e. appointing someone as one's own deputy. But, either way, it did not appear in *The Times* until a classified ad in 1895 announced that another new and startling trick had been added to the repertoire at the Egyptian Hall, 'England's Home of Mystery', but that 'Mr. Douglass Beaufort, the accomplished Professor of Sleight-of-hand, will to-day deputize for Mr. Devant, who is indisposed.'

Both *squiggle* and *squirm* appear to come from English dialect words meaning to move around like an eel (or maybe a worm). *Squirm* began to appear in print in Britain in the late nineteenth century: a letter writer to *The Times* in 1890 thought it would be a good word to 'express the progression of electricity'. But later in the decade it began to find its true destiny: as a word for the movement of politicians confronted by difficult facts.

Squiggle did not return to Britain until the 1920s. *Slush* is a more puzzling case: maybe it's not any kind of Americanism – one would imagine the English had always needed a word for sloppy snow, and the *Observer* used it confidently enough to describe what the crowds were standing in to see the King of Prussia's visit to London in 1842. We will return to the story of *lengthy* later.

This is just a snapshot of some fairly random examples. Like every human, every word has its own story, sometimes simple and transparent, sometimes complex and opaque. In addition to the words and phrases in the text, a full-as-possible list of other Americanisms now in current British use is in Chapter 8, starting on p. 201 with a further selection of words from Pickering.

One phrase Pickering missed out was *on paper*, as opposed to in practice: George Washington said it in 1795, thirty-nine years before the first British reference. And he could have added *cache* from the French *cacher*, to hide, which came out of the 1804 Lewis and Clark expedition into the west, and came to Britain about half a century later. He did include a fair few other words whose American credentials seem dubious.

Webster said his 1828 dictionary included only fifty actual Americanisms, though his definition was the one used in the constitution for presidents: they had to be native-born. These were mostly the basics, like *skunk*, *hickory* and *chowder*. Webster's cultural nationalism had faded by this time. He had made his declaration of linguistic independence in youth; the dictionary was his peace treaty. He now increasingly saw his work as reversing the consequences of the Tower of Babel (he had an obscure theory), having spent most of life building a new one.

However, at this stage British and American English were still very close together. And Lewis and Clark played a greater role in changing that than anyone chained to a desk. Because the settlers who followed the explorers into the West would just head on out there and plant themselves great rolling fields of vocabulary, as far as a man could see.

2

AHOY THERE!

When things got too hot for him at home politically, the English countryman and radical William Cobbett moved to the United States. This happened on two separate occasions, the first coming in 1792. He was not quite as enamoured of the new democracy as might have been expected. 'The country is good for getting money if a person is industrious and enterprising,' he wrote from Pennsylvania to an old friend.

> In every other respect the country is miserable. Exactly the contrary of what I expected. The land is bad – rocky – houses wretched – roads impassable after the least rain. Fruit in quantity, but good for nothing. One apple or peach in England or France is worth a bushel of them here. The seasons are detestable. All burning or freezing. There is no spring or autumn ... The people are worthy of the country – a cheating, sly, roguish gang.

Cobbett had to go back into exile twenty-five years later. 'There are two things ... which are almost wholly wanting here, while they are so amply enjoyed in England,' he wrote this time. 'The singing-birds and the flowers. Here are many birds in summer, and some of very beautiful plumage. There are some wild flowers, and some English flowers in the best gardens. But, generally speaking, they are birds without song, and flowers without smell ... No daisies, no primroses, no cowslips, no blue-bells and no daffodils.'

It was a little unkind; no doubt he was homesick. But it does touch on a particular distinction between the two countries, exacerbated during the push west, that is evident to this day. It can be summed up in two American words that still do not exist in the same way in British English, except perhaps in a property developer's PR brochure: *improvement* and *betterment*, often used in the plural. Both were noted by Pickering, though *improvement* may have been used in this sense in England from the Middle Ages by landlords seeking to enclose their lands to exclude the peasantry. *Betterment* ('an act of improving property, to an extent which enhances its value' – OED) looks like a pure Americanism.

As the settlers moved westward,[1] they chopped down forests, cleared and cultivated the land, built houses, towns and great cities, and shot and ate the native fauna, without pausing for rustic sentimentality or second thoughts. Thus the passenger pigeon went from being probably the most numerous bird on earth circa 1814 to extinction in 1914. Thus the bison (and the native American) almost suffered the same fate.

In the modern US, there is very little land that can be regarded as countryside, in the idealised English sense. There is land that people own, to improve or not as they please. There is agricultural land. There is still wilderness across the great shaggy continent, especially west of the Mississippi, though whether it should be allowed to stay that way is a matter of political debate. There are even, in pockets of well-heeled liberals, English-style NIMBYs. But there is an essential presumption that development = betterment which does not exist in crowded Britain. The aim of the computer game Sim City is to develop a large city from scratch by attracting as many people as

---

1 Indeed, right from the get-go.

possible without going bankrupt. A British version would try to keep them out.

This has its roots in the fear of the unknown that afflicted early settlers like Mary Rowlandson. American land, essentially, is there to be actively used, not passively admired as in Britain. For the pioneers, this was a matter of survival. The natives had to be neutralised; the fauna had to be eaten; the forests had to be felled. America had to be subdued before it could be shaped to the white man's needs. The alternative was death.

One telling indication of this seems to be the word *dirt* for soil, which has never taken hold in Britain. The implication of that word is that here is something vaguely unpleasant. The US is still not a country of gardeners the way Britain is.

Part of this difference is a function of the conditions. The American climate has none of the gentle inflections, the apologetic reticence, of the English weather. When it gets cold, it gets cold; when it is hot, it is hot; when it snows, thunders or rains, it does so with full, often frightening, gusto. There are hurricanes and tornadoes. Perhaps that helps explain the American character. They wear their emotions on their sleeves; if they like you they say so, and if they don't, they say that too. They are not wholly without euphemism, hypocrisy and dissimulation, but those characteristics too are on a grander scale compared to Britain's casual evasions.

Indeed, everything is on a grander scale, and not just the land and the weather: the beauty, the ugliness; the wealth, the poverty; the crime, the generosity; the problems, the solutions. To early readers back in little old England, this must have been a source of fascination, as it is now. And the vocabulary reflected this too. Using †*fall* instead of *autumn* seems to me one manifestation. American leaves really do fall, in heaps, often in a matter of days. In Britain it is a much gentler, more erratic process: subtly beautiful but less spectacular.

After 1800 a growing number of British visitors came to the US and many of them wrote about it in much-noticed books with varying degrees of enthusiasm or contempt. To readers back home the prime response must have been how exciting it all sounded. As it still does.

Certain other themes of these books were general, and still

applicable. The writers noted, mostly approvingly, the Americans' exceptional devotion to hard work and, less approvingly, the obsession with money. They noted that Americans ate a lot but without obvious enjoyment. 'They eat with the greatest possible rapidity, and then in total silence,' said Frances Trollope, mother of the novelist Anthony.

'I never saw any people who appeared to live so much without amusement as the Cincinnatians,' she added from Ohio. 'Billiards are forbidden by law, so are cards. To sell a pack of cards in Ohio subjects the seller to a penalty of fifty dollars. They have no public balls, excepting, I think, six, during the Christmas holydays. They have no concerts. They have no dinner-parties.' This undercurrent of workaholic joylessness can also still be observed.

'The most striking circumstance in the American character,' wrote the Scottish naval commander and traveller Basil Hall, 'was the constant habit of praising themselves, their institutions, and their country, either in downright terms, or by some would-be indirect allusions, which were still more tormenting.' Again that has not changed much.

The visitors also of course noticed the differences in language, as modern travellers still do. Among them was Charles Dickens, who made his first visit to America in January 1842, still short of his thirtieth birthday but a literary star ever since the serialisation of *The Pickwick Papers* in 1836. The result was his first full-length work of non-fiction, *American Notes*, in which Dickens got upset by American commercialisation and violence, as visitors still do, and also slavery and spitting, which have abated. He also had some fun with the vocabulary. In a manner we can now recognise as very Dickensian, he has a riff about an encounter with a waiter who, to Dickens's bafflement, keeps using the phrase **right away** when he ordered dinner.

'Right away?' said the waiter.

After a moment's hesitation, I answered, 'No,' at hazard.

'Not right away?' cried the waiter, with an amount of surprise that made me start.

I looked at him doubtfully, and returned, 'No; I would rather have it in this private room. I like it very much.'

Dickens only cottoned on when someone explained it meant

directly. The phrase *right away* was used in Britain as in 'getting right away from somewhere' but not to mean 'immediately'. And there is evidence that this secondary usage was for the rest of the century understood as a characteristic Americanism, as we might consider *Gee!* or *Say!*

Commander Hall told the story of visiting a girls' school in New York, where the mistress asked him to choose a passage for her pupils to read. He opted for Thomas Campbell's *Hohenlinden*:

The combat deepens. On, ye brave,
Who rush to glory, or the grave!
Wave, Munich, all thy banners wave!
And charge with all thy chivalry!

'On being asked my opinion as to how they exhibited,' Hall reported, 'I merely said that the girls read with a good deal of expression and feeling. But I suppose there was something in my tone which did not quite satisfy the good schoolmistress; for she urged me to criticise any thing I disapproved of.' The silly old fool took the bait.

'"Pray," said I, "is it intended that the girls should pronounce the words according to the received usage in England, or according to some American variation in tone or emphasis?"' The teacher insisted that the school was very hot on the subject and followed the dictates of the Englishman John 'Elocution' Walker, whose rulings were taught on both sides of the Atlantic. She hoped this met with his approval: 'Pray mention it, sir, if you think otherwise.'

So he did, and told her that where he came from, combat was pronounced *cumbat* and chivalry *shivalry*. Which was a combative response rather than a chivalrous one.

Backing down a bit, he added: 'We poor Scotch folks yielded up our opinions on all such points to the English.'

'You in Scotland may do as you like,' she replied magisterially, 'but we Americans have a perfect right to pronounce our words as we please.'

And herein lies the paradox. On one level, the Americans, still insecure, wished to be told what was right. On the other hand, pride and a wish for self-sufficiency led them in a different direction. These contending forces both grew in strength as the young men headed west. Here the conditions would be more extreme and even more thrilling.

The process inspired Mencken to glorious patriotic lyricism. These pioneers were

> youngsters filled with a vast impatience of all precedent and authority, revilers of all that had come down from an elder day, incorrigible libertarians. They swarmed across the mountains and down the great rivers, wrestling with the naked wilderness and setting up a casual, impromptu sort of civilization where the Indian still menaced. Schools were few and rudimentary; there was not the remotest approach to a cultivated society; any effort to mimic the amenities of the East, or of the mother country, in manner or even in speech, met with instant derision. It was in these surroundings and at this time that the thoroughgoing American of tradition was born.

Well, up to a point. Hereabouts several American linguistic habits took wing, including the practice of creating new compound words. It may actually have started in the early days of Massachusetts when the Puritan minister Increase Mather wrote of the **back-log**: a large log at the back of the fire to help keep it going (the metaphorical uses come much later). Now these were *back-settlers* in the *back-woods* of the *back-country*. Here also developed the unruly habit of making nouns from verbs and vice versa.

Certainly the westerners brazenly made up words for fun, revelling in *tall talk*. If you *hornswoggled* (cheated) someone, or *honeyfogled* (ditto) them, you might give them a *sockdolager* (knock-down blow) designed to *exflunctiate* (destroy) them unless they *absquatulated* (absconded) first. Well, *jee-whillikins!* Some of these exuberances did survive in the US, at least for a time, and some have even made it to the fringes of British English, e.g. **spondulix** and **skedaddle**. There was probably a great deal of *hornswoggling* and *skedaddling* out there on the wild frontier with Davy Crockett in his coonskin cap. And for the American language, vintage years of fecundity lay ahead.

But in Crockett's world human fecundity was also an issue: women were in short supply, and that would remain the case throughout the push towards the Pacific. In all the best western films, the hero may be the scourge of bad men and red men but he is no match at all for the schoolmarm.

Long before the Wild West of global imagination emerged, gently ferocious females like the one Basil Hall encountered took charge across the frontier and imposed standards of their own. Even before Victoria ascended the throne in England the values associated with her assumed extreme form right across America. This also had its roots in seventeenth-century Massachusetts, where profanity was punished, and not pleasantly. ('Joseph Shorthose, for profane swearing, was sentenced to have his tongue fixed in a cleft stick, and so to continue for half an hour.') Later, the punishment was mere exclusion from polite society but the taboos multiplied.

According to Lincoln Barnett:

During the 1830s words like *bitch, boar, buck, ram, sow* and *stallion* virtually disappeared. The Biblical *ass* became a *jackass* or *donkey*; the bull became a *cow-creature* or *seed-ox*; and *manure* became *dressing*. In the domain of human anatomy, *belly* and *bosom* were not to be mentioned and a *leg* became a *limb*. The word *seat* was for a while more delicate than *chair*, but when it came into use as *backside*, the French *derriere* supplanted the anatomical *seat* and the *chair* returned to the parlour. A lady was *enceinte*, never *pregnant*. And one never *went to bed*, one *retired*.

Long before that, *cock* had become **rooster**, a word hardly used in Britain until the Rolling Stones picked up the Willie Dixon blues song 'Little Red Rooster' in 1964.[2] When the English novelist Captain Frederick Marryat visited Niagara Falls in 1837, he committed a shocking *faux pas* by asking a young lady if she had hurt her *leg*; he

---

2 If Mick Jagger had wanted to sound really raunchy to Americans, he could have gone for 'Little Red Cockerel'.

was supposed to say *limb*. Visiting an academy for young ladies, he discovered that the piano not merely had four limbs but that they were dressed 'in modest little trousers, with frills at the bottom of them'.[3]

In some circles, *shirt* was banned and *lady* replaced *wife* ('too frankly sexual' – Mencken). *Bosom* was somehow considered more acceptable than *breast*, but when, in 1833, Noah Webster bowdlerised the Bible, he used *breast* to avoid saying *teat*. In Leviticus 21:20 he opted for *peculiar members* in place of *stones*, which was in itself the King James version's euphemism for testicles.

Astonishingly, delicacy appears to account for the general American abbreviation of cockroach to *roach*. I had assumed that was mere familiarity, but according to a note in an 1837 translation of Aristophanes: 'Cock-roaches in the United States … are always called "roaches" by the fair sex, for the sake of euphony.' Euphony, ha!

Alongside all this came the self-censored swearwords like **darn** and *dang* and **golly**. According to J.R. Bartlett, whose 1860 glossary was an updated, extended and less censorious version of what Pickering had started, the phoney genteelisms were even more pronounced 'beyond the mountains', where the bull ceased to exist except as a *cow-creature, male-cow* and even *gentleman-cow* – yes, out there on the wild frontier, where men were men and, according to Mencken, instant derision lay in wait for the slightest hint of affectation.[4]

***

On the one hand the American language was born free. It saw off an attempt, promoted by President John Adams, to set up a French-style national academy. Adams's baby was indeed born: the American Academy of Language and Belles Lettres was established in 1820 to 'determine the use of doubtful words and phrases' and

---

3 There has always been some suspicion that Marryat was being teased, but the reality was strange enough.

4 Against that, *bloody*, taboo in Britain until Shaw put it on stage in 1914, was never used as an intensifier in the US and had no shock effect.

establish a 'correct, fixed and uniform language'. But it withered in infancy.

On the other hand the language was everywhere in chains. The incorrigible libertarians spent their schooldays chafing under the constraints, not so much of Webster's 1828 dictionary but of what everyone called his Blue-Backed Speller. This went through a stagger-ing 385 editions between its publication in 1783 and Webster's death in 1843. Another book that managed to be a huge bestseller without ever being liked was *English Grammar* by Lindley Murray.[5]

The two of them, with some help from 'Elocution' Walker, imposed their rules on generations of American children, to great effect. Even the snootiest English travellers often praised American diction and enun-ciation, partly because the language was more unified, without Britain's beautiful patchwork of sometimes impenetrable local accents which were considered marks of Cain by the London and Oxbridge establishment.

From colonial days, literacy rates were much higher among white Americans than in Britain. And there remains to this day a much greater respect for dictionaries – which usually means the latest product from Webster's heirs, Merriam-Webster – than in Britain.[6] The National Spelling Bee, for children up to 15, is nationally tele-vised and treated as a major event. The last six words in the 2016 competition were *Mischsprache, tetradrachm, zindiq, euchologion, Feldenkrais* and *Gesellschaft*.[7]

On a less rarefied level, American spelling may be helped by the habit of pronouncing difficult words more phonetically. This was noted in a series of lectures in the late 1850s by the philologist (also a US diplomat and pioneering ecologist) George P. Marsh. He attrib-uted this to the 'universality of reading in America'.

'Americans incline to give every syllable of a written word a distinct

---

5 Murray was a Pennsylvania Quaker who moved to Yorkshire, aged 39, because he believed the climate was healthier. He lived to be 80.

6 My A-Level English teacher, P.J. Hobson MA, who once settled a classroom argument in his favour by announcing 'Dictionaries are wrong', might have been arrested for heresy in some of the sterner American states.

7 All twelve winners between 2008 and 2016, including joint winners in the last three years, were from families of South Asian migrants. The youngest was 11.

enunciation,' he said, 'and the popular habit is to say *dic-tion-ar-y*, *mil-it-ar-y*, with the secondary accent on the penultimate instead of sinking the third syllable, as is so common in England.' Marsh then added, rather tartly: 'There is no doubt something disagreeably stiff in an anxious and affected conformity to the very letter of orthography.' In other words there was still a subconscious fear of being monstered by self-appointed experts, probably English.

***

The influence of the London literatocracy diminished as the nineteenth century wore on, with the American centre of gravity moving westwards and the whole country growing in population, power and confidence. But the British elite still raged, with increasing feebleness, against the neologisms the new country created. Four, in particular, caused longstanding resistance.

Jefferson's *belittle* failed to make the cut even for Webster in 1828 and had a long journey towards acceptance. But by the 1880s the leader-writers of the *Manchester Guardian*, under the sway of the fastidious C.P. Scott, were using the word as blithely as if it had come over with the Normans.

And then there was *lengthy*, another word whose American origins are beyond reasonable doubt: the Dictionary of American English has a citation for 1689 from Massachusetts: 'I very much fear a dreadfull, lengthy, wasting Indian war.' Pickering, ever embarrassed about Americanisms, pronounced: 'This word has been very common among us, both in writing and in … conversation; but it has been so much ridiculed by Americans as well as Englishmen, that in writing it is now generally avoided.'

He spoke too soon, mainly because it is a damn fine word. It was not and is not an unnecessary synonym for *long*; it conveys the implication of *too* long. *Lengthy* was an especially apt word in the heyday of the verbose Victorians, when politicians and pedagogues rambled on interminably, and vicars had licence to bang on forever to a captive congregation, even when the summer sun was taunting them beyond the stained-glass windows.

British writers grasped *lengthy* with relish. 'The style of my grand-sire … was rather lengthy, as our American friends say,' wrote Sir Walter Scott in 1827.[8] 'He publishes what in America would be called a lengthy poem, with lengthy annotations,' wrote Robert Southey in 1838. The point was made most delicately by Mr Bennet in *Pride and Prejudice*: 'That will do extremely well, child. You have delighted us long enough.' But that was a lengthy way of putting it in itself. It was rather clever of the Americans to find a way of expressing the sentiment so succinctly.

British journalists also grasped it long before other Americanisms became general: *lengthy* was used in *The Times* in its very first year, 1785, when the paper was still called *The Daily Universal Register*. It could be a wonderful excuse for saving space: 'Mr Heneage, MP for Grimsby, in a lengthy and most elaborate speech, defended the Whig administration,' it reported in 1842.

No.3 on the list was †*influential*, which engendered less hatred than the other words and was certainly not born in America. The OED has uses back to 1570, mainly referring to the effects on earth of the heavens, natural or supernatural. But it seems to have been little used until it crossed the ocean and acquired a new, sinister undertone, implying political influence, and corrupt influence at that. Hence the modern American phrase, coined circa 1949, *influence-peddling*.

The very first use of *influential* in *The Times* is in a letter alleging 'secret influential authority from other quarters' in 1787. The word then apparently vanishes again in England before returning mostly as a neutral adjective, while retaining the hint of skulduggery in the US – a rare case of divergence.

Nothing whatever can match the arguments that took place in Britain in the mid-nineteenth century over the seemingly innocuous word †*reliable*, now living in contented anonymity in all our vocabularies. It was widely denounced as (a) American, (b) philologically improper and (c) useless – all argued with a vehemence that now beggars belief. In the language wars, the Battle of Reliable ranks with Balaclava and The Somme for bloodthirsty pointlessness.

---

8 While we're on the subject, Scott's books are rather lengthy too.

Sir William Craigie (1867–1957), the Scotsman who was an editor of the OED before moving to Chicago to edit the (normally reliable) Dictionary of American English, pronounced: 'This word was once thought to be an Americanism'. This brings us back to the recurring question of what we mean by an Americanism. *Reliable*'s first known appearance is in a Scottish work of 1569. But it was a great rarity until the nineteenth century.

The reference that allegedly proves its legitimacy as a continuing word in British English is from the young Samuel Taylor Coleridge in 1800: 'The best means and most *reliable* pledges of an higher object'. But Coleridge was actually reporting parliament at the time, for the *Morning Post*. It was a quote from the prime minister, the younger Pitt, who might have picked it up from anywhere. And the quote may not have been, well, reliable.

By 1800 reporters had recently been granted the right to take notes in parliament. But their working conditions were terrible: they had to queue with the public to stand with the throng and often never got inside at all so had to beg others to tell them what happened. 'I have not a moment's time, and my head aches,' moaned Coleridge. The reports seem to have resembled a precis at best, or more likely an imaginative reconstruction. *The Times* did not report the word *reliable*. So this tyro reporter may have misheard; he may have misremembered; very likely he was summarising in his own way.

In the 1790s, when revolution was in the air, Coleridge was obsessed with America, and in particular the scheme he cooked up with Robert Southey for a settlement there based on socialist principles they called 'pantisocracy'. Coleridge claimed to have been abused and threatened in a Welsh pub for proposing a toast to George Washington.[9] I reckon Coleridge was just overdoing his American pash.

In fact this early British debut of *reliable* looks like a complete outlier. In *The Times* and *Sunday Times* the word appears only in raw

---

9 Coleridge changed tack in later life. He once complained that the *Newgate Calendar*, the record of London executions, had at some point become unobtainable: 'as they had all been bought up by the Americans, whether to suppress the blazon of their forefathers, or to assist in their genealogical researches, I could never learn satisfactorily'.

overseas reports, nearly all from North America, until 1846. The *Man-chester Guardian* does have a couple of lonely references but after 1848 *reliable* pops up all the time, often in conjunction with *sources*. All of which suggests the characteristic migration pattern of an American word.

But still this one had a disreputable whiff. In his 1864 book *The Queen's English*, Henry Alford, prolific author and Dean of Canter-bury, complained: '*Reliable* is hardly legitimate. We do not rely a man, we rely upon a man; so that reliable does duty for *rely-upon-able*. *Trustworthy* does all the work required.'

From our perspective, this is arrant nonsense. Someone can be reliable without being trustworthy: they may turn up on time for work but still be suspected of raiding the petty cash. Or vice versa. And as the OED points out, in a rare piece of editorialising, a number of other words were already in use that took the *-able* prefix in the same way: *available*, *dependable*, *dispensable* and, appropriately enough, *laughable*.

The word's opponents did tend to tie themselves in knots. '*Rely-on-able* is too gross; but *reliable* is absurd. *Trustworthy* is English,' said a writer in the 1860 volume of that gloriously Victorian publication *The Literary Churchman*. The same year the same magazine, though perhaps not the same writer, described someone as 'probably more trustworthy, or, as our dreadful cockneys say, *reliable*'. In between, however, the phrase *reliable conclusions* crops up without apology or comment.

In 1877 the philologist Fitzedward Hall published a book with the catchy title *On English Adjectives In -Able With Special Reference To Reliable*, yet somehow never managed to come off the fence about the dreaded word: 'With no fairness can I be called its advocate. It is not the proper province of him who interests himself in philology, to do much more than assemble facts.'

The next word is †*talented*. In the 1830s it aroused the particular fury of the future prime minister Sir Robert Peel, who was convinced it was an American import. The *Philadelphia National Gazette* said Peel 'was right in protesting against the word, but wrong in his refer-ence. It is of London cockney derivation, and still more employed in

Great Britain than in America.' That was 1831. A year later the now very anti-American Coleridge weighed in: 'I regret to see that vile and barbarous vocable, *talented*, stealing out of the newspapers into the leading reviews and most respectable publications of the day. Why not *shillinged, farthinged, tenpenced* ... Most of these pieces of slang come from America.'

The OED suggests that Philadelphia was right to some extent: the dictionary has British references from 1500 to 1627, though it seems improbable that George Abbot, Archbishop of Canterbury, would have counted as a Cockney. The word then evidently disappears from written English, though the Irish orator Daniel O'Connell said it in 1813 and it crops up in other reports of speeches at the time. So it probably deserves its † as an emigrant–immigrant that came back from the US to Britain.

Finally, there is also the very strange case of *scientist*, a word that the world managed without for a surprisingly long time. When it did surface it was regularly accused of American parentage on the usual-suspects principle, and because it was much slower to gain acceptance in Britain. As late as 1890 the London *Daily News* called it 'an ignoble Americanism'. And it was firmly claimed for the US by Alistair Cooke in a BBC talk in 1935: 'Just about the purest American phrase you can say is *a reliable scientist*,' he asserted boldly.

However, *scientist*'s first public outing is now widely credited to the Cambridge University polymath William Whewell circa 1833, and it is almost certainly not an Americanism as such. Nonetheless, calling someone a *reliable scientist* could have earned you surprisingly dirty looks in the 1890s. From his home in Eastbourne the biologist T.H. Huxley proclaimed in 1894: 'To anyone who respects the English language, I think *scientist* must be about as pleasing a word as *electrocution*.'[10]

And *reliable* still generated extraordinary loathing. Another turbulent priest, this time an American, Bishop Cleveland Coxe,

---

10 The disdain for *scientist* is puzzling. But aside from the normal pedantry about Latin roots, the boundaries between science and philosophy were not yet clearly delineated, and it seems some people we would call scientists were reluctant to be pigeonholed.

denounced the word as 'that abominable barbarism' in 1886; and, as late as 1899, a letter writer to *The New York Times* insisted: '*Reliable* is still a vulgarism in English literary circles'.

***

The migration pattern of birds is famously and wonderfully mysterious even in an era when they can be tracked across the planet. The migration pattern of words is infinitely more baffling – especially in the nineteenth century when mass media as we now know them did not exist. But somehow the character of America, and its words, seeped into the British consciousness, with the help of New World pushiness and self-promotion.

In 1836 a life-size representation of a white American artiste, Thomas D. Rice, arrived at the Surrey Theatre, just south of the Thames, several months in advance of the man himself. The *pièce de résistance* of Rice's act was a song-and-dance routine long popular among slaves. Blacked up and dressed in tatters, he sang:

Fist on de heel tap,
Den on the toe
Ebry time I weel about
I jump Jim Crow.
Weel about and turn about
En do jus so,
And every time I weel about,
I jump Jim Crow.

News of Jim Crow had preceded him: imitators were performing their own versions in Britain soon after Rice became a star in the US in 1832. The man himself received enormous if not unanimous acclaim. The principal merit of the piece *Oh, Hush! or, Life in New York*, the *Manchester Guardian* reported, 'consists in affording an opportunity to Mr Rice, the American low comedian, to display his talents in exhibiting the characteristics of the lower order of Negroes'. The review concluded with dismay: 'The house overflows every night.'

By 1841 the social reformer Anthony Ashley Cooper (later the Earl of Shaftesbury) told the Commons that in Wolverhampton there were children with 'their minds as stunted as their bodies, their moral feelings stagnant', who in some cases had never heard of London, the Queen or Jesus. But they all knew Jim Crow.[11]

And then, in 1844, in strode America's greatest showman, P.T. Barnum, and his sidekick, 6-year-old Charles Sherwood Stratton, aka General Tom Thumb. Stratton lied about his age, or at least Barnum did: he doubled it to make his protégé seem even weirder.

Stratton was two feet tall, just as he had been when he was six months old. He could also sing, dance and do impersonations – and revel in the attention; he had already taken the US by storm. Barnum leased a fancy carriage and attracted matchless attention by parading the general himself on daily basis. The news reached the Queen, and a private performance followed at the palace, which was a great boon to ticket sales. Stratton returned to London as the General several more times, not necessarily adding much to the language but contributing a great deal to the public's gaiety and sense of America's freakishness.[12]

As far as the language is concerned, the power was still with the written word. And the most important influence of all in the first half of the century may have been a writer who was from not the US but Canada, is now almost totally forgotten (outside Canada), and in any case eventually moved to Britain and became a Conservative MP.

His name was Thomas Chandler Haliburton and he wrote stories about a small Nova Scotian town centred on the clockmaker, Sam Slick, who happened to be a Yankee. They appeared first in a local paper, and their teasing humour and simple wisdom just struck a chord. When the first volume of *The Clockmaker* came to Britain in 1837, the *Observer* predicted English readers would never understand

---

11 The phrase was to live on in the US as a code word for southern segregation long after Wolverhampton had forgotten about it.

12 This story is not necessarily an unhappy one. Stratton married a woman of his own height in 1863, and became exceedingly rich, reputedly even bailing out Barnum during a sticky patch. He died in 1883, at 45 and 3ft 4in. 'I adore my creator,' he once wrote. 'He has given me a small body, but I believe He has not contracted my heart, nor brain, nor soul'.

what Haliburton said. It was wrong. Slick touched a nerve about the outsider's perception of American characteristics: a bit over-shrewd in his business dealings and defiantly nationalistic ('The British can whip all the world, and we can whip the British!'). But he was also decent and kind and well-liked: 'It is done by a knowledge of soft sawder [flattery] and human natur,' Slick would say.

And the phrase 'as Sam Slick says' reverberated for a generation. It was attached several times in the papers to the term †*upper-crust*: the repentant *Observer* quoted him on this when the Queen opened the new Royal Exchange in 1844 and Haliburton gets the credit as the first user of *upper-crust* in both the OED and Bartlett's 1848 Dictionary of Americanisms. However, it also appears in a Northamptonshire glossary for 1854, so it is probably not an original Americanism. Nonetheless this does seem a case when the spread of a word can be attributed to a single writer.

In all, the OED cites Haliburton as a word source (not necessarily the first source) 349 times for words ranging from *absquatulate* to *yonecked*, many of which failed to travel or even survive, though others certainly did. We can probably give Sam Slick credit for popularising, if not inventing, ***beanpole*** (of a person), ***cave in, corker, lambasting, like a house on fire, lick*** (speed), ***like it or lump it, making tracks*** and ***that's the ticket***. He also may get some credit for ***large as life***, *mad as a hatter*[13] and *crying over spilt milk*.[14]

A turning point was coming. And if Sam Slick could have pinpointed the moment, he would have said something humorously swaggering to his Nova Scotian neighbours. Sometime in the late 1840s, around the 22 million mark, the population of the US overtook that of Britain. Two events seem to typify the change in the relationship this implied. The first was quite bizarre.

It involved the much-lauded English Shakespearean actor Charles Macready and his American rival Edwin Forrest, who were appearing in New York simultaneously in rival productions of *Macbeth*.

---

13 This certainly pre-dated Lewis Carroll: the makers of felt hats suffered from mercury poisoning.

14 Used by Jonathan Swift, but a century earlier.

Macready was the epitome of English poise and sangfroid; Forrest was the young nation's champion and its embodiment – rugged, over-exuberant and deeply insecure (earlier, he had turned up to hiss Macready at a performance in Edinburgh).

It was not just a personal feud. Their cause was taken up by American partisans, in print and on the street. In American cities theatrical disputes were the equivalent of British football or French politics: an excuse for a punch-up, a tradition that dated back at least to the Stamp Act riots of 1765. Theatre in general was a powerful medium for all classes in both countries, and Shakespeare was at its heart more, if anything, in the US than in little old Shakespeareland. It really mattered to the Americans who was the better Macbeth.

In 1849 Macready was playing at Astor Place, haunt of the upper classes. On 7 May Forrest supporters wrecked his performance by throwing everything except dead cats on the stage. Meanwhile, across town Forrest was being cheered to the rafters by his fan club – especially when he came to the lines

What rhubarb, senna, or what purgative drug,
Would scour these English hence?

Three days later the Forrestites rioted in Astor Place; the militia was called; they fired into the crowd; about two dozen dead.

Three years later and 3,000 miles away, it was London's turn to go berserk over an American writer. Nobody died this time. But by the end of 1852 the book's sales in Britain are thought to have topped a million; there is no way of being sure, because nearly all the copies were pirated. Even if you halve the figure, it is still astonishing in a country of 22 million people and far from universal literacy.

And that was just the start. There were 'paintings, puzzles, cards, board games, plates, spoons, china figurines, bronze ornaments, dolls and wallpapers'. And there were plays based on the text, often based very vaguely indeed – but dozens of them, each with different scripts, interpretations, characters and endings, like modern British pantomimes. And these productions reached out far beyond what we think of as the theatre-going classes, as Forrest had done to the football-fan Shakespeareans of New York.

The book was *Uncle Tom's Cabin* by Harriet Beecher Stowe, a completely American story using very American dialogue. The phenomenon was described, even in the staider papers, as 'Uncle Tom mania'.

Astor Place was an ending: of an era when America strove to beat the British at their own game, and got huffy if they could not outdo them. Uncle Tom was a beginning: of an era which has never ended, when every new American excitement would be seized upon by the world. Henceforth, the US would be happy to cede the lead role in Shakespeare to Britain. The British could have the past. The United States would dominate the future.

***

Uncle Tom played into various different aspects of British tastes and preferences in the mid-nineteenth century. One was that the Jim Crow phenomenon had mutated into a full-blown craze for black-face minstrel shows which lasted until the Civil War and beyond. They were just as popular in Britain and indeed lingered long after growing black consciousness did for them in the US.[15] Many of the classier songs were composed by the prolific New Yorker Stephen Foster – 'My Old Kentucky Home', 'Swanee River', 'Camptown Races', 'Oh! Susanna'. They remain part of the culture and, after the lyrics have been cleansed of racial epithets, the repertoire too.

At the Great Exhibition in Hyde Park in 1851 American exhibitors knocked British government officials, industrialists and the broader public back on their collective heels with displays of modern machines, like Colt revolvers and McCormick reapers. That was also the year Isaac Singer of New York patented the first practical sewing machine.[16]

---

15 *The Black and White Minstrel Show* remained on the BBC until 1978 and was still on stage in the provinces, in watered-down form, in the early 1990s.
16 Singer was a failed actor and had twenty-four children.

In 1858 the first transatlantic cable was connected, enabling American news to reach Britain in hours rather than days. Unfortunately, the cable broke almost at once, and it took another eight years to construct a serviceable replacement. The Civil War was fought in old-fashioned silence as far as British readers were concerned, and it took London five days to find out that Lincoln had been shot.

However, the new attachment to American novels, which began even before Uncle Tom, carried on. These books appealed not merely to British readers but to British publishers, since, as happened with Uncle Tom mania, the absence of international copyright agreements enabled them to go ahead without the tedious obligation of having to pay the authors.

Several of the biggest-selling nineteenth-century American novelists on both sides of the Atlantic are little known today, but they were equally little known to their readers' menfolk. Written by and for women, their books featured heroines who had to triumph over adversity to find a fulfilment which certainly involved both men and money but not at the expense of faith, purity, moral worth and self-reliance.

The most unstoppable of the writers was Emma Southworth, always known as E.D.E.N. Southworth.[17] Abandoned with two children by her own husband and beset by poverty and ill health, she began scribbling in the late 1840s; under the circumstances she did not need too much imagination for material or for the title of her first novel: *Retribution*. It was a huge success and the books kept coming; in 1877 there was a forty-two-volume collected edition, including her biggest winner *The Hidden Hand*:

'Oh, Mrs. Rocke, only last evening we were so happy – But if we have received good things at the hand of God, why should we not receive evil?'

'Yes, my child; but remember nothing is really evil that comes from His good hand.'

---

17 The initials (Emma Dorothy Eliza Nevitte) came when she was 5, as her father's dying wish.

Susan Warner's triumph, *The Wide, Wide World*, came in 1850. In 1854 came Maria Cummins's *The Lamplighter*, the uplifting story of the orphaned Gerty. ('Trash' – Nathaniel Hawthorne.) Fifty years later a survey of a Lancashire industrial community showed that the books most likely to be found inside the home alongside the Bible and *Pilgrim's Progress* included both *The Wide, Wide World* and *The Lamplighter*.[18]

None of these seemingly tiresome and didactic books added much to the British vocabulary, though Warner is credited with the first use of *floor-cloth*, as something to clean the floor rather than cover it. But they did heighten awareness of America among a huge chunk of the British population.

There were also books that must have crossed the gender divide. One was *Little Lord Fauntleroy* (1886) by Frances Hodgson Burnett, whose family emigrated from Manchester to Tennessee when she was a teenager. The title has passed into the language, although not necessarily in the way the author intended; Fauntleroy is remembered not as a brave, charming and compassionate all-American example to the aristocracy but as an effete prat. This was due to the illustrations, by Reginald Birch, showing him in black velvet and lace, even when riding a pony; thousands of late Victorian mothers insisted on dressing their embarrassed and perhaps permanently traumatised boys just the same. There was also *Ben-Hur*, by the soldier and politician Lew Wallace. This was another thundering bestseller, though even the author of the piece on Wallace in *American National Biography* calls it 'turgid'. The book's fame has long been eclipsed by the 1959 film.

As a poet, Longfellow, with his accessible tum-ti-tum rhythms, made more impact in Britain than Walt Whitman. The most enduring American novelists of the era, Herman Melville and Mark Twain, may also have been less influential than their reputation suggests. Twain was an early user of **shenanigan**, **pass the buck** and *rolling off a log* (in Britain, more often **falling off a log**) but seems to have played no major part in spreading them.

---

18 Special thanks to Dr Thomas Smith of the University of East Anglia for introducing me to this genre.

Twain's popularity derived above all from his place in the category known as the American humorists who, for reasons that now appear rather baffling, transfixed British readers in the mid-to-late nineteenth century. First came the *The Biglow Papers* by J.R. Lowell, a less winning New England-based variation on the Sam Slick theme; later there were the Artemus Ward stories by Charles F. Browne and, for children, the stories by Uncle Remus (aka Joel Chandler Harris): '*Brer Rabbit wuz gwine lippity-clippitin' down de road*'. In 1888 Matthew Arnold, in a celebrated attack on American culture and Twain in particular, in *The Nineteenth Century* magazine, complained that 'an addiction to the funny man' was 'America's national misfortune'. Modern readers might think the problem was that this stuff was just not very funny.

Did these books have an impact on the British vocabulary? The London editions of Lowell and Ward do have helpful glossaries provided by two well-placed authorities: Thomas Hughes, the author of *Tom Brown's School Days*, for the Lowell; and J.C. Hotten, an expert on slang, to decode Ward's self-conscious vernacular. Hughes thought British readers would not be aware of *grit* (as in *pluck*), which certainly made it to their vocabulary before 1900. Surprisingly he also included *blurt out*, *bust* (as in gone bust), *great shakes* and *whopper*, all of which were well used in Britain before this date. (A witness said 'he knows he's telling a whopper,' in a London court in 1834.) More convincingly, Hotten's list includes *tomarter*: '= tomato, a common table delicacy in the United States, partaken at almost every meal.' No wonder so many Britons emigrated.[19]

There was one category of writing on America that did touch the male imagination, and whose influence proved incalculable in creating the most powerful of all American mythologies. It harked right back to Mary Rowlandson and James Fenimore Cooper. It was an

---

19 Tomatoes were certainly known in Britain well before 1900, but only in the way that celeriac or calabrese are known today. There is a memorable passage in Flora Thompson's *Lark Rise to Candleford* trilogy, set in late-nineteenth-century Oxfordshire, about a pedlar trying to interest the villagers in his consignment of unfamiliar 'love apples'. Interesting that Ward called them *tomarters*, which is no longer the normal American pronunciation.

inescapable part of any 1950s pre-political-correctness boyhood. And to this day its legends lie deep in the global imagination. (Germany has a particular fascination with it all.) The Wild West was born not on horseback on the dusty trail but in the minds of men, some of whom had never been near the place.

Frontier themes were a staple of the dime novels that took off in the US in the 1860s. These would be translated into British English and formed part of the equivalent British craze, penny dreadfuls and shilling shockers. The most prolific and successful author was one Ned Buntline, which lightly disguised Edward Judson, one of the leaders of the Astor Place riots and always a bit of a scally. It was Buntline who, somewhere out west, met an army scout called William Cody, who told him his story, which was indeed pretty dramatic, though that was no reason not to embellish it further.

Buntline wrote a serial notionally about Cody for the *New York Journal*, though the anecdotes actually involved Wild Bill Hickok, not Cody, if they involved any real person at all. But hey. As the editor said in *The Man Who Shot Liberty Valance*: 'This is the West, sir. When the legend becomes fact, print the legend.' And Buntline taught Cody the value of that.[20]

For a while Cody spent his summers roaming the plains and his winters appearing back east in plays about men roaming the plains. By 1883 he had realised that doing it for real was worthless compared to doing it for fake, and so launched his Wild West Show. Four years later he headed for London aboard the steamship *State of Nebraska* along with '83 saloon passengers, 38 steerage passengers, 97 Indians [their place on the ship unspecified], 180 horses, 18 buffalo, ten elk, five Texan steers, four donkeys and two deer'. Foot and mouth regulations were waived by British officials, an early example of cultural cringe.

Buffalo Bill's show was to be the star turn of an American Exhibition that took up a huge site round Earls Court. His encampment was itself a major attraction, not least for the *upper-crust*, including Mr Gladstone and the Prince of Wales, along with the press, who

---

20 *American National Biography* says Cody was the subject of 550 dime novels in all.

could swallow the legends whole at a single bite. Cody, said the *Illustrated London News*, had shot 4,280 buffalo in a single year and in every pursuit on the frontier 'had achieved the distinction of being the bravest, the most thorough, the most active, the most chivalrous, and the most daring'.

Then the Queen, steeling herself to emerge from her by now long-established seclusion a month before her Golden Jubilee, requested a private performance. When the US flag was paraded in the ring, Victoria stood and bowed. 'We felt that the hatchet was buried at last,' said Cody. Victoria told him she would like to come again, and then she patted the painted cheeks of a pair of *papooses*.

The following month the prince appeared along with an assortment of visiting royals in town for the Jubilee. The kings of Belgium, Denmark, Greece and Saxony joined him in jumping aboard the Deadwood Stage while the Indians staged a mock attack. The prince, who had been taught poker by American diplomats, told Cody: 'You've never held four kings like these before.' 'Four kings and a royal joker,' replied the old gunslinger. Or so goes the legend. Thus here, in the heart of the British Empire and at its zenith, American confidence and classlessness were making their mark.

But as some historians have pointed out, the stars were not the bucking broncos or the red men or their papooses or even Buffalo Bill himself – but the Colt revolver and the Winchester repeating rifle, made by what was now known as the 'American System of Manufactures', which made it simple to produce precise, interchangeable parts.

The relationship between the two countries was now very different to the one which allowed the early-nineteenth-century British travellers to ponce around the infant country with their noses in the air. In the 1870s the transcontinental railroad enabled prairie farmers to get their crops to Europe at a competitive rate, sending British agriculture into a death spiral. Industrially, if Americans did not invent every single novelty, they always knew how to exploit them.

The US had vast acreage, a wealth of natural resources and a seemingly endless supply of cheap labour from the huddled masses yearning to breathe free (also exploitable). Plus, never forget, there was an ethos of hard work and positivity. All this made America's destiny obvious to any astute observer.

To many Londoners, Americans seemed even richer than they actually were, because those who travelled – like the modern Chinese – were the wealthy ones. They came as representatives of the new elite. The scions of the faded aristocracy regarded them with relish: one in ten of all marriages by peers or their sons between 1874 and 1910 were to Americans; they had a preference for either heiresses or chorus girls.[21]

Other Londoners regarded the big-shot visitors with the cold contempt of the underdog. 'Our trunks are supposed to be full of money,' complained one American in a letter to *The Times* after a stay in a posh hotel, 'and it is conjectured that my mission in life is to distribute that money among the surplus population of this "happy land".' The letter was signed simply A Victim.

A Victim did appreciate one waiter who paid 'a delicate compliment' to his nationality. He said he would *hurry up* breakfast and bring it *right away*. The implication is that these were still regarded as Americanisms and were known as such by worldly young men who planned not to spend their lives as waiters. Maybe this one was a keen Dickensian. It is hard to know exactly when these two phrases were given their British passports but *hurry up* was creeping into the papers by the late 1870s and *right away* had certainly been naturalised before the end of the century.[22]

The US was already making precise, interchangeable parts for the English language. And before the end of the nineteenth century, dozens more words coined – or popularised – in America, appear to have spread to Britain, passed their initial sale-or-return period and were starting to bed down within the national conversation. They are collected on p. 203.

In *American Notes* Dickens does a riff on one of the words in that

---

21 Lord Randolph Churchill opted for an heiress, Jennie Jerome. Just seven months after the marriage, in 1874, she gave him a son who became quite famous.
22 *Hurry up the cakes* was a catchphrase used by customers in New York restaurants from about the 1830s.

list – *fix*: 'It is the Caleb Quotem[23] of the American vocabulary,' he wrote, continuing:

> You call upon a gentleman in a country town, and his help informs you that he is 'fixing himself' just now, but will be down directly: by which you are to understand that he is dressing. You inquire, on board a steamboat, of a fellow-passenger, whether breakfast will be ready soon, and he tells you he should think so, for when he was last below, they were 'fixing the tables': in other words, laying the cloth. You beg a porter to collect your luggage, and he entreats you not to be uneasy, for he'll 'fix it presently': and if you complain of indisposition, you are advised to have recourse to Doctor So-and-so, who will 'fix you' in no time.

Dickens was susceptible to Americanisms before he set foot there. In *Pickwick Papers* he mentions a speech being 'unusually lengthy'; *Oliver Twist* (1838) has a *mighty fine* and there's an unusual use of *precious* as an intensifier in *The Old Curiosity Shop* (1841): 'blessed if he could make out whether he [Kit] was "precious raw" or "precious deep"'.

In 1886, when Dickens was no longer around to fight back, he came under attack from the American *reliable*-hater, Bishop Cleveland Coxe, who blamed him for picking up what Coxe considered to be the worst of the American language, making sport of it, and thus infiltrating it into British English:

> This writer came to America in search of the grotesque, and by putting everything he heard in tap-rooms, or among backwoods-men, into his books, he has debased his mother tongue. He sold his editions and raised a laugh from Land's End to Berwick-upon-Tweed, but mark the consequences. The slang which amused boys in the great schools, passed with them into the universities.

---

23 From a jolly piece of doggerel by George Colman the Younger (1808): 'I'm parish clerk and sexton here, / My name is Caleb Quotem / I'm painter, glazier, auctioneer / In short, I am factotum.'

At first they used these words and phrases with a smile equivalent to aerial quotation marks; but very soon the smile disappeared and the words were employed in serious speech. Great Nemesis! I have heard Americanisms in England which I have never heard in America.

But if people in Britain thought the American language was grotesque why on earth would they copy it? It seems quite obvious why Dickens and his Victorian readers latched on to Americanisms: they found in them a freshness, freedom and vigour that British English of that era often lacked. When a politician used an Americanism in an otherwise solemn speech the notation *[laughter]* quite often stands out amid the greyness of the reports.

Simply using a phrase like *greased lightning* made a politician sound a bit of a devil, but not too much of one, like a modern vicar saying 'silly arse' or 'Blimey'. In an era when there was a much bigger gap than there is now between formal and informal discourse, Americanisms provided a relatively safe but rather exotic means of bridging it. That's why they caught on.

***

As every British schoolboy used to proudly declare, the credit for inventing the telephone belonged to the Scotsman Alexander Graham Bell, in 1876 – though Bell had long since gone to Canada and then the US, and later became an American citizen. The word *telephone* is much older, and was applied to a primitive contraption that could convey fog signals by compressed air forced through trumpets. *The Times* used the term – without embarrassment, hyphens or quotation marks – in 1844.

However, there was no doubt which country felt more at home with the new instrument. The ubiquitous American Thomas Edison soon invented a better telephone than Bell, using a carbon microphone, while simultaneously inventing the phonograph and the first practical light bulb. And American newspapers were languidly abbreviating telephone to *phone* from at least 1880 while, across the

Atlantic, the *Westminster Gazette* was still stiffly calling it a 'phone' in 1899.

Edison also won the battle about how to start a phone call. There was a serious problem about what to say when picking up the receiver when you had no idea who was at the other end. Since humans acquired speech, conversations had habitually begun with both sides having a rough idea who they were about to address. Not now. Was it a man or a woman? A friend or a stranger? Old or young? Socially superior or inferior? Secret lover or some desperate young man in a Bangalore call centre under orders to steal your life savings?

This would have been a particular problem for the British, with their habitual social unease. But every language would come to require a neutral word that could cover all telephonic eventualities, and each language had to find its own way round the problem. Edison started using *Hello*, which was already part of English but used more often to attract attention than as a routine greeting. Bell proposed *Ahoy*.

Very soon the women employed to make the manual connection between the two instruments became known, first in the US then in Britain, as *hello girls*. The first ahoy girl is still awaited, though Bell, bless him, continued using *Ahoy*.

Did *Hello* win because *Ahoy* was ridiculous, or do we think it's ridiculous because *Hello* won? Hard to say, but throughout the nineteenth century the Americanisms that permeated the British language did so largely on merit, because they were more expressive, more euphonious, sharper and cleverer than their British counterparts.

Edison's victory was a symbol, a harbinger: the American language would soon acquire new weapons to assist its spread. And the contest would no longer be a fair one.

Americanisms that arrived in Britain before 1900 but were not included in Pickering's collection are listed starting on p. 203.

3

YOU AIN'T HEARD NOTHIN' YET

It was 1901, which was generally regarded in Britain and America as the first year of the twentieth century. The Germans had got in first and greeted the dawn a year earlier:[1] the Kaiser marked the moment with a bellicose address to his troops in Berlin, which was a more accurate indicator of what was about to happen than the pious optimism of the anglophones.

As a turning point, 1901 proved more appropriate: before January was over came the death of Queen Victoria, who embodied a single century in the popular imagination more than anyone else in history. In September the very nineteenth-century figure of William McKinley was shot dead (the third assassination of an American president in thirty-six years), to be succeeded by the youngest of all presidents, the energetic and very twentieth-century Teddy Roosevelt.[2] In December a 27-year-old Italian, Guglielmo Marconi, waited in Newfoundland and received a wireless message in Morse code sent from Cornwall.

---

1 As all but extreme pedants did at the start of the twenty-first.
2 Roosevelt was 42; John Kennedy 43.

Also that year, an editorial writer in the *New York Evening Journal* set out what he perceived as the agenda for the new century:

The nations of Europe, and especially the English, wonder at the success of the American people. If any Englishman wants to know why the American race can beat the English race in the struggle for industrial precedence, let him stand at the Delaware-Lackawanna station, in Hoboken, from seven until nine in the morning.

It is one rush to business; it is one rush all day; it is one rush home again. The gauge on the American human being stands at high pressure all the time. His brain is constantly excited, his machinery is working with a full head of steam ... The American succeeds because he is under high pressure always, because he is determined to make speed even at the risk of bursting the boiler and wrecking the machine.

The Americans getting on the trains from Hoboken to New York were known as *commuters* (holders of commutation tickets), a word that did not become general in Britain until the 1950s. The only commuting that went on at all in Britain in 1901 was the somewhat random process by which the Home Secretary decided whether or not to commute a death sentence to life imprisonment.

The Hoboken station image, however, was picked up by the British editor and controversialist W.T. Stead in his book published the same year, *The Americanization of the World*. He also used a quote from that other quintessential Victorian, the former prime minister, William Gladstone, from 1878: 'It is America who ... will wrest from us that commercial primacy. We have no title. I have no inclination to murmur at the prospect. If she acquires it, she will make the acquisition by the right of the strongest; but in this instance the strongest means the best.'

Stead's aim was to secure a union of English-speaking states 'in the interest alike of the peace of the world and the liberties of mankind'. As far as political institutions were concerned, he had no doubt who would have to give ground: 'It is we who are going to be

Americanized; the advance will have to be made on our side; it is idle to hope, and it is not at all to be desired that the Americans will attempt to meet us halfway.'

Already, as Stead noted, the takeover of British companies and even castles was advancing fast. One American magazine ran a picture of the Houses of Parliament with the inscription: THE RESIDENCE OF MR JOHN B. GRABB, OF CHICAGO. And the Yanks were coming to the heart of London in reality as well as satire. A new underground line, the Central London Railway, opened in 1900, initially from Shepherd's Bush to Bank, backed by American money.

American railroads and British railways had their own vocabulary right from the start, as they do to this day. But on the Central the carriages were known, in the American manner, as *cars*, and they ran eastbound and westbound rather than up and down – up meaning towards the centre of London – which was used across the British railway network. Both these usages became the norm on the Underground. The new trains also had leather straps for standing passengers to hold, American-style. The term *strap-hanger* (now largely obsolete) had appeared in *The New York Times* in 1899 and reached its London namesake six years later.

The year 1900 also featured an American called Charles Tyson Yerkes (rhymes with *circus*) becoming chairman of the proposed Charing Cross, Euston and Hampstead Railway – what London now knows as the Charing Cross and Edgware branches of the Northern Line. Before he died in 1905, Yerkes also set about creating the Bakerloo and Piccadilly Lines and electrifying the District.

This was the culmination of an, um, interesting career. Yerkes's 2006 biography was entitled *Robber Baron* and revealed that the bed in the Louis XV room of his Manhattan mansion was decorated with a 'voluptuous nymph, nude and provocatively posed'. He had spent seven months in a Pennsylvania penitentiary and brought all kinds of aggressive and dubious American business practices to staid imperial London.

According to the railway writer Andrew Martin, Yerkes's trains also had guards called *conductors*, as in the US; an American system of electric power; American *elevators* and *escalators*; and American-style hours of operation – not quite the twenty-four-hour service of New York, which would take more than another century to reach London, but at least nineteen or twenty hours a day. Previously, many lines even closed for a 'church interval' before lunchtime on Sunday. Many of Yerkes's backers were American. They lost most of their money – someone had to pay for the nymph – and the tube system eventually reverted to *guards*[3] and *lifts*. But the London Underground as we know it was substantially Yerkes's creation.

The Americans were everywhere now. In 1909 Commander Robert Peary claimed to have reached the North Pole and sent what the *Manchester Guardian* called a 'delightful' telegram to his wife: 'Have **made good** at last; have the old Pole.' The paper's Miscellany columnist pointed out that, while *making good* one's words, promise or position had long been common in Britain, Peary's intransitive use was novel, but might catch on. And so it did.

'Lately we have become very apt pupils of American phrase makers,' the column continued, throwing in as further examples it's **up to** someone to do something; **up against** an opponent or a problem; and **out for**, as in blood. It concluded: 'Our recent readiness to adopt Americanisms is not an unhealthy tendency if we adopt them not as mere novelties and slang, but for their liveliness and force. Perhaps it would be a still healthier sign to make a few new idioms for ourselves.'

This was an eminently sensible point. Over in the book columns, however, reviewers were chuntering on about Americanisms in the spirit of their pre-Victorian forebears. There was no arrogance or passion in the comments any more; these were just routine grumbles, as though about misprints or the weather. Their heart was no longer in the fight. And often the words they hated were not necessarily Americanisms at all.

In 1906 the *Guardian* reviewed *Vikings of the Pacific* by Agnes Laut, a study of the explorers of the American West Coast. 'Miss Laut

---

3 Before they were abolished. Where guards remain on the national rail network the companies are now inclined to call them *train managers*, which is US-style title inflation.

writes a somewhat hysterical style,' sniffed the anonymous complainant, 'and her use of Americanisms is to be deprecated. The words *dare* (for daring or courage) and *respectable-ize* (for the act of making neat) are hardly fitted for the historical writer.' True, the words are not elegant and they did not catch on. On the other hand, Laut was American (to be precise, Canadian) and was writing about an American subject. She was entitled to write in American (or at least Canadian).

It was very common and more legitimate for reviewers to complain about translations from foreign languages that were aimed at American readers rather than British ones.[4] In 1911 *Das hohe Lied* (Song of Songs), a novel by the German writer Hermann Sudermann, was withdrawn in Britain after complaints were made to Scotland Yard about the sexual references in the translated version. The publisher canvassed various prominent authors for their views. 'If I were inclined to be flippant,' replied Eden Philpotts, 'I should say that the only things obscene therein were the Americanisms of this translation.' Thomas Hardy also complained about 'the rawest American' of the words rather than the raw sex. And in 1913, a new version appeared to deal with all the objections.

Even the American ambassador, Whitelaw Read, had a go about Americanisation of the language: 'The degradation would be less threatening if we in England had a little less cordial admiration for American slang,' he said in a speech in 1906.

That same year came the first edition of what is regarded as one as the classic works on the language, *The King's English* by the Fowler brothers, Henry and Francis. Their position on Americanisms in general was firm, clear and (in my judgment) sound: 'Americanisms are foreign words and should be so treated. To say this is not to insult the American language.' In particular they deal sternly but fairly with the ever-recurring argument about Americanisms being 'good old English'. It is true, they said, that *I gesse* [aka *I guess*] is used by Chaucer, 'but though it is good old English, it is not good new

---

4 This is a problem that has worsened as the gap in size between the American and British markets has widened.

English. If we use the phrase ... we have it not from Chaucer, but from the Yankees, and with their, not his, exact shade of meaning'.

The Fowlers then veered off into matters of personal taste, as one does. They actually preferred *fall* to *autumn*. But they disliked ***standpoint***, ***right along*** and ***just*** (meaning quite or indeed), which have squeezed through their objections into everyday English.

They also had a villain, a most improbable one, so improbable that in an Agatha Christie novel, he would undoubtedly turn out to be the murderer. They started by praising his greatness as a writer and as a patriot. Then the denunciation began. 'His influence is probably the strongest that there is at present in the land; but he and his school are Americanizing it.' In the conservatory, with the silken rope, the murderer's name ... was Rudyard Kipling.

Actually, I believe the Fowlers had the right man for the wrong reasons. Their objection was to Kipling's style which, they said, 'exhibits a sort of remorseless and scientific efficiency in the choice of epithets and other words that suggests the application of coloured photography to description; the camera is superseding the human hand'. They picked out one sentence: 'Between the snow-white cutter and the flat-topped, honey-coloured rocks on the beach the green water was troubled with shrimp-pink prisoners-of-war bathing.'

It is certainly a bit overegged, with the four different colours. According to the Fowlers, this constitutes the 'brief and startling exhaustiveness' that they denigrate as efficiency. But that is not Kipling's real crime. The evidence for that is in the OED, where he is quoted as a source for a word 4,450 times, which knocks Sam Slick's 349 into a cocked hat. In a remarkable number of cases, Kipling is the first British source for what was until then an Americanism.

Kipling was widely travelled, not least in the US; he lived in Vermont for several years in the 1890s, a period which produced *The Jungle Book*, *Mandalay* and 'Gunga Din'; his spirit was in the tropics while the New England snows piled up outside his study window. But his life was in America, and not surprisingly he picked up some of the language. Dickens's use of Americanisms was knowing and deliberate; in Kipling's case it looks subconscious.

He certainly played some role in spreading ***back number, bite the*** *bullet*, *crowd* (meaning set of people), *cut corners*, *hogging*, *monkey around*, *paint the town red*[5] and *plumb* (as an intensifier). These are not useless words and phrases – there will be plenty of those later. Nor was he especially influential: Kipling used the word *commuter* without the British taking advantage for another half-century. There was another, even more improbable, writer coming up behind who had a far more serious effect on the way English was spoken. We will talk about him shortly.

Many of the Americanisms that reached Britain as the Victorians morphed into Edwardians came from new American-led technologies and innovations. The language of motoring, like that of train travel before it, went its own sweet way in the different countries, and the same happened with another new technology: in 1877 Edison invented the *phonograph*. Ten years later Emile Berliner, a German migrant to the US, came up with the *gramophone*, which used discs instead of cylinders. Although Berliner's technology prevailed, the Americans generally stuck with Edison's word while the British did not.

However, in the Edwardian era, the British started to get the idea about *radiators* and *refrigerators* even if they could not afford to buy them. The British also acquired a taste for *department stores*, and began to understand the concept of *big business*, even though they were not especially good at it.

The cultural forces that would reshape the English language soon enough were just gathering strength at this stage. Blues music attracted public attention from around 1910; the tango was the hot dance of 1913. The lexicographer Susie Dent has retrospectively listed a Word of the Year starting in 1904, when she chose the adjective *hip* in its modern meaning. There is no sign of it reaching British English until much later but the American writer George Hobart in 1904 certainly does have a character saying 'Are you hip?'. *Blues* was Dent's word for 1912.

For 1913 it was, startlingly, *Celeb*. This, the OED confirms, was first

---

5 He actually used the phrase 'paint the town vermillion', which is better than shrimp-pink.

recorded among undergraduates at Smith College in Northampton, Massachusetts in two separate copies of the *Smith College Monthly* in 1907 and 1908. Growing up in Northampton, England half a century later, I swear I never heard the word. Not that we came across many celebs.

Celeb, however, was born at the wrong moment for fast trans- mission. Dent's word of the year for 1914 was *Cheerio*, a chillingly apt choice. This is surely not an Americanism, nor did Americans need it as much as the British that year. The first reference in the OED is from a letter written by Rupert Brooke in November 1914: 'Cheeryo! (as we say in the Navy)'. He died of an infection six months later. The second reference is from the song 'Good-bye-ee' dated 1917, by which time the lives of millions of other young men – some of them as handsome and gifted as Brooke himself – had been destroyed: 'Bonsoir, old thing! Cheerio! Chin-chin! Nahpoo! Toodle-oo! Good-bye-ee!'

***

In July 1916, as the Battle of the Somme raged beyond the ocean, President Woodrow Wilson addressed the first World's Salesman- ship Congress in Detroit. His audience comprised 3,000 of America's growing class of executives, managers and salesmen, much of the rest of the world being otherwise engaged.

The president was in inspirational mood. 'Lift your eyes to the horizon of business ... let your thoughts and your imaginations run abroad throughout the whole world.' He had practical advice too: 'Study the tastes and needs of the countries where the markets were being sought and suit your goods to those tastes and needs.'

Then his speech took wing: 'And with the inspiration of the thought that you are Americans and are meant to carry liberty and justice and the principles of humanity wherever you go, go out and sell goods that will make the world more comfortable and more happy, and convert them to the principles of America.' Three months earlier, the old Irish Republican motto 'England's extremity is Ire- land's opportunity' had been used to telling effect during the Easter Rising. Now Wilson was saying that Europe's extremity was America's opportunity. It was becoming, in Victoria de Grazia's phrase 'a great imperium with the outlook of a great emporium'.

During the war itself, American language probably had less influence in Britain than at any other time in the twentieth century. The US did not declare war until April 1917 and its troops only passed through Britain in numbers for a year, mostly rapidly. The neologisms of the war were minted nearer home, though *whizz-bang* was used in the US to mean firework long before it became a German shell.

In 1927 W.E. Collinson, who was Professor of German at the University of Liverpool for forty years, wrote an extremely useful guide to the changing nature of English based mainly on his own authentic-sounding recollections. He believed that during the war the British found time to absorb *attaboy*, *beat it*, *a big noise*, *a dead cinch*, *dope* (for drugs), *hunch* (an inkling), *hot air* (human not balloon) and *stunt* (performed by aviators and newspapers).

Other words and phrases that appear to have shed their American origins and been accepted in Britain before 1920 are on p. 201.

***

No one really knows how many people died in the First World War, even to the nearest million or so. And the consequences touched everyone: Britain became an entirely different place. Everything that felt remotely Victorian went out of fashion, from oratorios to facial hair. The young women gained new confidence, having been forced into workplaces where females had never previously set foot.

And they needed that confidence: they could no longer sit back, simpering and swooning, waiting coyly for the next dance; the ratio between the sexes had been drastically altered. So the old conventions broke down, including linguistic ones. Eliza Doolittle's cry of 'Not bloody likely!' would no longer cause the shock it did when *Pygmalion* was first staged in 1914 even if, in genteel homes, it would still be referred to as 'Not Pygmalion likely!'

When the whizz-bangs fell silent, the United States was in control of the blasted field: its economy unruined, its currency strong, its ambition boundless. US investment in Europe doubled in the 1920s and American brand names also became part of the vocabulary: Ford, Kodak, Woolworth's.

When America entered the war Wilson had put one of his aides, George Creel, in charge of an inchoate propaganda machine, selling the war to the folks at home and dropping leaflets behind enemy lines, but also establishing a continuing policy of national PR: sending the film stars overseas on goodwill missions and bringing journalists over to the US to be awestruck.

In Weimar Germany for instance, in the words of the cultural historian Richard Pells, America was summed up by the word *Fordismus*, in theory just a means of mass production, but also 'a savage but riveting and sometimes contradictory mixture of skyscrapers, slums, urban violence, organised crime, smoke-belching factories, Puritanism, sexual licentiousness, and raw human energy unmatched in the Old World'.

Between 1914 and 1945 the Old World, with a brief interlude in the 1920s, produced a series of horrors on a scale unmatched in human history. The US had a capacity to produce real-life dramas of its own, but of a type that could be comfortably and profitably fictionalised. Short of a storyline after the Civil War and the Wild West, they came up with the well-meant lunacy of prohibition, with its boundless opportunities for mayhem. But, since they faced no existential threat, the Americans also had plenty of chances to develop their new role as craze-makers to the world.

Britain, with its increasingly common language, was especially susceptible, and within a year of the war ending American influences permeated the country: the young were drinking *cocktails* and listening to *jazz*; the girls were discarding their whalebone, putting on *lipstick* and make-up, and bobbing their hair. And for the next decade successive American dance crazes would flood the country like great waves off the Atlantic, most memorably the shimmy, the Black Bottom and the Charleston, denounced by the *Daily Mail* as 'a series of contortions without a vestige of charm or grace, reminiscent only of Negro orgies'.

Increasingly, these were performed inside a *palais de danse*, a term that on the face of it represented an example, increasingly rare, of a borrowing from France. In fact it came straight from Chicago, where the first *palais* was opened in 1913 by an imaginative entrepreneur who thought the place would sound both sexier and classier with a French name.[6]

Barely six months after the Armistice there was one unquestioned achievement for Britain. The aviators John Alcock and Arthur Brown flew from Newfoundland to Ireland, completing the first non-stop transatlantic flight. As they crossed the Galway coast looking for a landing place, they were spotted by an audience of two: an Australian soldier on holiday and a local farmer's boy. 'We didn't do so badly, did we?' Alcock said after they landed.

The fliers collected a £10,000 prize from the *Daily Mail* and knighthoods from the king. But their names never quite left their mark on the world's consciousness. Alcock was killed when he crashed in fog only six months later; Brown lived on to enjoy a modest celebrity. Their names still crop up occasionally in pub quizzes, in Britain at least.

Eight years later, in 1927, another pilot, alone this time, took off from Long Island. Here is Alistair Cooke's account of his flight:

> The plane ... wobbled and bounced into the heavy skies, and that night forty thousand baseball fans in New York stood and prayed for its pilot. In Tokyo, at their midnight, people swarmed into the streets. The stock exchanges of London, Berlin, and Amsterdam interrupted regular quotations with the word – that there was no word. As the second night came on in Paris, an appeal went out to everybody who owned an automobile – which might be from seventy to eighty thousand, maybe – to head for a landing field at Le Bourget and line up in two files, switch the headlights on and thus create a visible shaft of white fog. Into it, thirty-three hours after just missing the telephone wires on Long Island, the strange plane trundled and stopped. It was engulfed by one hundred thousand Parisians. When they lifted the pilot out of the cockpit, if he had said he was Alexander the

---

6 The phrase was never used in France. A French dance hall became known as *un dancing*, borrowed from English and pronounced (more or less) as it would be in English. My thanks to the academician Sir Michael Edwards for this magnificent titbit.

Great, they'd have believed him. All he said was: 'I am Charles Lindbergh.'

Lindbergh came home to naval salutes, a ticker-tape parade up Broadway and *Time* magazine's first Man of the Year award. He also had a dance named after him: the Lindy Hop. He was probably the most famous man in the world until Hitler took power. Was his achievement substantially greater than Alcock and Brown's? Objectively, no. But these two flights represent the defining victory of American theatre over British understatement. And this was inseparable from the development of the language. The British essayist Basil de Sélincourt summed it up:

> The English of the United States is not merely different from ours, it has a restless inventiveness which may well be founded in a sense of racial discomfort, a lack of full accord between the temperament of the people and the constitution of their speech. The English are uncommunicative, the Americans are not. In its coolness and quiet withdrawal, in its prevailing sobriety, our language reflects the cautious economies and leisurely assurance of the average speaker. We say so little that we do not need to enliven our vocabulary and underline our sentences, or cry 'Wolf!' when we wish to be heard. The more stimulating climate of the United States has produced a more eager, a more expansive, a more decisive people.

But for most of the 1920s most people in Britain would still never have heard an American voice. If you worked in a great country house, in Harrods or Selfridges, or in a smart West End hotel, then yes, especially in that decade when American tourists became ever more visible. Otherwise most Britons would have had no first-hand idea what an American sounded like – at least until the early days of what the British, unlike the Americans, preferred to call a *wireless*, rather than a ***radio***.[7]

---

7 This finally changed with the arrival of the transistor radio, even though it was, unlike its predecessors, externally wireless.

And even then American voices would have been comparative rarities, once the freewheeling early days gave way to the monopoly of the BBC under the stern leadership of John Reith. There was no certainty that British broadcasting would take the distinctive and much-admired course it has done. And had the corporation's pioneering director-general been a more relaxed character, it is highly likely that the Americanisation process would have proceeded much faster than it did. As things turned out, the BBC was, and to a considerable extent remains, a bulwark of British distinctiveness.

Yet even so, the British voice was changing, and it may have started near the top. Robert Graves and Alan Hodge, in their social history of the interwar years *The Long Weekend*, said that in that period 'the "Mayfair accent" changed remarkably from an over-sweet rather French lisp to a rasping tone that had traces in it of Cockney, American and Midland provincial'.

The phrase 'Mayfair accent' is not often heard these days. The accent itself is less often heard. Instantly it conjures up the notion of an old-fashioned young man about town, probably silly and feckless, perhaps in a monocle, most likely played by the late Ian Carmichael, or Hugh Laurie before he reinvented himself – doubtless attended by an all-knowing butler. If there is a Typhoid Mary in the Americanisation epidemic of the 1920s the name of the No.1 carrier must be the creator of Bertie Wooster and Jeeves, P.G. Wodehouse.

Wodehouse first visited the US in 1904, aged 22. He wrote in his memoirs that he had always yearned to go there and saw it as a 'land of romance'. He immediately immersed himself in New York gangland culture, or at least the New York papers' accounts of it. Forever after, he either lived in the US or travelled there regularly, except in the period when, unable to escape from France, he was detained by the Nazis. After 1947 he was in America permanently, owing to his unfortunate decision, under duress, to make a series of light-hearted broadcasts about life as a captive, which were interpreted back home as treachery.[8]

Thus his imaginary England remained forever pickled in the

8 He was given a forgiveness-knighthood a month before he died, in 1975.

increasingly distant past, which, artistically, added to the delight of his later work. But as far as the direction of the language was concerned, he was always in the forefront. And indeed the essence of his prose was a mixture of Edwardian Mayfair slang, slightly mangled classical and scriptural allusions, his own dexterous wordplay and the latest Americanisms, all blended together with infinite charm. And the characters remained consistently beguiling and endearing over an astonishing span that lasted from 1915 to 1974. Dear old Plum.

However, in the particular matter of this book's narrow concerns his contribution, like his wartime broadcasts, may not have been entirely helpful. Wodehouse stands accused of being a prime mover in smuggling from America to Britain several hundred separate foreign words. He is quoted in the OED in 1,550 different entries, including dozens of American-bred words in which he was the first recorded user in a British context.

Various charges have been dropped owing to conflicting evidence, but more than three dozen look clear-cut. They are listed on p. 214.

The accused is obviously guilty, but there is a great deal to be said in mitigation. Many of these phrases may well have been in verbal use before Wodehouse put them in print: there was a far greater difference between what was said and what was written until about the 1960s. Part of his skill was to adapt demotic language into his books. And even before his exile, he had spent so much time in the US he probably lost any sense of what was American and what was British. Furthermore, m'lud, he was far from the only offender. Kipling we know about. But John Galsworthy, Conan Doyle, H.G. Wells, Dorothy L. Sayers ... they were all at it, if less voraciously.

In 1922 there was also an American literary sensation, when the UK edition of Sinclair Lewis's book *Babbitt* was published. *Babbitt* caused a huge impact with its desolate depiction of the amorality and vapidities of provincial American business and family life. But its vocabulary, the London publishers decided, was such that sheltered British readers needed a glossary, as in mid-Victorian times. This contained 128 words and phrases. Maybe a third have now long vanished, even from the furthest recesses of the Midwest; another third have never really travelled beyond the US, though would probably be understood easily enough in context.

The rest have passed lastingly into British English, although in many cases they still retain that little giveaway hint of an American accent. Some transferred by the end of the 1920s, perhaps with Lewis's help. Indeed, it is possible the glossary compiler was a bit behind the times even in 1922. *Babbitt* has deservedly remained in print, but without the glossary. Still, this list is a fascinating snapshot, and can be found on p. 215.

✳✳✳

What President Wilson cannot have fully envisaged is the extent to which his Babbitt-style salesmen would be helped in their quest to sell gadgets and *widgets* by an industry expressly dedicated to selling the American way.

Before the Great War the United States was only just starting to exert itself in the newfangled business of motion pictures. In 1907 the French company Pathé sold twice as much film footage in the US as all the home-grown companies combined. This started to change even before Europe's collective decision to commit suicide, and by 1917 the European film industries had pretty much collapsed, leaving America dominant in the market, as it would be for the following hundred years and, very likely, the next hundred years too.[9]

The public began flocking to the cinemas, and the stars – Douglas Fairbanks, Mary Pickford and Britain's own Charlie Chaplin – were mobbed when they visited London in the years after the Great War. Perhaps the public wanted not just to see them or touch them but to hear their voices, which was still technologically impossible through the medium of film.

The subtitles[10] of the silent era constituted an art form in

---

9 A position exemplified by the contemptuous Oscar handed out each year for 'Best Foreign Language Film', just after the make-up award and some time before the one for sound mixing.

10 Or to be precise, intertitles.

themselves – of a very particular kind, written by a tribe known as the 'came-the-dawners', for their most famous cliché. Looking back in 1942 the pioneering (female) film critic C.A. Lejeune said that the art of dialogue had not moved on much from the days 'when black letters on a white ground whispered "Oh, what one little glass of wine will do!" and white letters on a black ground promised, "Came the dawn."' What went on between wine and dawn remained unclear but the young man in the back stalls holding his neighbour's trembling fingers might have hoped she got the right message.

That much was universal. But the captions were written in American, and often caused a mixture of amusement, bafflement and irritation to British cinemagoers. 'Beatrix Esmond goes nix on the love-stuff' was one example which was widely quoted, being some way from the style of William Makepeace Thackeray, whose work was being mangled at the time. 'You've dribbled a bibful, baby,' in response to an outburst from a discontented heroine, was not very Victorian either.

It was through the captions, according to Professor Collinson, that the British picked up *uplift*, *highbrow*, *lowbrow*, *get wise*, *make a getaway*, *beat it*, *joint* (a bar) and *some* as an intensifier. And – a real sign of the future – *guys*. They also learned to understand that *stiff*, *boob* and *mutt* described some of the characters they were watching, and that the films constituted *sob-stuff* and *mush*, although these words stayed in Britain relatively briefly.

The influence of the silent films was not just verbal. The work of the Irish painter Mick O'Dea has been much influenced by the poses struck by the combatants in the Irish wars of the early 1920s. The way they wore their clothes, the facial expressions, the way they wielded both their cigarettes and their weaponry – the British and the Irish alike were all trying to pretend they were fighting the great American civil war of the 1920s, between G-men and bootleggers, rather than Ireland's brutal and messy imitation.

Hollywood's impact in the silent era, despite all the limitations, was still enough to alarm the British government. Throughout the decade the British film industry tried to make films of their own to appeal to the domestic audience. But American producers began selling their films in blocks: if cinemas wanted the latest transatlantic hit, they also had to show the rest of the product range, clogging the screens and denying access to home-grown competition. Just in case that plan faltered, the Americans started buying the cinemas.

In 1927 parliament imposed a quota system that made it a legal requirement for cinemas to give full-length British features 15 per cent of the screen time. Sure they showed them – first thing in the morning, usually. The films became known as 'quota *quickies*', made as cheaply as possible to fulfil the requirement. If they were promoted and shown in the evening as a supporting feature, the *Daily Mirror* reported, they were sometimes hooted off the screen.

Even so, in the 1920s the older generation appeared to take a mildly indulgent, good-humoured view of the youthful insistence on talking American. Too many of the young were dead; it could hardly hurt if the survivors had a little fun. In 1929 the *Manchester Guardian* held a competition for readers to offer their favourite slang phrases. These did not have to be American, though most were. Indeed, the paper gently lamented the complete absence from the entries of the old First World War slang – *Blighty, get the wind up* and *gone west*.[11]

Instead readers offered selections from the *Babbitt* glossary: *tight-wad, hitting the hay, lounge lizard, bonehead* and *tea hound* (a lounge lizard prior to cocktail hour). The prize (one guinea) for the most expressive list was awarded to D. Summerfeld of Levenshulme for

pain in the neck
†*get away with it*
let in on the ground floor
bump off
spill the beans
and *bats in the belfry.*

---

11 Which one might assume to be an Americanism, but evidently was a euphemism from the trenches. *Go west, young man*, the famous nineteenth-century advice attributed to Horace Greeley, most certainly is American, but one hardly used in Britain. In modern business-speak *go south* is used as an indicator of trouble, based on the direction of the graph. This has spread to Britain but, for climatic reasons, not comfortably. *Go south* is what most of us yearn to do.

This last certainly sniffs of musty English slang, possibly dating back to Chaucer. After all, do those gleaming American churches have bats, or even belfries? Nonetheless, the OED's opening citation is for the American author George W. Peck in 1901; the next three are also American; the first English reference I can find is in a 1917 copy of the *Daily Express*. *Let* (or *get*) *in on the ground floor* is another odd one, given that American elevators/lifts show the ground as being the first floor. But it had been around in the States since at least 1864. So this looks like a clean sweep for the US of A.

But 1929, when few British cinemas were yet wired for sound, was a time when Americanisms could still be treated lightly. Over the next few years, the US economy entered into the deepest and most lasting crisis in its history while Britain suffered more spottily. Hollywood, however, was not begging, and the advent of the talkies turned the century-long rumbling about Americanisms in Britain into something like a national emergency, at least for the *bien-pensant* classes. American slang was no longer the province of Mayfair or the *Babbitt* readers; it was gushing down the social scale.

In a sense Wodehouse and Lewis may represent the last gasp of the old means of philological travel. Until the mid-to-late 1920s printed words, including those written by the came-the-dawners, were by far the most powerful form of transmitting new words and new concepts. A list of Americanisms that arrived in the 1920s, beyond those used by Wodehouse or Sinclair Lewis, is on p. 216.

Compared with what was to come, that was a mere trickle. Ever since 1820, American words had settled in Britain because the American language had proved itself livelier, cleverer, suppler, more adaptable. Now that was about to be enforced by raw power. And it marks a point of no return.

***

The world changed for ever on the night of 6 October 1927. At the Warner Theatre on Broadway Al Jolson uttered the most consequential line in the history of the big screen. It was an ad lib.

The film was *The Jazz Singer*. It had been a long time coming:

plenty of studios and inventors, including Edison, had tried and failed to develop a technology that solved the problems of both amplification and synchronisation. Finally, Warner Bros found a system called Vitaphone that was serviceable enough, and decided to make a full-length film with sound. It was never intended to be a proper talkie: just a silent film with music.

But the old hoofer Jolson was not satisfied with that. In the words of his biographer, Michael Freedland: 'The mike was switched on and, as the orchestra struck up the opening chords of his first number, "Toot Toot Tootsie, Goo' Bye", with the (amazing this) sound of china and cutlery being moved behind him, Jolson broke in with those historic words, "Wait a minute, wait a minute, I tell yer, you ain't heard nothin' yet."'

The rest is history, usually oversimplified. *The Jazz Singer* was not an immediate game changer, particularly not in Britain, where it did not arrive until a full year later. The audiences were reasonable, the critical response patchy. 'Many shortcomings,' said the *Observer*'s critic. 'Not the least of these is a pronounced lisp, and a sort of bronchitic resonance.' The *Sunday Times* hailed it as a revolution but insisted that it would still not kill off the silent cinema. The *Daily Express* got to the nub of it: 'I grew very tired of the American voices, the jazz tunes and the Yankeeism of it all, Oh, for some English voices!'

Well, he hadn't heard nothin' yet. Jolson's impromptu intervention was left in the final cut and indeed delighted the studio so much that an extra scene with dialogue was added. However, Warner Brothers had something up its sleeve: when *The Jazz Singer* came off after a month, it was succeeded in the Piccadilly Theatre by a proper talkie, *The Terror*, a film adaptation of a Scotland Yard drama by Britain's own Edgar Wallace, the hottest name in crime fiction. They thought the British would love it.

'Preposterous nonsense … insufferable boredom … interminable twaddle' (*Express*). 'The pauses between each metallic Americanism are so prolonged that the element of suspense is entirely absent' (*The Times*). Even the once-supportive *Sunday Times* now changed sides: 'Ludicrous.'

There were two separate problems. Firstly, the film was obviously a stinker in itself. Secondly, the presentation of London bobbies in American-cop uniforms spouting American-cop jargon and using American-cop procedures was seen as a national insult, one the studios would take more care to avoid in future.[12] Thirdly, there was the sheer shock of an evening's immersion in the American accents and dialogue generally. It was unfamiliar even to Fleet Street's film critics; imagine what it might have felt like in Bradford or Bolton.

That autumn both Britain's national and specialist cinema press began to discuss the impending failure of the talkies, and speculating that this American humiliation might be the springboard for the revival of the British film industry.[13] They were confusing the message with the medium. *The Terror* may have been a terrible film, but there was nothing wrong with the talkies. Even as they turned wishful thinking into words, Jolson's follow-up *The Singing Fool* was starting to wow audiences in the US, and it soon did the same in Britain.

Still, the British continued to complain about 'the squawkies': 'Oh that American twang!', 'very bad catarrh or some nasal defect', 'If only these American artists would take a course in elocution'. And *Picturegoer* magazine spoke for many of its readers in May 1929 when it editorialised: 'American movie magnates, drunk with instantaneous success at home, have not yet fully realised what they have done. They have largely destroyed the greatest and most valuable attribute of motion picture art – its internationality.'

On the continent, this would indeed pose a problem, resolved in the medium term by the Nazis conquering most of Europe and banning all American films, and in the longer term by (a) dubbing and (b) the growing realisation that foreigners jolly well had to learn English.

The British were more easily subdued. In 1929 a promising young director called Alfred Hitchcock was making a silent feature for British International Pictures called *Blackmail*. It was already in production when the studio decided it needed to respond to the Hollywood

---

12 *The New York Times* said it was like giving New York police officers lines like 'I say old chap, lend me a bob to buy some fags.'
13 The British have always been keener on meaningful silences than the Americans.

challenge by adding some dialogue. The posters were aimed at the very heart of Middle England:

THE FIRST FULL LENGTH TALKIE FILM MADE IN GREAT BRITAIN.
SEE IT HEAR IT. OUR MOTHER TONGUE AS IT SHOULD BE SPOKEN!
100% TALKIE. 100% ENTERTAINMENT.

As Mark Glancy points out in his seminal guide to the period, *Hollywood and the Americanization of Britain*, it was neither quite the first nor was it 100 per cent talkie, 'but *Blackmail* suited the mood of the moment so perfectly that no one seemed to notice or care'. Also, Hitchcock was rather good at his job, and the film was a huge success. The audiences may also have failed to notice the other subterfuge: the lead actress, Anny Ondra, was Czech, and did not quite speak English 'as it should be spoken'. So her part was dubbed.

Hollywood prevailed in the end of course, and ten years later, just before the outbreak of war, Hitchcock would pack his bags and head west. Whatever the London critics might have said, British cinema also had to deal with an accent problem: even the home audience did not want to hear everyone talking like Gussie Fink-Nottle. An equilibrium was eventually established whereby actors like Ronald Colman, Clive Brook and Cary Grant could go west and sound acceptable to everyone. And the British decided they quite liked American voices, whether theirs was the way the mother tongue should be spoken or not.

***

Authority was mortified. Mr C.H. Gray, headmaster of Diss Grammar School, complained that his pupils were finding it hard to understand a page of English: 'the vocabulary of the modern pupil was infested with barbarisms, vulgarities and Americanisms'. Rev. C.H. Parsons, head of Finchley Grammar, urged parents to help the school cut out 'the slovenly habit of using Americanisms picked up from talking films'.

Miss E.R. Gwatkin of Streatham Hill High School actually used the word *debunk* in her presidential address at the Association of Head

Mistresses' conference. She was then attacked, indeed debunked, by Miss M. Muir of Bridlington High: 'Our whole soul revolts against … the soulless inventions of such vulgarities as *debunk*.'

The Chief Constable of Wallasey, Mr J. Ormerod, reporting an increase in crime in his annual report for 1932, said: 'I cannot refrain from commenting on the pernicious and growing habit of youth in using Americanisms with nasal accompaniment to appear, in their own vernacular, "*tough guys*". On one of my officers going to search him a young housebreaker said to him "*Lay off*, cop".'[14]

Mr Ormerod went on:

'*Oh yeah!*', is a frequent answer to charges, and we are promised '*shoot-ups in the burg*' and threatened with being '*bumped off*' by these would-be *racketeers*,[15] who are mere boys and who have never been away from their home towns. I am grateful to the Watch Committee for recently preventing an exhibition of films depicting incidents in the careers of wasters like Al Capone and Jack Diamond. I fail to see what earthly good can be derived from these films.

The grand total of burglaries in Wallasey in 1932 was seven.

Mr A. Douglas Cowburn, the Southwark coroner, asked a constable who was giving evidence: 'How were the brakes on this car?'

'OK, sir,' replied the constable.

'Don't talk about OK,' said Mr Cowburn sharply. 'You are in the King's court, so use King's English.'

The constable then said the brakes were all right.

During the 1931 election campaign the Conservative leader Stanley Baldwin made a speech at a school in Worcestershire supporting the campaign for the protection of Britain's trade, adding: 'My personal reason for being a Protectionist is that I may help to banish from this country the American language.'

---

14 'Lay off thy bloody hands.' – Christopher Marlowe. The boy may have been quoting this, in which case it was not an Americanism.

15 This is definitely an Americanism, even if *racket* is not.

In 1936 even the King's English changed. In the first broadcast of his short-lived reign Edward VIII began: 'It has been an ancient tradition of the British monarchy that the new Sovereign should send a written message to his peoples. Science has made it possible for me to make that message more personal, and speak to you all over the *radio*.'

It had, since the first Wireless Telegraphy Act, been customary in Britain to refer to the newfangled sound device as a wireless. 'Radio has been gaining ground,' admitted a mildly peeved *Manchester Guardian* columnist after the King's speech, 'and it obviously achieved a great victory yesterday.' Perhaps that's why Baldwin, re-installed as prime minister, was so anxious to get rid of the King when the abdication crisis broke.

However, Alistair Cooke, in one of his own early broadcasts from America, pointed out that Baldwin himself had used *bestseller*, *backslider* and *a party dogfight* in quick succession in the House of Commons. Indeed we are all backsliders – though it looks to me that neither *backslider* nor *dogfight* is actually an Americanism.

***

In 1935 America's most celebrated journalist, Henry Louis Mencken, paid one of his occasional visits to London. The purpose was primarily therapeutic, following the death of his wife. Nonetheless he was able to survey the scene with satisfaction, indeed with something of the swagger of a victorious general smiling as he looked over the blighted landscape and cowed populace of the enemy capital he had just entered in triumph.

Mencken was a great man of his time, though not always a big one. He was a writer of immense talent, energy, range and striking originality, and an aphorist to match Dr Johnson or Oscar Wilde. His judgments, though always vigorously expressed, were erratic (which is in the nature of journalism), often petty and vengeful (which is merely a journalistic vice) and sometimes completely on the wrong side of history. In particular, his enthusiasm for his own German heritage led Mencken to immerse himself a little too deeply in some of the, um, more controversial manifestations of Teutonic culture.

In 1916 he persuaded his employers, the *Baltimore Sun*, to send him to Germany to report the war. The United States was still neutral; Mencken emphatically was not: the advert the paper ran to trumpet their star turn's trip made this very clear. 'MENCKEN IS NOT NEUTRAL. He is pro-German.' Mencken arrived in Europe in December 1916. The Germans gave him treatment to match his ego and allowed him to go to the Russian front and come under fire, a coveted rite of passage for any war journalist.

Less helpfully, within weeks the Kaiser announced unrestricted submarine warfare against all shipping. He hoped to force Britain into submission; instead he forced the US into the war. Mencken had to get out fast, take a circuitous route home, get rid of some embarrassing documents and keep a very low profile for the duration.

So he immersed himself in non-journalistic projects. These included the expansion of some *jeux d'esprit* he had collected on the way Americans speak, and turning them into a book called *The American Language*. It was published in 1919 and instantly popular in a way that astonished both author and publisher.[16] Mencken's stated aim was to point up 'certain salient differences between the English of England and the English of America'. One may speculate that at least part of his unstated aim was to work out his own contempt for Britain in a manner that did not involve unwelcome visits from the FBI or some of his raucously anti-Hun Baltimorean neighbours.

It mutated into something much more important than that. Mencken received a vast postbag of corrections, amplifications and additions which turned into a second edition and then a third. By 1935 he was preparing the fourth edition, and by now, helped by the wisdom of crowds, it had turned into a classic, a work of scholarship hugely enriched by Mencken's own verbal sizzle.

However, in one respect Mencken had lost a little focus. The title was crucial: the thesis was that the American language needed to be treated as something separate from and equal to British English, and that the languages were bound to draw further apart. But Mencken partially reversed the thesis, which he had every right to do because

---

16 Now wouldn't that be nice?

the facts were changing. Far from drawing apart, the languages were merging, on American terms.

He admitted that he had been wrong in an article for the *Daily Express* in his previous visit in 1930. Or rather, he said he had not known quite how right he was. The weight of American numbers and the superior quality of its language was now making itself felt even in London. After the Great War, he proclaimed: 'the old lofty confidence, the old pride, the old postulates of infallibility … were quietly abandoned' and the British realised that the language of 'their old lackeys, the loud-mouthed, abominable Yankees' was actually better.

> There followed the invasion of the talkies, and the dreadful deed was done … The Englishman, whether he knows it or not, is talking and writing more and more American. He becomes so accustomed to it that he grows unconscious of it. Things that would have set his teeth on edge ten years ago, or even five years ago, are now integral parts of his daily speech … In a few years it will probably be impossible for an Englishman to speak, or even to write, without using Americanisms, whether consciously or unconsciously. The influence of 125 million people, practically all headed in one direction, is simply too great to be resisted by any minority, however resolute.

There was a fuss of course, as he intended. But he had understated the truth: the British were already unconsciously using Americanisms introduced decades earlier.

When the fourth edition of *The American Language* appeared in 1936, he was, amidst the near-800 pages of erudition, less judicious in a reference book than he had been in a popular newspaper column, giving full vent to the anti-Britishness that had helped damage his reputation twenty years earlier.

'To the common people,' Mencken wrote, referring to American common people, 'everything English, whether an article of dress, a social custom or a word or phrase has what James M. Cain has called "a somewhat pansy cast". That is to say, it is regarded as affected, effeminate and ridiculous.'

This was, at the very least, an oversimplification of some complex attitudes. Then he put the boot in: 'The American soldiers who went to France in 1917 and 1918 did not develop either admiration or liking for their English comrades; indeed, they were better pleased with the French, and reserved their greatest fondness for the Germans.' And how, one wonders, did he divine that? From his old press minders in the Kaiser's high command? Or while cowering in his Baltimore bunker?[17]

He was, however, hitting at a sore spot when he wrote about the extent of the variations in English that hinged wholly on the class system. And one of Mencken's undoubted achievements was to create a greater awareness among the non-lexicographical community of the extent to which Americanisms were not invented but derived from the ancient past. 'Perhaps the new locutions will turn out, like many "Americanisms", to be old locutions that have been living in retirement,' wrote St John Ervine in the *Observer*. 'Some professor may yet discover that "*OK, Chief*" was first lisped by children dressed in woad, and who knows that Ethelred the Unready was not accustomed to remark "*Hello, big boy*" or "*I get you, baby*" to his friends.'

Very soon after that, there was a report of a new discovery in the Paston Letters, that remarkable survival documenting the life of a well-connected fifteenth-century Norfolk family: the chatelaine Margaret Paston had written after someone had reneged on a business deal: '†*I am through with him*'.

***

It was easy enough for Mencken to attack the English for being effete and decrepit; it was harder to make the allegation stick against Australia, a country about which he knew even less than he did England, where he was at least familiar with the environs of the Savoy Hotel. Yet Australia was going through similar angst to the British about American influence, especially once the talkies arrived.

---

17 In the 1930s Mencken was regarded as soft on Hitler, if not quite smitten.

In fact, there was an extra dimension because there was a triangular tournament going on between what Australians of that era loved to call the King's English, the new American slang and the dinki-di Aussie vernacular. Stories about the impact of American on Australia's language drew a huge response locally, as in Britain, and authority figures could be every bit as fogeyish.

Mr F.W. Berne, the defendant's barrister in a fraud case in Sydney, suggested the whole affair was a *frame-up*. 'Please speak good English,' interrupted Judge Curlewis. 'I object to being addressed in the language of the criminal classes of the New York Bowery.'

In the early days of talkies a government minister even said a watch was being kept on the quality of English in imported American films, a decision defended by Father L.F. Murphy of St Ignatius College, Sydney, who may not have been a very dinki-di Aussie. 'The American talkie is exerting the worst possible influence on Australian speech,' he said. 'We are not a highly educated people. Our resistance to destructive influences of this nature is therefore much lower than English resistance.'

Another American voice was whispering in youthful ears in both Britain and Australia. It belonged to Dorothy Dix, a pioneering agony aunt who was well over 70 by the time the *Daily Mirror* started featuring her daily syndicated column in 1935. Nonetheless she adopted a progressive, understanding and non-censorious tone which influenced future generations of advice columnists. That tone, however, was an American one, and was not translated as a concession to British readers.

Dix used a lot of words that would have been familiar enough to her movie-mad readers: she talked about the complex issues of *dating* and *petting*; the problems of dealing with *wise-crackers* and *gold-diggers*. She used some words that would have been less familiar, such as *mis-steps* and the British archaism *pocket-book*.

Sometimes the questions were also in American. Dear Miss Dix, 'Will you tell us what you think of a boy who will let a girl acquaintance casually treat him to a *soda* or a *package* of cigarettes or a *show*? ... – TWO BOYS, OF CARDIFF.' 'New times make new customs,' said Miss Dix sagely.

But was the Americanisation process in Cardiff so far advanced that teenagers were drinking soda not pop, buying packages not packs and seeing shows and not films? Or were the letters actually amalgams of those received in what was surely a pretty huge postbag, designed to let Dix tackle whatever subject took her fancy that day?

The evidence, strangely enough, comes from parliament in Australia, where Dix was even more widely read than in Britain. In Canberra a fawning parliamentary question planted on a pliant back-bencher by the whips so the minister can make a pronouncement is known to this day as a Dorothy.[18]

British and Australian youngsters in the 1930s hardly needed more encouragement to talk American. By 1939 the average Briton went to the pictures twenty times a year – newborn babes, the bedridden old, enclosed nuns and convicted prisoners included – so most teenagers would have been going once or twice a week. 'Girls were noted for self-consciously adopting Hollywood accents, which they thought gave them "extra smartness and tone", but boys, too, deployed Americanisms to give themselves extra confidence,' according to the social historian Melanie Tebbutt.

The showing of the musical *Broadway Melody* at Barrow Coliseum in 1929 was said to have brought a whole new language to an introverted corner of England: '*OK baby*', '*Gosh oh gee*', and '*Hiya babe*'. And elsewhere it was reported that to avoid the difficult business of framing sentences when approaching girls, nervous boys would take refuge in lines from songs. '*Who's taking you out tonight?*' '*Pardon me, pretty baby, is it yes, or is it no, is it maybe?*' '*I don't know why I love you like I do.*'

The anthropologist Marcel Mauss said in 1934 that Hollywood had changed Britain's deportment and posture, 'even the way of entering a room, shaking hands and sitting in a chair'. Which was helpful if the pretty baby said yes (or more likely *yeah*) and wanted to pursue the other great interwar craze of heading down the dance hall and perhaps going *jitterbugging*.

---

18 A few Antipodean old-timers with a taste for rhyming slang also still use 'a Dorothy' as slang for a six in cricket.

The *Mirror* columnist Patricia Pearse roused herself to a full bold-capital frenzy: 'Pictures published in American magazines, and daily flooding this country, show the drugged eyes and parted lips of these men and women as the music and dancing gets hotter and hotter, and excitement mounts. America calls this craze an express of gladness ... **I CALL IT MASS HYSTERIA.**' After a short period of relative calm she concluded: **'WE MUST NOT – WE WON'T – HAVE A RACE OF JITTERBUGS!'**

Britain's defences against American cultural invasion were even more Captain Mainwaring-ish than those against Nazi invasion, but there was a little pushback in the late 1930s. The hot new dance craze of 1938 was not the jitterbug, despite the *Mirror's* frantic attempts to make it sound irresistible; it was, of all things, the impeccably Cockney Lambeth Walk, from the British musical *Me and My Girl*. It was even a hit in benighted Germany, and for a while the joyous (indeed rather Yiddish) *Oi!* at the end of the chorus became almost as universal as *OK*.

'British dance music was more restrained, less spontaneous than its American counterpart,' wrote Tebbutt, and the dancers often covered their embarrassment with a hint of self-parody. On the dance floor, British inhibition was one factor preventing total Americanisation. It was noted in the 1920s that the Charleston in Britain was altogether more sedate than in the US. And just before the war a group of surprisingly effective counter-revolutionaries, the dance teachers, resolved 'to stamp out freak steps' – and managed to ensure that what they called 'the English style' became briefly dominant in the ballrooms.

There was a recognition among musicians that the British had slightly different tastes. 'The Britisher must have a song to sing – something simple and easy to learn,' said the US-born, UK-based pianist Charlie Kunz. On the whole, the British preferred their music sweet rather than hot, he added, and they liked a dash of music hall comedy in the mix as well. Hence the popularity of Gracie Fields and George Formby. And just to make sure the British kept some of their insularity, members of Britain's Musicians' Union, whose job opportunities had been savaged as music hall declined and the talkies booted live music out of cinema, worked hard to keep American performers out of the country.

Young people wealthy enough to afford a car to get to the palais and drive down the local lovers' lane afterwards did so in cars built more often by British-owned Austin Morris than by American-owned Ford. Above all, Britain had one massive line of defence against unbridled Americanisation: the BBC. Unlike Stanley Baldwin, who was merely prime minister for seven years, it could do something. And it was full of internal anguish about how to balance its responsibilities. Gerald Cock, the head of outside broadcasts, had warned in a report in 1929 that the BBC monopoly was not a secure defence against 'the Transatlantic octopus', adding: 'It is even possible that the national outlook and with it, character, is gradually becoming Americanised.'

The controller of programmes, Cecil Graves, chuntered about presenters using American formulations like 'We bring to you' and 'We offer you'. He also had a particular loathing for the crooners, the new singers like Rudy Vallée and Bing Crosby, who half-whispered into the microphone as though rocking a newborn babe, rather than belting out numbers in the old way. One might have thought such stars were made for radio, but Graves wanted this 'particularly odious form of singing' barred.

The BBC's hierarchs were not idiots. They felt strongly, like the rest of the establishment, that British broadcasting should not rush down the path of babble and pap. Perhaps they shared the general old-fashioned British distaste for American influences that were all too often black and/or Jewish. They were aware that the BBC could learn much from American techniques, and it did. But they were by no means in complete control of the situation.

Competing transmissions were beamed in from neighbouring countries, and were particularly popular on Sundays, when the BBC had extra Reithian self-denying ordinances in force. The names of the rival stations lingered on dials of old-fashioned wirelesses into the 1950s and beyond, to the bafflement of post-war children: Toulouse, Hilversum, Normandie, Athlone. Above all, there was Radio Luxembourg, which began regular broadcasts of an unnervingly

American-looking schedule from the pushy little statelet in 1934: 'We are the Ovalteenies / Happy girls and boys!'

'Unfortunately,' the Postmaster-General told the Commons in 1937 when asked to Do Something, 'this is not a case where Britannia rules the waves'. A Labour MP then drew laughter and cheers by pointing out that millions of people preferred Luxembourg 'to the dull programmes of the BBC'.

One can see his point. Take 8 p.m. on Sunday, 6 August 1939, the last bank holiday weekend before the war, and what we would now call *prime time*. The BBC had two networks: the National and Regional services. Listeners in the south-east had a choice of programmes from holiday resorts, Blackpool and Ramsgate: one was a service from a Baptist tabernacle; the other a service from a Catholic abbey. The infant television service blacked out its pictures for the duration and broadcast the sound feed from Blackpool. Not surprisingly millions – a majority, according to some sources – did go in for dial-twiddling.

The schedules were not always so bleak. In 1938 the BBC's big music-and-comedy hit was *Band Waggon*, starring Arthur Askey and Richard Murdoch; the following year it was joined in the schedules by Tommy Handley's *It's That Man Again*, which became the symbol of humorous British defiance of the Nazi threat. Connoisseurs of wireless days, however, point out that the Askey–Murdoch double act had a certain quickfire Americanism about it, and that *ITMA* was influenced by the *Fred Allen Show*.

The very term *band waggon* is an interesting hybrid. Webster had long since taken the second G out of *waggon*, and he prevailed in the US. He was actually in line with Dr Johnson in this, though not with common British usage. The British became gradually more confused, so much so that a street in Barnet, on the northern edge of London, had signs saying Waggon Road at one end and Wagon Road at the other (and Google Maps still reflects the confusion).

A *bandwagon*, meaning the wagon carrying the band in a procession, often at election time, was a pure Americanism, as was its figurative use as something one might jump on. The BBC used the American word with the British spelling: a very British compromise. Music in the late 1930s, both on and off the BBC, typified the same awkwardness. There was a comeback in the popularity of British-composed tunes, led by the partnership of lyricist Jimmy Kennedy and composer Michael Carr, who had a series of hits. These included, in 1935, 'Roll along, Covered Wagon'. Note the spelling and indeed the words, which are 100 per cent American up to the chorus:

Wipee-teeyi, old timers,
heading for your ranch house door

Four years later Kennedy and Carr delivered the all-time classic 'South of the Border'. Ah, yes: Down Mexico Way. Kennedy was an Ulsterman, from Omagh. It would have scanned just as well if he stayed home in County Tyrone and written

South of the Border
Down Ballymore Way

Punch had a cartoon around this time showing an effete dinner-jacketed and obviously English singer with a cad's moustache leaning into a radio mike singing: 'For we're tough, mighty tough, in the West.' Perhaps he meant Somerset.

***

Hollywood's power in this era was such that words could just appear from nowhere. 'Almost everybody's a ***doodler***,' Gary Cooper told the judge in the 1937 film *Mr Deeds Goes to Town*. 'People draw the most idiotic pictures when they're thinking.' And thus ***doodles*** and ***doodling*** passed instantly into both American and English, there being no previous word for the practice.[19]

Presumably †***quit*** also arrived via the cinemas by endless repetition, rather than a single revelation. It was not a new word in Britain but had disappeared except in specialist senses. It was normal to

---

19 A doodle in the song 'Yankee Doodle' was something similar to a noodle, a bit of a simpleton. The word has also served as slang for both penis and the sex act.

quit a rented house and, in *The Times*'s hunting reports, a fox would often 'quit covert'. But the phrase 'quit his job' did not appear in the *Observer* between 1838 and 1968, although it did make the more informal *Daily Express* in 1938.

The two most useful historic guides to which words should be treated as Americanisms in this era came from two scholars who employed a good ear, sound memory, scientific methods and long experience of both countries. The first, *An American Glossary* by Richard H. Thornton, appeared in 1912. The second, by Herbert W. Horwill, was published in 1935. It was called *A Dictionary of Modern American Usage*, a conscious homage to H.W. Fowler's English equivalent in the 1920s. It was less ambitious in its scope, and intended primarily to assist in 'facilitating intercourse between England and the United States'.[20]

Three lists of Americanisms that arrived in Britain before the Second World War start on p. 217. Take a very deep breath before reading. The sheer weight of them is staggering.

---

20 Many young people have also crossed the Atlantic with this in mind.

4

ONE, TWO, THREE O'CLOCK, FOUR O'CLOCK ROCK

Britain went to war with Germany again in September 1939. The first seven months of eerie quiet between Hitler's invasions of Poland and Norway were described as *the phoney war* even at the time. This was an Americanism, attributed to Senator William Borah of Idaho, an elderly isolationist and Anglophobe. *Phoney* itself was also American, though it was said to have been around in Britain since at least 1920.

But for most of 1940 and 1941, as Britain became increasingly alone, endangered and preoccupied, the nation was forced back on its own resources in every respect. This included the need to use its own linguistic inventiveness to describe its situation, although when the secretary to the Overseas Trade Department, Robert Hudson, warned that Britain would not be able to borrow to meet its needs as it did in the first war, he explained: 'This, to use an Americanism, is a *cash-and-carry* war.'

And, even though careless talk was said to cost lives, new words continued to burrow their way into the language, as impervious to the emergency as rabbits or woodworm. *Blitz*, after all, was imported straight from the enemy.

And by now, the process by which all foreign, which meant

mainly American, words made their home in Britain had acquired a ritualised quality. In print or in formal discourse they would at first be accompanied by an escort, a disclaimer like the one used by Hudson: 'To use an Americanism' or something arch like 'as our American cousins put it', perhaps, or 'as they say across the pond'.[1]

The attributive escort would soon drop away but the would-be migrant word remained in the quarantine of inverted commas, as though it were a hot coal being handled with tongs. In the case of a compound, it might also be hyphenated as an extra security measure. Then one by one these protections would disappear until, within a few years, it would be fully naturalised. It would lose any trace of a foreign accent, and only a few aged pedants would even remember a time when it was not part of the language.

Take *haywire*, originally a purely North American term that meant exactly what it implies: 'Wire for binding bales of hay, straw, etc.' By the early twentieth century it had come to imply to Americans a certain rustic hopelessness: as the US Forestry Bureau Bulletin explained in 1905: '*Hay wire outfit*, a contemptuous term for loggers with poor logging equipment.' And it began to be extended to any inefficient operation, where things appeared to be held together with bits of hay wire.

The *Manchester Guardian*, as it then was, disdained the word for another twenty-six years. But then in 1931 a story about music on the plains included the phrase (placed within quotation marks) 'a hay-wire joint', described as being part of 'the peculiar idiom of the West'. In 1937 a romantic comedy called *Hotel Haywire* was released in British cinemas, which may have been significant.

In 1941 the *Guardian*'s bridge correspondent kept the explanation and the quotation marks but ditched the hyphen: '"all haywire", as the Americans quaintly put it'. In another bridge column a year later a different writer dropped the health warning but restored the hyphen: 'the bidding might stop or "go hay-wire"'.

By 1943 a columnist offering light comedy from the domestic

---

1 The term *over the Great Pond* is recorded from America in 1642, but sailors may have used something similar before that, so perhaps it is not an Americanism.

front got the word twice in the opening paragraph in a manner that suggested the word had now reached the more genteel Manchester suburbs: 'My telephone, I am charmed to say, has gone hay-wire. I do not quite know what "gone hay-wire" means, but then I do not quite know what my telephone is doing.' By the 1990s the now Manchester-less *Guardian* was using *haywire* on average once a fortnight. It is unlikely that any of the writers or subeditors ever thought of it as an Americanism.[2]

And any wartime slump in the word-import business was rapidly repaired. Indeed, the trade got a fillip after the US entered the war in December 1941 and began sending troops to Europe. This time Britain was not just a staging post, it was at first the only available destination. Between 1942 and 1945, 3 million US service personnel came to Britain for varying lengths of time.

Now the British people could not just hear American voices, they could touch the owners of them. Indeed, in the case of large numbers of young women, they could touch them, and be touched back, very intimately. It was not just that the Yanks were, as the saying went, 'overpaid, oversexed, and over here'; British menfolk were often somewhere else. And if the young GI in the dance hall did not necessarily look like a movie star he sure as hell, to the untrained ear, sounded like one. 'Pre-eminent was the impression of American wealth,' wrote David Reynolds. 'Material wealth also fostered cultural values.' And the Americans were often skilful exponents, and willing teachers, of the uninhibited dance hall routines that made British men so self-conscious. None of this went down well with either Britain's cultural guardians or the absent boyfriends and husbands.

The US forces were not spread evenly across the country; there was a concentration round the East Anglian airbases. But anyone deprived of American company at close, or very close, quarters was able to get an enhanced helping of American culture from the radio. In 1940 a special station was set up: the BBC Forces Programme, which in Auntie's family history can be seen as mother of the post-war

---

2 This writer certainly didn't. I used it six times myself in the *Guardian* between 1984 and 1990, mainly to describe the state of English cricket.

Light Programme and granny of Radios 1 and 2. It was originally aimed primarily at the expeditionary force in France and had a schedule that did make some concession to soldierly tastes: the Sunday services, for instance, were cut to ten minutes.

After the British retreated from Dunkirk the programme was retained and, after the Americans arrived, catered for them too, including their own comedy shows, featuring the likes of Bob Hope and Jack Benny, plus the baseball scores. The British, though baffled by the baseball, did like the rest of the American stuff. And when the US Army set up its own station, the American Forces Network, the BBC insisted on limiting the competition by restricting the Americans' broadcasting range while at the same time coming under pressure to keep giving the long-suffering British what they wanted.

Sir William Haley, the director-general, was worried that American comedy 'might become a Frankenstein'. One of his senior officials, Norman Collins, pointed out that if British troops chose the records for the music programmes, 90 per cent of them would be American.

Despite the shared tastes, the War and Navy Departments in Washington thought it necessary to issue a patronising little guide to the forces about their strange hosts:

> The British are often more reserved in conduct than we are … So if Britons sit on trains and busses [sic] without striking up conversation with you, it doesn't mean they are being haughty and unfriendly. Probably they may be paying more attention to you than you think.
>
> The British may have phrases and colloquialisms that might sound funny to you. It isn't a good idea, for instance, to say 'bloody' in mixed company in Britain – it is one of their worst swear words. To say 'I look like a bum' is offensive to their ears, for to the British this means you look like your own backside.

Cheery reports from the North African front implied that, on neutral ground, the fighting men of both countries were resolving the linguistic problem for themselves. In a speech to Congress in 1943 Churchill announced that the British had agreed to call their lorries *trucks* in exchange for the Americans filling theirs up with petrol rather than *gasoline*.

And the Associated Press war correspondent Daniel De Luce reported that the British were more inventive in making the war zone user-friendly. The British had captured Longstop, Banana Ridge, Grenadier Hill and The Bou; the Americans took Hill 609. The route to the British front line was via Charing Cross, Piccadilly Circus and Hindenburg Corner; the American route just used the signposts left by the former French colonists.

My sense is that the war in itself was not such a massive conduit for the transmission of Americanisms as has sometimes been suggested. After all, such contact as there was between the actual soldiers from different Allied forces in some theatres would have been no match for the mass media. Also, much of what emanated from the US in this war was not the zippy, zappy lingo that had been worming its way into British brains, willing or unwilling, for more than a century. The newest parts of the American language mostly comprised the titles of federal government bodies with initials that refused to form easy acronyms. They then issued orders couched in the language that came to be known as *gobbledygook*.

The word must be credited to Maury Maverick, a Texan politician who had become chairman of the Smaller War Plants Corporation, a name which was in itself an illustration of the problem. In 1944 he finally exploded and issued an instruction to his staff, barring terms like *pointing up*, *dynamics*, *finalizing* and *effectuating*. And he warned: 'Anyone using the words *activating* or *implementation* will be shot.'

Maverick later wrote that he got the idea at some meeting he attended at which he listened to a windbag spouting jargon. 'Perhaps it came to me in a vision,' he mused. 'Perhaps I was thinking of the old bearded turkey gobbler back in Texas who was always gobbledy-gobbling and strutting with ludicrous pomposity. At the end of this gobble there was a sort of gook.' Maverick became a hero but left no legacy. It took a while for the full range of gobbledygook to be exported to Britain, but that *eventuated*.

In October 1945, Herbert Horwill, author of *Modern American*

Usage, wrote a sad little postscript. In the book his tone had been neutral and dispassionate. Now, in an article for the *Manchester Guardian*, he invoked the imagery of war, arguing that, while Britain was no longer in danger of a German invasion, there was still the American threat. 'We have enrolled no Home Guard to meet it. Indeed, it has been assisted, quite unwittingly, by a number of Fifth Columnists, so to speak, among ourselves. It has been a silent infiltration, and it has gained ground little by little, without any fighting on the beaches or in the country lanes.'

Horwill claimed that the role of Hollywood had been overstated; he was not much bothered by slang. He was more worried by books, newspapers and magazines[3] – and the BBC, 'which daily makes Americanisms familiar to its multitude of listeners'. And he had been assiduously squirrelling away BBC Americanisms from news bulletins and talks.

In addition to his previous lists of words that had parachuted in, he had heard of outposts *keeping their eyes skinned*, of a Burma campaign being fought *on a shoestring*, of six trains being *scheduled* to leave daily, of Allied aircraft *stepping up* their attacks on Japanese bases and of crowds *milling about* on VE day. And that Germany's transport was all *haywire*, a defeat to which he was not yet ready to reconcile himself.

In British newspapers he had come across *go-getting*, *mistreated* (instead of *maltreated*), †*contraption* (which has West Country ancestry) and even *bugaboo*, though that one was swiftly arrested and deported. He also got cross about the increasing practice of intensifying a verb by appending what he insisted was an unnecessary adverb not a preposition: *close down*, *test out*, *check up*. He was also offended by lists like that one, without a linking *and*.[4]

The judges were still on the case too. In the closing months of the

---

3 He probably meant what were known as the Yank mags: *Fight Stories*, *Action Stories*, *Crime Stories*, *Western Short Stories*, rather than the *Times Literary Supplement*. They were sold for tuppence or so to boys and undereducated men, having allegedly been brought in as ballast on merchant ships. The female equivalents of these were more likely to be home-grown.
4 Doesn't bother me.

war Mr Justice Birkett, sitting at Chester Assizes, got snotty with an expert witness, drawing attention to his use of *finalize* in the expert's report. 'Where did you get that from?' demanded the judge. 'It is not English. It is not in the dictionary.' This witness would not be cowed, however. 'We use strange words,' he replied, 'as is done in law.'

Horwill's article coincided with the publication of a supplement to Mencken's magnum opus, which included an updated collection of Americanisms that had passed into British English, as sent to Mencken by his army of snouts (or fifth-columnists). A major source was the writer H.W. Seaman, who told him that *peanuts* had now completely ousted *monkey nuts;* that *grouch*, *pull* (meaning influence), *lay off* (desist), *once over* and *pin-up girl* were all now in common use; that kids were writing 'So-and-so is a *sap*' or 'a *sis*' on walls; and that the nursery term for a train was no longer *puff-puff* but the American *choo-choo* (presumably because mum had been listening to Glenn Miller's 'Chattanooga Choo Choo') – and that 'no English dramatic critic would shrink from writing of a *flop*'.

Mencken had some understandable fun catching Americanisms from the lips of starchy British politicians. Before the war, Neville Chamberlain and other appeasers adapted the word *jitterbug* to indicate a pro-war alarmist. In turn, Clement Attlee, as Leader of the Opposition, accused Chamberlain 'of trying to put *sob stuff* over the House'. The PM said in reply that he was 'a *go-getter* for peace'. Chamberlain, said Mencken, 'was very fond of Americanisms, and occasionally used them more or less correctly'.

Mencken also told a story about Dorothy L. Sayers, who as a novelist is one of the leading stragglers behind Wodehouse for the award in the Importing Most Americanisms into Novels category. In 1942 she wrote the script for a BBC series on the Life of Christ, broadcast by the BBC on Sunday afternoons in *Children's Hour*, and was promptly attacked in the London evening paper *The Star* by a nonconformist priest from Balham, Rev. James Colville, for using Americanisms like *hop it*.

A few matters arise from this which Mencken did not mention. Firstly, the conformist view, expressed by the *Church Times*, was that the production was 'tremendously impressive' in every respect.

Secondly, the whole idea was to make the story accessible to young people by putting in modern language. Thirdly, it seems unlikely that *hop it* is an Americanism. Fourthly, there might have been a more pertinent criticism.

This was summed up in the *Daily Express*'s otherwise highly favourable review of the first episode, which showered praise on the 'sincerity, reverence and controlled beauty' of the writing but added: 'Simon, fisherman by profession, speaks not in the rough fisherman's tongue you would expect, but in the accents of Balliol. The disciples might be any group of earnest young undergraduates devoted to their spiritual leader.'

Here lay the real problem with the BBC. Yes, it was in some ways (and still is) a conduit for crass and careless Americanisation, but most of the time it is a unique standard-bearer for Britishness. Its notion of Britishness at that time was a limited one, however, and its role as a unifying force was hampered by its inability to surmount the country's social and regional stratification.

In 1926 the corporation had set up an Advisory Committee on Spoken English under the chairmanship of Robert Bridges (Eton and Oxford), the poet laureate and a founder of the Society for Pure English. The aim was to ensure that the BBC norm, for announcers in particular, should cause minimum offence, and the committee opted for 'educated English'. This was not exactly Mayfair English but it was a great deal nearer Mayfair than Middlesbrough. 'Unwisely, however, the corporation began to think it was determining the English of the future,' in the words of the historian Ross McKibbin. 'The more overt became its intention the more controversial was the policy.' It was much mocked and, in the rougher papers, much abused.

Claud Cockburn (Berkhamsted School, along with Graham Greene, and Oxford) would later make the point that the appeal of America was that it appeared more democratic. At the time the writer Compton Mackenzie (St Paul's School and Oxford) said the BBC exuded a 'finicking, suburban, synthetic, plus-fours gentility'. As a modern historian, Martin Pugh, summed up: 'Working people in Britain enjoyed and consumed American entertainment because it did not treat them as second-class citizens.'

The baton was picked up in the 1940s by George Orwell (Eton and University of Life), which was another indicator that even the critics came from the same narrow background, however hard they worked to escape it. In his essay 'The English People' (published in 1947) Orwell explained the appeal of Americanisms:

American has gained a footing in England partly because of the vivid, almost poetic quality of its slang, partly because certain American usages (for instance, the formation of verbs by adding -*ise*[5] [sic] to a noun) save time, and most of all because one can adopt an American word without crossing a class barrier. From the English point of view American words have no class label.

This applies even to thieves' slang. Words like **stooge** and *stool pigeon* are considered much less vulgar than words like *nark* and *split*. Even a very snobbish English person would probably not mind calling a policeman a ***cop***, which is American, but he would object to calling him a *copper*, which is working-class English. To the working classes, on the other hand, the use of Americanisms is a way of escaping from Cockney without adopting the BBC dialect which they instinctively dislike and cannot easily master. Hence, especially in the big towns, working-class children now use American slang from the moment that they learn to talk.

✳✳✳

In the years after the First World War Britain felt American influence more closely than ever before. After the Second it must have felt further away, as the number of GIs diminished. There was no question now about who ruled the world: the British Empire was creaking arthritically towards its deathbed. Conditions at home were bleak: in many ways deprivation was greater than during the war. Austerity was the watchword, under a government pursuing policies as near to socialism as Britain has ever seen. The luxury goods of America were not even available, never mind affordable.

---

5 Or, indeed, -*ize*.

American entertainment was more dominant than ever, though, and now it even stretched into the ancient British domain of the theatre. The hottest tickets in London were for American musicals – *Oklahoma!*, *Annie Get Your Gun* – and even American plays – *Death of a Salesman*, *A Streetcar Named Desire*. Across the country, the grand tradition of music hall was withering; battered by the cinema and wireless, it waited only for television to strike the fatal blow. However, the impresario Val Parnell took a gamble and in 1948 signed a little-known young comedian to revive the old ways with a one-man show at the London Palladium.

He took the place by storm. *Life* magazine called the reaction 'worshipful'. 'As the Forties ended,' wrote the social historian Harry Hopkins, 'it seemed that the long-vacant throne of king of the British music hall had been filled; that the missing successor to the line of our great popular comedians, Dan Leno, Harry Lauder, George Robey and the rest, had been found. And that he, too, was an American.' His name was Danny Kaye.

In Britain, this was merely another phase in a long journey towards subservience. Other countries with less experience of the process were now being drawn in. In Japan America's conquering heroes were not trying to teach the Japanese to play baseball – they already did that – but to play it the American way, adventurously and argumentatively, not spiritually and respectfully. This was only a partial success.

In Europe they were to trying to persuade the French to drink Coca-Cola, which the French had not been doing enough for the company's liking, and in 1949 moves were afoot to build a new factory in Marseille. Permission was denied: the Ministry of Finance said it would be disastrous for the balance of payments; there were problems over the secrecy of the ingredients; opponents said Coke was addictive; its presence would ruin the wine industry; there were rumours that a Coke advert was planned for the facade of Notre Dame. Perhaps, in the spirit of the Comte de Buffon, someone blamed Coke for stunting Americans' growth.

The powerful French Left was particularly vehement in its opposi-tion, and it took four years for the matter to be resolved. Jim Farley, the head of Coca-Cola Export, put the case this way: 'Coca-Cola was not injurious to the health of American soldiers who liberated France from the Nazis so that Communist deputies could be in session today.' Guess who won – although Coca-Cola to this day is less ubiquitous in France than in most other countries. And the Franco-American relationship would continue to be tortured: a counterpoint to Britain's willing submission.

One person was well placed to judge just how much Britain had changed: a real-life Rip van Winkle. Monica Baldwin had joined an enclosed order of nuns in 1914 and, though she had long been disillusioned, did not re-emerge until 1941. Her memoir, *I Leap Over the Wall*, published in 1949, created a sensation. In it she described having tea with two old friends, Gay and Barbara, after her re-emergence: 'Perhaps what startled me most was the constant recurrence of words which not even a man would have used before girls when I left school. *Lousy*, for instance, and *mucky, guts, blasted, bloody* and *what-the-hell*.'

None of these can actually be counted as an Americanism, though *lousy* had definitely acquired a mid-Atlantic accent. And the combination of them was evidence of something more than the passage of time. The influence of America, as a force towards directness, informality and perhaps even liberation, was unmistakable.

More Americanisms that came to Britain in the 1940s can be found on p. 222.

More Americanisms that came to Britain in the 1940s can be found on p. 222.

***

In 1953 the Egyptian philosopher Zaki Najib Mahmoud went into a New York *movie theater* to watch the first film made in Cinerama, which used a huge curved screen designed to give the audience a sense of something like complete immersion. It certainly worked for him. The film, *This is Cinerama*, was designed to show the technology to best effect: perhaps Mahmoud was overwhelmed by the stirring images of the shaggy continent that dominated the film, and the patriotic hymns that accompanied them. 'Henceforth,' Mahmoud announced like a prophet, 'God has destined these people to lead, and us to follow. He has destined them to produce, and us to consume.'

Cinerama proved to be a cinematic dead end; there were technical issues. More importantly it was launched into a plummeting market: the television era was under way. Mahmoud was right about which nation was doing the leading; it just was not going to happen much in Cinerama.

I was a child of the 1950s. The first line from a song I can remember was 'Davy, Davy Crockett, King of the Wild Frontier'. Our default game was Cowboys and Indians, and no one wanted to be the Indians. In my memory we always had a television, and I can hardly remember the screen not being filled with a western: *Roy Rogers*, *Hopalong Cassidy*, *The Lone Ranger* (rather austere), *The Cisco Kid* (jolly), *The Range Rider* and so on and on.

Later I would be allowed to stay up and watch the American series that dominated the early days of ITV, like *Dragnet* ('Just the facts, ma'am') and *77 Sunset Strip*, which mainly seemed to comprise handsome young Edd Byrnes as Kookie perpetually combing his hair in the blinding light of a black-and-white Los Angeles.

It was an English childhood, not an American one. But by now America occupied a peculiar place in British culture. It was distant and unattainable, yet utterly fascinating. There was something in the relationship that matched the way Australians of that era referred to the Britain they had never seen as 'home'.

America was not home: it was very, very foreign – a weird place full of great flashy cars with teeth, and strange half-understood dangers. Fearful yet beguiling. There were even rumours that the Yanks had colour TV, but older boys said it didn't work very well.

The year 1953 had not just Cinerama but the Coronation as well, the event that famously turned TV in Britain from the radio's gawky and unconsidered younger sister into a domineering superstar. Joe Moran, who chronicled Britain's telly-watching in his book *Armchair Nation*, thinks that the loosening of hire purchase restrictions a year later was probably a more significant development. But one way and another, around that time British television became a genuine mass medium, and then THE mass medium.

The BBC had only a brief window to enjoy a monopoly of it. Independent Television began in London in September 1955, and then spread across the country. It was not that there had been any great demand for an alternative to the BBC; the nation was too enthralled with the novelty in the corner to complain. But the Conservatives had returned to power in 1951, six years after their crushing defeat by Labour. With Winston Churchill presiding from an increasingly ethereal height, the Tories were anxious mainly just to stay there and not upset anyone. However, the more go-getting commercial types in the party saw an opportunity, and pushed through the idea of a competing advertising-led TV channel.

The opposition to this idea was widespread and sometimes virulent. The horrified former head of the BBC, Lord Reith, compared the introduction of 'sponsored broadcasting' to smallpox, bubonic plague and dog racing. In the event ITV did not have sponsored programmes: the bill's proponents were forced to accept so many amendments and compromises that what emerged was something more like the BBC-with-knobs-on than anything American. As one US commentator said: 'The British have decided to paint the gaudy thing a sombre grey to blend in with the general fog.'

Perhaps the main influence on this knew nothing of his contribution. His name was J. Fred Muggs. The mascot of NBC's *Today* programme, he was a chimpanzee[6] who popped up to entertain US audiences during the *longueurs* in the Coronation ceremony. When, that is, NBC were not showing commercials 'advertising goods from cars to a deodorant', in the words of a horrified *Daily Express* reporter.

The BBC protested that all three of the American networks had broken their promise to handle the occasion with dignity. One of the proposed changes to the bill as it went through the Commons, designed to protect royal occasions from desecration, was described by its proponent as the 'J. Fred Muggs amendment'.

The new channel did not seem grey to the British. It was faster paced, more informal, less respectful, particularly in its news coverage. Its programming – both home-grown and American – slaughtered the BBC in the ratings without quite displacing it in public affection.

---

6 … and perhaps still is. In 2013 he was reported alive, aged 61, well and living in Florida with his girlfriend.

Reith's creation was forced to adapt and sharpen up; amid its for-mulaic pap, ITV, forced to accept both public responsibility and a devolved regional structure, had outbreaks of creativity and daring to which American TV did not aspire. The outcome was not a sombre greyness but what was agreed, for the next thirty years or more, to be 'the least-worst television in the world'. And this was almost certainly true.

But it was the bits between the programmes that made the most immediate impact. ITV was allowed far less advertising time than the American norm, and Britain's ad agencies were forced to grope their way towards what became a new art form: the thirty-second commercial. 'At the start we imported quite a lot of US people to help us cope, but mostly what they knew was of no direct relevance at all,' recalled Jeremy Bullmore, later chairman of J. Walter Thompson.

These ads were heavily reliant on jingles, earworms that remain lodged indelibly in the brain though everything else has gone beyond recall, including many of the products.

> *You'll wonder where the yellow went, when you brush your teeth with Pepsodent.*
> *Take a tip, take a Bristol. Take a real cigarette, that's a Bristol.*
> *The Esso sign means happy motoring, call at the Esso sign.*
> *One thousand and One cleans a big, big carpet. For less than half a crown.*
> *This is the luxury you can afford. Buy Cyril Lord.*

These jingles were emphatically not American. Advertising was still not globalised, though inside the industry there was talk of inter-national takeovers. And many of the ads were made by high-quality directors like Lindsay Anderson and, later, Ridley Scott to fund their riskier endeavours.[7]

In the US, the major advertising breakthrough of the 1950s came when a new brand of cigarettes was given a thoroughly British name, but a very unBritish slogan: 'Winston tastes good like a cigarette

---

7 Scott created the famous Hovis advert.

should'. The insistence on using the demotic *like* rather than the grammatical *as* produced a gratifying furore among grammatically minded Americans so loud that it propelled the new brand into a lasting position as a market leader. Walter Cronkite, the American broadcasting legend who was then hosting *The Morning Show* on CBS, trying to compete with J. Fred Muggs in the breakfast market, refused to say the line. Because of the grammar, not because smoking killed people.

But it was American-ness that British advertisers were selling: a world of consumer goods and labour-saving devices that the British saw on *I Love Lucy* and instantly coveted. Leaving aside the TV that they presumably already had, that still left a fridge, a washing machine, a car, a phone and central heating. The generations that had been through the war had acquired an unsentimental streak. They had done hard work, suffering and endurance, thank you, and were keen on solutions that would make life easier. And their television sets dangled them.

'There's too much said about these poisonous sprays,' said Percy Thrower, the BBC's reassuring gardening expert, advising viewers to get busy with the DDT and paraquat to rid themselves of insects and weeds. His DIY counterpart, Barry Bucknell, told viewers how to cover over their period-fireplaces and other nasty old ornate features. He was so popular he had to employ ten secretaries to deal with the 35,000 letters he might receive each week.

My parents' generation had had their share of cold and draughts: in the 1950s the great homes of the aristocracy were often demolished; manor houses might be worth less than a nice modern suburban detached; country cottages crumbled. 'You can't stand in the way of progress,' the grown-ups would say, even if it meant a motorway going through their garden. That phrase was not necessarily an Americanism, but it was a very American sentiment. Davy Crockett would have said the same.

Everywhere old British traditions were starting to wither: music halls were closing; pub life was beginning its slow decline; attendances at cricket (and at that stage football) matches were falling fast;

even cinemas now began to close,[8] but slowly – for teenagers they did still offer a haven from parental scrutiny. Almost all clubs and hobbies found themselves battling the new obsession for staying in, although sales of knitting wool flourished, to support the one hobby that combined nicely with the telly. For a nation obsessed with home, hearth and privacy, TV was a technological development that really catered to its tastes.

Yet the image of Britain did not reflect any of these changes. Once again American tourists began to arrive, though few went in the opposite direction. They were lured by a British Tourist Authority campaign in American magazines that promoted every cliché imaginable, from beefeaters and castles to hollyhocks and any thatched cottage still standing. The adman behind it, David Ogilvy, was unrepentant when attacked for not showing the gritty, progressive new Britain that the government liked to believe was emerging: 'No American is going to cross the briny ocean to look at a power station,' he wrote later.

Ogilvy also tried to counter lingering American perceptions. His surveys showed that potential visitors expected their British hosts would be 'polite, cultured, honest, straight-forward, clean and moral' but also 'aloof, intolerant and doleful'. So in his ads the British were always real charmers.

One reason for being doleful was that half the families in the US had incomes above £2,000 in the mid-1950s; the figure in Britain was 3 per cent. This was partly because Americans continued to work harder – which is why their holidays were always rushed. They also produced more. In 1948 a bizarre-sounding body was set up called the Anglo-American Council for Productivity, which had somehow emerged from the Marshall Plan and the Attlee government. The American solution to Britain's problems involved the three S's: standardisation, simplification, specialisation. But neither management nor unions were enthusiastic.

Two successful films released by Ealing Studios in 1953 summed

---

8 In my home town, Northampton, a dozen eventually went down to a single screen before the development of multiplexes transformed the economics.

up Britain's sentimental vision of itself. One, *The Titfield Thunderbolt*, was about a campaign to save a broken-down old branch line from being closed by British Railways and a rapacious bus company; the other, *The Maggie*,[9] was to save a small Scottish cargo boat from being put out of business by an American tycoon. Money wasn't everything, you see.

It was no doubt a confusing time to be a teenager, but then it always is. Richard Hoggart, in his much-admired (though perhaps more cited than read) 1957 book *The Uses of Literacy*, was scathing about the teenage boys who hung round the *jukeboxes* in the milk bars, playing American records: 'with drape-suits, picture ties, and an American slouch ... this is all a peculiarly thin and pallid form of dissipation, a sort of spiritual dry-rot amid the odour of boiled milk ... a myth world compounded of a few simple elements which they take to be those of American life ... They have no aim, no ambition, no protection, no belief.'

What they did believe is that, unless they wangled their way round it, they would face two years of national service, a requirement that ended in 1960. Given what the next cohort of teenagers would start getting up to, perhaps Hoggart might have been less censorious. If the milk-bar kids were modelling themselves on Americans, they would not have been the cheeky, confident, sassy Yanks of the 1930s talkies, but the strong, silent types of the westerns, or the real-life tragic heroes like James Dean and Buddy Holly. The heyday of American slang had passed. After all, who wants to imitate their parents' catchphrases?

But the one-way obsession with America endured. 'The Man from Laramie' went to No.1 in the charts, as sung by the very British Jimmy Young, in 1955. And it was pretty obvious that no one would get to No.1 in the States by singing 'The Man From Leighton Buzzard'.

Then came the brief popular frenzy which woke Britain's teenagers from their lethargy and set the tone for much that would follow. In 1954 Bill Haley & His Comets, an ex-country singer and his backing group who looked and dressed like wine waiters, recorded a simplistic

---

9 The name would eventually acquire a certain retrospective irony.

but lively song called 'Rock Around the Clock' as a B-side. It took a year for it to become the first great international rock-and-roll smash, and that was largely due to it being used over the opening credits in the film *Blackboard Jungle*.

It was 1956 before anyone over about 21 took any notice in Britain, when Haley and the Comets starred in their own film ('It's the whole story of rock and roll,' said the publicity). This was also called *Rock Around the Clock*, and at that point the spiritual dry rot turned to something that seemed altogether more threatening. Suddenly, the term **rock and roll** began to appear in print, but because of what was happening in the cinemas not on the jukeboxes.

Across Britain, audiences got up from their seats, started *jiving* and/or wrecking the joint. In Burnley, after several disturbances, the chief constable and his deputy turned up and sat in the stalls in case of trouble. In Manchester a manager was sprayed with a fire hose. In South London cinemas refused to show the films on Sundays, which is when the problems were worst. An official at the Trocadero cinema, Elephant and Castle, said: 'We have been instructed to show the film *Gun Fury* instead.'

So that was OK then. Though authority had a general sense that it was something to be deplored, few of the jivers, fire-hosers, their parents or the police officers were likely to be aware of the background to the term *rock and roll*. 'The roots of rock music stem directly from sexual imagery,' wrote the slang expert Jonathon Green later, 'thus the 1922 song title, "My Man Rocks Me (With One Steady Roll)".'

Even fewer might have taken notice of the word ***around***, which in a phrase like *Rock Around the Clock* is an Americanism. Someone on *The Times* did though, and insisted on calling the film *Rock Round the Clock*. I suspect *around* only became anglicised through song titles, from 'Love is Just Around the Corner' (1934) to 'I Get Around' (1964).

Other harbingers of the new youth culture began to arrive, but slowly. The pioneering TV pop music programme *Cool for Cats* made it onto London ITV late in 1956, and across the network the following summer. But in 1959 the jazz musician Humphrey Lyttelton still had to explain to an audience at the Buxton Festival that *cat* was

American for *bloke*, especially if that bloke was a jazz musician, or at least an enthusiast, and that *cool* meant relaxed.

A *square* was somewhat harder to explain, especially as the orchestral conductor Sir John Barbirolli had just been called one, and was part of the discussion. Sir John did say politely that he was 'always anxious to learn something about what is going on in the world of music'. *Uncool* had made it into print by 1960. Many of these words that reached British teenagers in the late 1950s – including *groovy* and *chick* – had been around the American jazz scene for decades, largely popularised by the band leader Cab Calloway. But Halifax was a long way from Harlem in those days.

Americanisms were still spreading, and the usual suspects grumbled about them: Sir Linton Andrews, editor of the *Yorkshire Post*, complained in 1956 about reporters using words like *balding* and *gangling*. 'Do not "going bald" and "lanky" meet our needs?' he asked, addressing the Bradford English Society.[10]

The imported words of the 1950s were mostly in keeping with a bland decade, though some arrived with a fanfare. In September 1952, in the midst of the Korean War, *The Times*, still a paper deeply suspicious of innovations, suddenly discovered a new addition to its vocabulary:

'*GIMMICKS*' FOR KOREA: NEW DEVICE ON U.S. JET FIGHTERS

Washington, Sept. 8

Mr Finletter, Secretary of the Air Force, told a Press conference today that a new technical device – a 'gimmick' as he called it – on the F-86 Sabre jet fighter, soon to be tried in Korea, will give the United States a 'very great technical advantage' over the Russian MIG. 'With this new "gimmick," or whatever you call it, more MIG-15s are going to go down and more F-86s are going to stay up,' Mr Finletter said. Details of the new device will not be released 'until the Communists have learned of its capability'.

---

10 Probably not, I would say. *Balding* may have been one of the clipped adjectives spread through *Time* magazine.

Two reports later that month hinted, first, that the gimmick was working, and then that maybe it was not even being used. Never mind the weapon, though, *The Times* loved its shiny new word, although it had been around in the US since the 1920s, originally 'as a device for making a fair game crooked' (OED); and it had very occasionally popped up in US reports in less fussy British rivals. It appeared fifty-seven times in all in *The Times* before the 1950s were out, and that was before the paper started becoming a bit more gimmicky itself, putting news on the front page and other such fripperies.

Another addition to British life were *blue jeans*, though they were nowhere near as ubiquitous as they would become. The concept cannot have been wholly unfamiliar, even if the *Babbitt* glossary compiler felt that way three decades earlier. But they were not part of a bourgeois wardrobe; they were something perhaps worn by British working men, though more often by eccentrically informal foreigners.

The cloth, 'Jene fustian' was recorded in 1567. The first OED citation for *blue jeans*, from the *Illinois Gazette*, is dated 1823. A Frenchman wore blue jeans to compete in the shooting at Bisley in 1903. In 1919 the *Daily Express* reported on the Duke of Abercorn leaving his ancestral home to emigrate to South Africa, and speculated that it may mark a trend towards 'marquises in their shirt sleeves and earls in blue jeans'.

Mrs Howard Hawks, having been voted best-dressed woman of the year, talked from Los Angeles of wearing 'wild shirts and blue jeans' (though presumably not in public) in 1945. In 1951, Prince Philip, bright young thing that he was, was reported in blue jeans at an evening of country square dancing in Ottawa. And in 1953 girls in blue jeans were spotted on the Thames at Battersea. And so the rough beast of modern British everyday fashion slowly emerged, slouching towards Chelsea to be born. An American slouch, that would be.

British domestic life was also slowly picking up foreign influences. There are two more words that had long been well understood in Britain but only as alien concepts. They were alien for the same reason: the weather. One was *patio*, which often made it into travel-page articles from abroad but was little considered as a garden feature before Basil Spence optimistically included patios in his plan to rebuild the Glasgow slums in 1959.

It is not absolutely clear whether the word came direct from Spain, where a patio was an inner courtyard, mainly shady, or the US, where it was an outside terrace. But the British patio developed along American lines, so the word probably spread from the US, rather than from pioneering package holidaymakers. Especially as the first dictionary citation is, yet again, from P.G. Wodehouse, in a letter written in 1931.

The other word was *barbecue*, which first crossed the Atlantic in 1697, usually meaning a raised wooden structure used for either cooking or sleeping, safe from ground-level dangers. The Americans had rapidly adopted the modern idea of a barbecue as an outdoor party. In 1769 George Washington attended one and 'stayed all night'. And in the twentieth century, the royal family kept attending them on tours to countries with suitable climates.

However, reports of British barbecues are more elusive until the mid-1950s. The US Air Force held one at Denham in 1955, a characteristically low-key affair, featuring 1,200lbs of Argentine beef. In June 1956, *Ideal Home* magazine featured a guide to barbecue entertaining, which may have started the modern trend and established the pattern that normally makes British barbecues a triumph of hope over experience: 1956 was an infamously wet summer, even for those not sprayed with fire hoses.

Other American words and phrases that made it to Britain in the 1950s can be found on p. 223.

✳✳✳

At intervals American journalists would pronounce on whether or not Europe as a whole and Britain in particular had fallen entirely under America's spell. In 1955 Art Buchwald of the *Washington Post* received an announcement from Lyons Corner House, the by now falling giants of British eating out, that they were opening a Wimpy Bar by Leicester Square. This was described as 'atomic-age catering': 'No cutlery is needed … All drinks are served in bottles and will be drunk with a straw … All sugar is wrapped. Napkins are paper. It seems to be an idea that many housewives will want to copy, since it cuts the washing up.'

For the avoidance of doubt, the announcement then explained what a hamburger was. 'One of the nicest things about Great Britain is that it has remained aloof from any atomic age innovations,' Buchwald mused sadly.

In 1960 there was a further culinary development. This time the publicity handout began 'It's gay; it's exciting.'[11] The *Observer* sent the food writer Cyril Ray to sample the Ox in Flames, 'Britain's first American drive-in,' sited on the road from London to Hastings, complete with what may well have been Britain's first *parking lot.*

He was not impressed: 'Although the hot dog … only looks, feels and tastes like plastic, the knives and forks provided actually are, which is very hygienic, but rather hard to handle, what with plastic being flexible.'[12] A woman asked for vinegar to put on what were described as *French fries*, but there was none. 'I've never been much of a one for pouring malt vinegar over my food but, as I sawed at a rubbery frankfurter that didn't taste with a plastic knife that wouldn't cut, I could see what she meant,' Ray concluded. 'Geographically the Ox in Flames, on the Farnborough by-pass, is between Elmer's End and Pratt's Bottom. You could say much the same gastronomically.'

***

In the early 1960s my brother Richard and I were avid readers of the *New Musical Express*, which always printed the American charts as well as the British ones. In 1962 a British group, The Springfields, actually reached the US top 20 with their fairly unremarkable recording

---

11 This is an indicator that *gay* had not yet changed its meaning. As code among American homosexuals it dates back at least to the 1920s. It then spread into the subterranean British homosexual subculture before entering the mainstream on both sides of the Atlantic in the late 1960s. So the modern use is an Americanism, but of a very particular kind. The *Manchester Guardian* has at least three mentions in the 1950s that look as though they might have been clues to the initiated.

12 *Deal with it*, as we say now.

of 'Silver Threads and Golden Needles'. Such things simply did not happen. It was like the day Northampton Town knocked Arsenal out of the Cup.[13] A year later a British heavyweight, Henry Cooper, knocked down the loud-mouthed rising star of boxing, Cassius Clay (later Muhammad Ali) in a fight at Wembley. Knocked down, not out; Ali went on to win. But, still, wasn't that something?

Against that, Elvis Presley, the greatest star of the early 1960s, never bothered to tour England.[14] It was like living in a New Zealand of the North. Through the 1950s, there had been a growing awareness that Europe might also be cool: Vespas and Lambrettas, Gauloises and Gitanes, Sangria and Asti Spumante; fondue and quiche; Audrey Hepburn walking down the Spanish Steps with a gelato … anywhere but Britain.

Many of Britain's most important, if not well known, talents were getting out. These were the scientists emigrating in the phenomenon known as the *brain drain*, whereby American companies and even government departments wooed what the popular papers then always called Britain's *boffins* (from RAF slang) to go and work for them for much better money in much better surroundings in a more optimistic country. The slang, for once, might have been British; the gain was America's. 'It is a compliment I would rather do without,' grumbled Lord Hailsham, the Science Minister. He blamed the weakness of American education, and hoped for the day when 'there may be an adequate interchange between our country and theirs, and not a one-way traffic'.

And then suddenly everything changed. 'Young people driven by ambition have always travelled from the outlying provinces to the city,' wrote the cultural historian Peter Conrad. 'It is an imperative of natural selection, a means of establishing your place in the pecking order. In an Americanised world, this journey of self-promotion extends beyond national borders and vaults across oceans.' For the

---

13 Later that year 'Stranger on the Shore' by Acker Bilk and 'Telstar' by The Tornadoes both reached No.1 in the US and the novelty began to wear off.

14 It later emerged that Elvis's sinister manager, 'Colonel' Tom Parker, might have had his own reasons for not leaving the US, since he probably had no right to be there in the first place.

scientists that meant getting out; others mounted a short-lived but stunning counter-attack.

The pioneers were the photographer David Bailey and the model Jean Shrimpton, who went to New York in 1962 for a feature in American *Vogue*. Bailey rejected the obvious Manhattan backdrops and took the pictures of this ethereal, protean, unselfconscious beauty amidst the unconsidered earthly clutter of the wintry city: fashion as documentary. She had a teddy bear as a prop. It could have gone either way, but the magazine decided to love it. Diana Vreeland, the presiding goddess, welcomed the pair into the office by roaring at an assistant: 'STOP! THE ENGLISH HAVE ARRIVED!'

In October 1962 'Love Me Do', a single by an unheralded, eccentrically spelt foursome from Liverpool, got into the lower reaches of the charts, earning them a brief profile in our copy of the *New Musical Express*. In 1963, the year of satire, the Profumo scandal, the Great Train Robbery and the invention of sexual intercourse (©Philip Larkin), the Beatles took Britain by storm. The American contribution to the year's momentousness was the assassination of President Kennedy. In February 1964 Liverpool conquered New York. 'Fringed, frisky and friendly … the most devastating male quartet since the Four Horsemen of the Apocalypse,' said Donald Zec, showbiz correspondent of the *Daily Mirror*.

Thousands saw them take off from Heathrow; thousands greeted them in New York. Walter Cronkite compared their landing to D-Day. Two days later millions watched them on *The Ed Sullivan Show*: 'a record-setting 73 million,' according to the official Ed Sullivan website, 'making it one of the seminal moments in television history … people still remember exactly where they were the night The Beatles stepped onto Ed Sullivan's stage'.[15] Which is interesting, since that's what the British say of hearing the news about JFK. By April they were not just in the US top 20, like the Springfields, they were Nos.1, 2, 3, 4 and 5.[16]

---

15 Mostly at home, watching TV, one imagines.

16 This was a quirk. Music industry politics meant that Beatles records were not released in the US in 1963, which intensified the frenzy when it finally erupted.

In their wake came many more, most notably the Rolling Stones. All of this, still immortalised on Wikipedia as the British Invasion, constituted a cultural, musical, sociological and even to a small extent geopolitical phenomenon. The US cultural establishment in general was going through one of its periodic phases of Anglophilia. In Hollywood, British actors were much in demand, socially and professionally. 'If you were a leading Brit star who spoke in those delicious tones you were the No.1 catch of all the famous dinner hostesses,' Zec recalled in 2016.[17] 'Laurence Harvey had merely to open his mouth and Mrs Samuel Goldwyn would swoon all the way to the smelling salts. He would wait till coffee then give the adoring diners a basinful of Oh for a Muse of Fire, and he could eat free for a lifetime.'

In the winter of 1965–6 Roger Miller had a transatlantic hit with the ridiculous 'England Swings' ('Like a pendulum do / Bobbies on bicycles two by two.') Then, after *Time* magazine ran its famous Swinging London cover in April 1966, the whole thing began to implode, and Carnaby Street became the least cool place on the planet to visit until the Hard Rock Cafe chain arrived.

But nothing in the modern Anglo-American relationship goes one way westward. Musically, the Beatles and, even more so, the Stones were themselves influenced by rhythm and blues, which they re-fettled and re-exported. Linguistically, the Beatles' lyrics had elements from deepest England, throwing in the Isle of Wight ('When I'm Sixty-Four'), Blackburn, Lancashire ('A Day in the Life'), semolina and pilchards (mixed together in 'I am the Walrus') and even politicians ('Taxman': Mr Wilson and Mr Heath).

However, unless you invest in a style of thoroughly self-conscious Englishness, as, say, Ian Dury did, it is extremely difficult to sing any form of rock and roll without lapsing into American, as the Beatles did from the start: 'She Loves You, Yeah, Yeah, Yeah'; 'I Wanna Hold Your Hand'. 'Ticket to Ride' was an American-style *one-way* ticket, not a British *single*. There was a short-lived fashion for American groups to take ye olde English names like the Town Criers and the Beau Brummels. But it was the reverse influence that was more durable.

---

17 Shortly before his 98th birthday.

This was even more true of the Stones, who were generally more difficult to introduce to one's parents. Mick Jagger helped sell the word *rooster* to urban England (they remain cockerels in the country-side) by investing 'Little Red Rooster' with a raw sexuality that was deliciously ironic when you consider the word's censorious origins.[18] The Stones' lyrics were overwhelmingly American in a way that was reputedly far too much for Brian Jones's father, a church organist in Cheltenham: 'There's enough of these Americanisms around,' he told his doomed, brilliant, wayward boy. 'Couldn't you just sing "I Can't Get Any Satisfaction"?' However, the same story is told about Paul McCartney's father: 'Couldn't you just sing "She Loves You, Yes, Yes, Yes?"' So this is either a pattern or an urban myth. But a pattern is not impossible: parents across Britain were thinking the same.

The music of the mid-1960s was heard primarily by British youth, especially in southern England, from the pirate radio stations quartered in ships and disused forts off the East Coast at a time when the BBC, hampered by union-imposed restrictions on 'needle time', broadcast a bare minimum of pop music. The pirates existed in a rather thrilling edge-of-the-law twilight, like marijuana and teenage sex, displaced Radio Luxembourg and infuriated both the BBC and the government, which legislated against them and, in 1967, paved the way for Radio 1.

The pirates' style was essentially American. My own favourite DJ was the late Tommy Vance (born Richard Anthony Crispian Francis Prew Hope-Weston in Oxfordshire), who had worked in both Canada and the US, and had a pleasant if Americanised voice and a genuine taste for the music. Vance had stints on the two most popular pirate stations, Radio Caroline and Radio London, and later worked for the BBC, as did many of his former shipmates. And thus the British Invasion mutated instead into part of Britain's Americanisation process.

***

This most flamboyant and heedless of decades had started with a

---

18 See p. 45.

controversy that convulsed, if not the world exactly, then at least the normally hushed cloisters of American lexicography. In 1961 the American firm of G&C Merriam – now known as Merriam-Webster – published the eagerly awaited volume officially known as *Webster's Third New International Dictionary*, otherwise *Webster's Third* or W3, lineal descendant of the sacred 1828 book.

The editor, Philip Gove, dropped any Websterian notion that he had any business or ability to command the language; he was very much a descriptivist. His most notorious inclusion was that of *ain't*, spoken and sometimes written in the US since at least the eighteenth century and in south-east England since time immemorial. Gove included various other words too, though he teetered and faltered when confronted with the great taboo of *fuck*. He was denounced as 'subversive' and 'permissive', which was an appropriate way for anyone to begin the 1960s.

If this flashy decade has any deeper meaning, it marks a dividing line between the age when long-established societal orthodoxies were largely unquestioned and the age when they weren't. There was, we had been told, a right way and a wrong way – or at the very least a good and a bad way – in music, religion, dress codes, hairstyles, politics, sexual behaviour, grammar and vocabulary. At various stages in the 1960s all these began to break down.

The American role in this process changed somewhat over the course of the decade. At first, its youthful new president, John Kennedy, was seen as the embodiment of optimism and hope. But then JFK was shot, and then Martin Luther King, and then Kennedy's younger brother Bobby. The streets, the ghettoes and the campuses were beset by rioting. Kennedy's successors became wholly bogged down by the mismanaged war against Communism in Vietnam and shipped off their young men to be killed, maimed or traumatised.[19]

Vietnam was the most public of all wars. The innocent Americans had not yet learned that the correct approach to combat is to keep all the horror secret and then declare victory. Instead, the media were

---

19 But not those scared and savvy enough to evade it: Bill Clinton, George W. Bush, Dick Cheney, Donald Trump …

allowed unprecedented and unrepeated access to the entire theatre. The early communication satellites beamed the pictures across the world and the war was as visible in European homes as in American ones, if nowhere near as real, since their boys were not involved. Harold Wilson, Britain's prime minister of the time, was constantly abused for supporting his closest ally's endeavours, and got no credit for skilfully evading any obligation to send troops.

The effect was a return to something of the sense of inferiority and distance Britain experienced in the early part of the decade. It was not that anyone wanted to be sent to Vietnam as such, but one did wonder (and this one still does) what it might have been like to experience something more challenging than a British university at the end of the 1960s. We protested as well, though no one was conscripting us; Mayor Daley's Chicago police were not beating us up; we did not live in Russia or China or Africa; we had student grants not loans; and lived the most liberal, comfortable and free-from-fear life of any generation in history, before or since. God knows what we were thinking. Perhaps on our shades-of-grey little island we just needed a taste of America and its stark primary colours.

***

And more people did get a taste of it. In 1961 David Ogilvy, the adman who had sold a tea-cosy version of Britain to American tourists, was awarded the contract to do the same in reverse. His approach this time was utterly different; the perception was that the US was impossibly expensive for British travellers: 423,000 Americans visited the UK in 1961 – only 43,000 went the other way. Ogilvy set out to persuade the British that they could have an American holiday and spend only £35 a week.

This was indeed possible, even in New York, provided one enjoyed the diet and lifestyle of a nineteenth-century Russian peasant. The new US travel office off Oxford Street was 'inundated', reported the *Observer*, and British travel to America indeed took off. There was a blip between 1966 and 1970 when the cash-strapped Labour government imposed a £50 limit on taking cash out of the country, which even under Ogilvy's figures would allow only a nine-day trip.[20] But it was only a blip, and the new flow of tourists would come to have immense consequences for Britain's language.

In the late 1960s words were being coined in the US, because that's where things were happening, and bedding down simultaneously in all forms of culture. That included the noun *happening*, 'a largely improvised or spontaneous performance intended as artistic display', a word which lived fast and died young, and also *long hot summer*, often cited as a cause of ghetto riots, though less of a problem in a country with short cool summers. *Hippie* dated back to the 1950s in the US and arrived in Britain later; the hippies took *acid*, *pot* and *hash*. But most other bits of drug terminology stayed out of mainstream use.

There were also the terms that came out of the Vietnam War, like *escalate* (a back-formation from *escalator*) on the one hand and *peacenik* on the other. *Hawks* were for escalation; *doves* were peaceniks who did not smoke pot. And then there was *draft dodger*. Although the term *draft* had not been used as a synonym for conscription in Britain, it rapidly became recognised during Vietnam, because it was in the news constantly and was certainly widely known by 1968, when Simon and Garfunkel released *Bookends*, containing the whimsical number 'Punky's Dilemma' and the lines 'Old Roger, draft dodger / Leaving by the basement door'.

Nonetheless, when the BBC did a version recorded by session musicians, someone insisted on protecting the audience from the Americanism and calling him 'Old Roger, tax dodger'. Last year a friend of mine referred to an Englishman in the First World War as 'a draft dodger'. So the world turns.

Other Americanisms to reach Britain in the 1960s are on p. 225.

---

20 The limit did not apply in the Sterling Area, which was basically the remaining colonies and the Commonwealth, plus and minus a few, the minuses including Canada.

5

STEPPING UP TO THE PLATE

In June 1978 Dr Robert Burchfield, the chief editor of the OED, gave an address to a convention of American librarians in Chicago: not the obvious forum to start a major international controversy. However, Burchfield used his speech to make both a diagnosis and a prediction.

Burchfield said he was convinced that 'the two main forms of English – American English and British English … are continuing to move apart, and that existing elements of linguistic dissimilarities between them will intensify as time goes on'. He also said that the two main forms of English would become mutually unintelligible within 200 years.

At a press conference afterwards Burchfield explained that 94 per cent of Britons had never visited the US and nearly 90 per cent of Americans had never visited Britain, and that the mass of people was more powerful than the mass media. British English would retain its ancient character, he thought, because American English changed so fast.

The following Sunday the Irish polymath Dr Conor Cruise O'Brien responded in the *Observer*, with a column headed WHEN LORDS OF THE WORD GET IT WRONG. Burchfield's argument, he said, 'consists of a gallery of unexamined assumptions and ignored relevancies, forming together a prospective non-sequitur of sublime proportions'.

Barring nuclear war or the like, O'Brien argued, divergence was highly improbable: 'Nobody who watches children, in any part of these islands, looking at and listening to *Sesame Street* and *Kojak* is likely to feel that American forms of English are beginning to progress towards unintelligibility on this side of the Atlantic.'

Sion Haworth of London W3 weighed in helpfully in a letter to the *Guardian*, saying he found Burchfield's forecast reassuring: 'At this moment in time, as an observer of the sentence construction situation, I can only conclude that our native tongue is in a drifting condition towards a state of equality with American English, and should have completed manoeuvres into a docking mode with a temporal spectrum of ten years.'

Later that year, in *Encounter* magazine, Burchfield called in aid the discrepancies that were already appearing between the languages in the separate states of East and West Germany. Since East Germany ceased to exist just over a decade later, this was not a very well-chosen example. Indeed, now that a fifth of Burchfield's two centuries have passed, one can assess that in the prognostication steeplechase, he is lying a bad third behind O'Brien, with Sion Haworth of London W3 in front.

It was not even necessary for any time to elapse before sensing that Burchfield was talking rot. As I was told by someone who was on the OED editorial staff at the time: 'I don't think anyone agreed with Bob Burchfield when he said it. He just liked to make provocative statements.'

Burchfield was an Oxonian of great erudition, and one assumes someone else booked and paid for his flight to Chicago. So one way and another he may not have noticed what was happening to transatlantic travel in general. In September 1977 the buccaneering entrepreneur Freddie Laker began operating flights from Gatwick to New York for £59, which even at 1977 values was insanely cheap, particularly compared with the amounts airlines had previously charged.

Laker's established rivals had to compete, grudgingly. By chance this coincided with a surge in the sterling/dollar exchange rate: from early

1979 to mid-1981 the pound was permanently above two dollars, at one time almost touching 2.5, which made it cheaper to leave London for a weekend in New York than one in Paris. David Ogilvy's idea of spending £35 a week almost began to look plausible, though not quite.

Five years later Laker went bust, but he had established a pattern of cheap and cheerful travel that paved the way for the likes of Ryanair and Easyjet, though they did away with the cheerful bit. He also got a generation of what would soon become known as *yuppies* accustomed to holidays in the US. While there they began to absorb the language. This did not permeate quite as far down the social scale as 1930s Hollywood slang had done, but it gave a great many people who would go on to make careers in the media, politics and other positions of influence a thorough brainwash.

And hundreds of thousands of other Britons started flying off to Disney World for their summer holidays, astonished by the excellent value – though nowhere near as astonished as the locals were by the sight of people insane enough to take a holiday in Florida in its unspeakably hot August.

The low dollar reflected a dismal decade for the US. America's normally boundless self-esteem took a constant battering in the 1970s: the Watergate scandal; the oil crisis; the final collapse of South Vietnam; the fall of the Shah of Iran and the subsequent capture of fifty-two American hostages – embarrassment piled on embarrassment. It was not an especially perky decade in Britain either, but our expectations were lower.

The fear of nuclear holocaust which, as O'Brien said, might have given Burchfield victory, had diminished since the early 1960s. But, on a daily basis, Britain and the US felt less safe. †*Mugging* was an old English localism, long dormant. But both the crime and the word rippled back from New York early in the 1970s. It was also the decade when *hijacking* began to be used primarily to describe the deeply unpleasant armed takeover of an aircraft. This displaced its earlier use of capturing a consignment of bootleg liquor or a vanload of banknotes, crimes at the jollier end of the gangster spectrum, which might explain its upbeat name.

Relatively few words made it across the Atlantic in the 1970s. One of them was *counterculture*, which became a catch-all term for the whole hippie, druggie, love-and-peace thing before it began to fade from public consciousness. The counterculture veered off in various directions, one of them being what was mostly known at first by the Americanism *women's lib* before the phrase (though not its intention) faded away to be replaced by a word that would have been familiar to the suffragettes: *feminism.*

Another spin-off was the environmental movement, which was also American-inspired, in part by *Silent Spring*, Rachel Carson's 1962 book exposing the dangers of pesticides. The 1960s had other preoccupations, and the word *ecology* was little used outside specialist scientific circles until late in the decade; *environmentalism*, first recorded by the OED in the *Washington Post* in 1966, did not appear even in the *Guardian* until 1973. *Green* in this sense also emerged in the 1970s, though it seems to be a rare Germanism, from West Germany's pioneering green party, *die Grünen.*

There was, however, a particularly British nostalgic middle-class element amid the more earnest aspects of this. Country houses, and cottages in particular, came back into a fashion that has never gone away. Some of it was rather male orientated. There was a renewed taste for real ale and village cricket, neither of which had any connection with America. Indeed, the decade was not just a comparatively thin time for the export of Americanisms; several of the words reflected America's gloom.

A list of Americanisms to reach Britain in the 1970s is on p. 225.

*** *

Within two and a half years of Burchfield's speech the political pendulum in both Britain and the US had swung dramatically to the right. Margaret Thatcher became prime minister in 1979; the following year Ronald Reagan was elected president. Together, they formed the strongest partnership of transatlantic soulmates yet witnessed. It was all very Hollywood. They were, so it seemed, the joint masters of the universe: he the muscly but genial frontman; she the hard-as-nails brains of the operation. And indeed their joint reign that dominated the 1980s was the harbinger of a new and very different era: the collapse of the Communist bloc followed by an epoch of capitalist triumphalism.

This Anglo-American political victory also brought in its train total dominance for the English language. Even after the Second World War it was still possible to ignore the various signals and pretend that English and French were still in some kind of rough parity. After the Berlin Wall collapsed the victory of English was complete.[1]

In 1992 Henry Kahane, an American-based expert on Romance languages, traced the history of No.1 languages since the dawn of civilisation. First there was Greek and then Latin which, even after Rome fell, remained Europe's means of administration. Next came French, spread through 'the chivalric culture of medieval aristocracy'. The Renaissance produced 'the educated courtier who combines the two traditions of the humanist and the knight; Italian is part of his equipment'. But by the eighteenth century French had become the courtly language again.[2] And one might say it retained its foothold in diplomacy, fashion and fancy restaurant menus at least until the *beau monde* was succeeded by the jet set.

Now once again there is an undisputable global language, fulfilling the dream of the late Victorian and Edwardian reformers, who invented Esperanto, Volapük, Ekselsioro, Mondlingvo and the rest to try to meet this very need. But their inventions came to naught: the future global language already existed. 'Ours,' concluded Kahane, 'is the day of American English.'

Not English, you will note. One version of it.

***

We will shortly start to discuss what is really going on inside the grand and sprawling mansion that constitutes the House of English:

---

1 This is not hindsight. It struck me by the Brandenburg Gate in 1990 as the East Germans voted in their first free election and I listened to a busker warbling 'Naads in wide sadin, neh-va reachy vee-enn'.

2 Even in Britain, during the reign of the non-anglophone George I.

the blocked pipes; the defective wiring; the whiff of drains; the fundamentally abusive relationship between the head of the household and the rest of the family; and the constant incursions on to the neighbours' property. But for the moment, let's just admire the magnificence of the facade. Seen from any angle it is undoubtedly impressive and intimidating.

When gazing at any stately home, one has to remember that at some point in history a member of the family must have had some combination of skill, luck and unscrupulousness. The entrepreneurs who made the eighteenth-century Industrial Revolution were primarily British; for the last 150 years they have mainly been American. The major advances in telecommunication came from one country or the other, and thus the language of telegraphy, shipping and most especially aviation – where Babel would have caused regular catastrophes – became English. And that was even before the computer and internet revolutions.

There are also the qualities of the language itself: full of simple monosyllables, absorbent and protean. As the scholar Jacques Barzun explained, English is quite simply far more suited to be a global language than either German or any Romance language: 'It possesses two vocabularies, nearly parallel, which carry the respective suggestions of abstract and concrete, formal and vernacular. A writer can say *concede* or *give in*; *assume* or *take up*; *deliver* or *hand over*; *insert* or *put in*; *retreat* or *fall back*.'

He continued: 'French, having lost much of its brisk medieval vocabulary during the Latinizing vogue of the Renaissance, has been left with very formal-sounding words for everyday use – for example *comestible* and *consommation* for cases in which we would say *food* and *drink*.[3] As for German, said Barzun, its 'lumpy compounds and awkward syntax' make it seem as though you are hearing the same thing three times over.

Russian, of course, is far more difficult to learn except in infancy; Chinese exponentially more so. But in English, beginners can flail

---

3 Indeed, the linguistic rituals involved in simply buying a morning croissant in provincial France are only slightly more informal than a cotillion in Jane Austen's Bath.

around on the nursery slopes without fear of breaking their necks. No one has to worry whether inanimate objects are masculine or feminine; the tenses are relatively straightforward and no one cares much if you get them muddled. Sure there are some fiddly spellings, but half the natives can't spell either and in any case the computer will do it for you. As a world language, English works.

At the start of the twentieth century, German still had strong claims to be the language of science. But that was killed off by the First World War, even before Germany committed reputational suicide in the Second. As a contender French has died much harder. But the inexorable nature of the process can be seen in the development of a supranational Europe.

Britain stood aloof from the initial process of forming the European Coal and Steel Community, which began with six countries (France, West Germany, Italy, Belgium, Netherlands and Luxembourg) in the 1950s. The Germans, in the atmosphere of that time, could not possibly be seen to be forcing their language down anyone's throats. So French became the unofficial working language by default.

However, as what became the European Union grew in numbers and scope, that position became untenable. This was not primarily due to the accession of Britain and Ireland in 1973. It was because most of Scandinavia and much of Eastern Europe also joined. Before long nearly all Europe's officials and parliamentarians were people who spoke English – some perfectly, some haltingly. But only a minority spoke French.

Official translations were always available in Finnish, Maltese, Slovenian and twenty-one other languages. But anyone who wanted to persuade, plot or even pass the time of day in Brussels or Strasbourg with a random representative from another country really had to speak English. That is in an organisation without any American presence, and which is due soon to have no British presence either. Brexit is expected to have minimal effect on Europe's language, except that Britain will have no direct influence on it.[4]

---

4 France and Germany both decided that *Brexit* would be regarded as masculine. This was perhaps the only aspect of the issue which was not a problem for Britain.

A similar pattern took hold in almost all international gatherings. English also rules at the United Nations, even though there are five other official languages, not least because its HQ is in New York and the staff have to understand basic English simply to get to the office and survive in the city.[5]

The Olympic Games normally take place with three official languages: English, French and that of the host country. Inside the Beijing Olympic Stadium in 2008 commentary alternated between Chinese and English, with a minimal contractual-obligation smattering of French. At a press conference, a French journalist demanded fairer treatment from Jacques Rogge, the then president of the International Olympic Committee. He was brushed aside with contempt. (I heard it happen.)

Rogge is a Belgian, born in Ghent in Flemish-speaking Flanders. In the late 1990s my wife and I visited Antwerp, the biggest city in Flanders and once a largely French-speaking city. She asked a woman for directions in her fluent French, and was greeted with scowling silence which appeared to indicate not incomprehension but disgust. So I tried in English. That did the trick.

On the first night I ever spent in South Korea, in 1987, I wandered down to an evening market not far from the centre of Seoul. I had no point of contact: no one spoke a word of English; the signs were incomprehensible; even the food was bafflingly foreign. Now, throughout the country, English is practised as if it were the state religion. The official language of the world's newest country, South Sudan, is English, although it had sixty-eight indigenous tongues to choose from.

Across the world there are linguistic flashpoints where English offers a non-contentious demilitarised zone. Any back-channel discussions between Israelis and Arabs necessarily take place in English. In India the main language, Hindi, is first among equals; but a Bengali, say, would never use it to speak to a Tamil. 'English is an essential language in India,' said Salman Rushdie. 'Not only because

---

5 At the UN the official version of English, in theory at least, is actually British English: documents are supposed to have British spellings.

of its technical vocabularies and the international communication it makes possible, but also simply to permit two Indians to talk to each other in a tongue which neither party hates.' Even in peaceable Switzerland, when a businessman from German-speaking Zurich talks to a counterpart from French-speaking Geneva, I am assured that it is now normal for them to meet on the neutral ground of English.

Members of the burgeoning Chinese bourgeoisie send their sons and daughters to English public schools, knowing that they will get a huge educational advantage even if they learn little except the language. There they adopt English names, as do many of their stay-at-home compatriots, who will often come later to the language schools. Those clustered in Oxford and Cambridge are especially popular with students of all nations, since the difference between the statements 'I studied *at* Oxford' and 'I studied *in* Oxford' may lose something in translation.

At demonstrations across the planet, protesters habitually use slogans in English, knowing that way they can get attention from the world's news media instead of just talking to themselves. In the Arab Spring of 2011 the words GO OUT MUBARAK were crayoned on a man's forehead in Tahrir Square, Cairo. Not the way we would have phrased it, but we got the point. Young Indonesians are said to use English expressions with each other for romantic purposes, not just because English is thought to sound cool but because it helps free them from religious and cultural inhibitions.

These last examples might be taken as offshoots of a related but different phenomenon: Globish, which is not just a word and a sort-of language, but a business opportunity and a trademark. It was invented by Jean-Paul Nerrière, a Frenchman and a former IBM executive. It has a vocabulary of 1,500 words, which are deemed to be enough for random conversations between strangers in airport lounges and what must be pretty basic business negotiations. Jokes, metaphors and acronyms are all taboo.

Nerrière's observation was that non-native English speakers in such meetings communicated better with each other – in English – than their British and American counterparts. He is trying to sell the product to native speakers too. As his website (START NOW – just

$49.95) says: 'One of the big problems with companies is that their English speakers speak TOO MUCH English for the people they work with.' Indeed, he appears to see himself not as a friend to English but as a kind of guerrilla fighter on behalf of its enemies: 'Globish will limit the influence of the English language dramatically,' he told Robert McCrum. It is already happening, according to the writer and former interpreter Frances Edmonds. 'My interpreter colleagues have noticed that international forums nowadays have been hi-jacked by "international" individuals, all of whom speak some approximation to the English language we know and love,' she told me. 'They all seem to understand each other in this pidgin language and nod reassuringly. The only problem is that no native English speaker ever has a clue about what is being said or agreed.'

It is certainly true that anglophones are facing serious problems of success. Foreign language teaching is slowly collapsing in Britain and the US because (outside the Hispanic-tinged south-western states) it is far from obvious what language students might sensibly learn. And arrogance is breeding complacency. Fewer and fewer anglophone tourists now even bother to learn the handful of pleasantries (*bonjour, por favor, grazie, Guten Abend*) that might make a waitress or a shop-keeper regard them with a fraction less contempt.

In Orihuela Costa, the expat-dominated town that has sprung up on the Costa Blanca south of Alicante, many of the incomers hardly learn a solitary word of Spanish. The Britons there were nearly all enthusiastic pro-Remainers when Britain voted to leave the EU in 2016, and distinctly nervous after the result went the other way. But most display little interest in their surroundings.

The more obliging the hosts, the worse the problem. In Scandinavia and the Netherlands, where English is understood almost universally, this merely makes the locals more mysterious to outsiders. Visitors too easily ignore their hosts' ability to retreat into their own language to say what they really think. This phenomenon has been noted in business negotiations too: it is very disconcerting indeed to Anglo monoglots if the other side suddenly start muttering among themselves in Japanese.

There are also occasional reports from universities in Wales about

English students feeling insulted when Welsh-speakers switch mid-conversation into their own secret code. In most such situations, the English have their own secret weapon: they can always slip into their own impenetrable patois, irony, which never translates into American. Unfortunately, this technique does not work with the Welsh, who can speak perfect ironic themselves.

***

The British have never had greater need of irony because, just like the Australians,[6] New Zealanders, Irish, anglophone South Africans and the poor forgotten Canadians, they find themselves in the strange situation of being both beneficiaries and victims, masters and servants, rulers and ruled. Their language suffices but they do not own it.

Looking back, we can see that the wave of Americanisms that travelled to Britain, from about 1820 to 1920, mostly involved the importation of words that were in some way useful: the young American language was vibrant and vivid where British English was often ponderous and ossified. For the next two decades American slang was the height of fashion: a means of irritating one's parents and impressing potential partners.

From the war to the 1970s American words were accepted primarily because they reflected new technologies, new problems, new beliefs. They came because the US was the most progressive country on earth and the wellspring of originality.

The situation now is very different and altogether darker. Britain's major problem was not, as 52 per cent of its voters imagined, that it had ceded control of its politics to Brussels but that it had handed over control of its culture and vocabulary to Washington, New York and Los Angeles. Britain is a country which, at vast expense and to no obvious purpose, insists on having its own nuclear weapons, the use of which is unimaginable. But the billions and billions of words spoken and written every day are increasingly dictated from

6 The most fluent of all ironists, being the nation who turned *bastard* into a term of endearment.

elsewhere, and protest is restricted to a few chunters from nostalgists, mostly elderly.

Quality control has all but disappeared. No longer do we embrace the words that might improve our vocabulary, and reject the rest. And far from there being two languages, as both Mencken and Burchfield proclaimed, they are merging. The bombardment of American has become so incessant that most British people no longer have the capacity to distinguish between one English and another. This is especially true of the young, who have no long-term memory. But it is increasingly true of us all.

A migrant who emigrates as an adult to another English-speaking country will not normally change their accent (unless they have deep insecurities). But in time their voice will change colour at the edges as it embraces local usages: it would sound absurd if it did not. If they stay long enough, they will become desensitised to the less obvious distinctions. Yet an American in London or an Englishman in Washington (or Glasgow) will still be readily identifiable.

Now the British are starting to become migrants in their own country. Alistair Cooke told the British on air from the US in 1935: 'Every Englishman listening to me now unconsciously uses thirty or forty Americanisms a day, however much he is opposed to American idiom in principle.' Now that figure might be three or four hundred. Maybe more for a teenager, if they use that many words in a day. This has become a crisis of self-imposed serfdom.

A nation that outsources the development of its own language – the language it developed over hundreds of years – is a nation that has lost the will to live.

***

In 2002, US president George W. Bush supposedly told Tony Blair: 'The trouble with the French is that they don't have a word for *entrepreneur*'. It is a quote that still floats around the internet. This of course does not remotely prove he said it, merely that it sounds so doltish he might have said it.

Well, I am inclined to believe that Bush did say it, because the story was denied by Blair's press secretary, which in that era was always a reliable guide to the truth. Whether Bush said it or not is a mere detail, however, because there is a much more surprising possibility. The statement itself might have a grain of truth.

The word *entrepreneur* dates back to France to the thirteenth century, and in Britain, as *entreprenour* – 'one who undertakes, a manager' – to at least the sixteenth. By the early nineteenth century it had taken on the French spelling in both Britain and the US and usually referred to what we would now call an impresario; newspaper references are confined to someone staging plays or concerts. It seems to have been used a little more broadly in France to mean the owner of a small business: *le patron* of a cafe or *un entrepreneur de pompes funèbres*, an undertaker.

Sometime in the late Victorian era the Americans broadened the word still further, to embrace its modern meaning. In 1888 *The New York Times* used it – cautiously, with inverted commas – in a review of a book called *The Art of Investing*, in a context that made it clear that in the US *entrepreneur* was assuming its modern meaning, implying not just running a business but taking risks to expand it.

In Britain the old theatrical meaning also faded away and the American usage began to take its place, but it was not an everyday word. It was understood in business circles, and one learned to wrap one's tongue around those rolling syllables doing A-level economics, but it was little used in public.

That began to change in the late 1970s as the then Labour government shifted away from anything that smacked of socialist solutions, and public discourse turned towards the revitalisation of capitalism. But the prime French meaning remained unchanged. My French–English dictionary translates it as *contractor* and the official Academy dictionary definition begins '*personne qui dirige une entreprise commerciale*'. It represented the European concept of a businessman: someone who tries to make a solid living by running a restaurant or garage, say, or maybe two, but not 200; someone who fears bankruptcy above all else, not willing to court it on the off-chance of a jackpot.

In Britain, though, things were starting to change fast. The

Guardian and the *Observer* used the word *entrepreneur* 104 times in the 1950s, 328 times in the 1960s, 1,282 times in the 1970s, 4,131 times in the 1980s and 5,962 times in the 1990s. It now had nothing to do with the theatre, nor making a solid living. It was about getting rich. In France, it has begun to assume that meaning as well, but more grudgingly. The revolution was coming, and at its heart was a dream as American as cherry pie and a word as American as *palais de danse*. This was not the revolution students talked about amid a haze of dope in the late 1960s.

***

In September 1976 the BBC began showing the comedy series *The Fall and Rise of Reginald Perrin*, which ranks alongside its contemporaries *Fawlty Towers* and *Porridge* in popular affection amongst the best-loved British sitcoms. Its starting point – it freewheeled wildly later – showed the great Leonard Rossiter playing Reggie Perrin as a typically bored husband/commuter/middle manager in a typically hopeless British company, plotting his escape by faking suicide.

The programme was notable for its catchphrases, and among Reggie's colleagues were two enthusiastic young men, Americanised ahead of their time, who would greet each daft new idea with the exclamations 'Great!' and (a very unAmerican) 'Super' and the occasional 'Success City, Arizona!' (or variants). The third and final series ended in January 1979, though repeats are never far away.

Four months later Margaret Thatcher became Britain's first female prime minister. Outside the door of 10 Downing Street she quoted St Francis of Assisi: 'Where there is discord, may we bring harmony'. Well, that was a whopper; discord was all part of the masterplan.

And the masterplan was carried through. There have, as of early 2017, been five British prime ministers since Thatcher: three Conservative, two Labour; all have governed in the Thatcherite spirit: here and there would be an amelioration or a political feint, but the principles remained unchanged. Intellectually, the belief that unalloyed American capitalism is the answer to every problem is showing signs of following Marxism into the dustbin of history. Politically, at the start of 2017, it was more entrenched than ever.

In the City of London of 1979 bowler hats and furled umbrellas were falling out of fashion as uniform but there were still men in top hats marching through the streets to deliver obscure pieces of documentation between offices, as Alex Brummer, the City Editor of the *Daily Mail*, recalls; and a quarter of the Bank of England's staff were engaged in monitoring every purchase of foreign currency by businessmen as part of the exchange control laws. Brummer left London at the start of the 1980s to work in the US. By the time he came back at the end of the decade, the City had changed utterly, and so had the country. The business landscape was a lot less like Reggie Perrin's world and a lot more like America. And the vocabulary changed with it.

The centrepiece of the process was the sudden 1986 change known as Big Bang, which involved computerisation, simplification and Americanisation of the central function of the City: the process of buying and selling shares. Inevitably, this involved the adoption of American vocabulary: the role of *jobbers* on the stock exchange was abolished and they were replaced by **market makers**; *brokers* became **brokerages**; *merchant banks* became **investment banks**; *dealers* became **traders**.

The changes helped London reclaim its role as a vital global financial centre, and thus as its business became more internationalised, it was inevitable that much of the jargon would be borrowed from the world's major economic power. So in due course the City adopted a secondary layer of financial Americanisms, in which London simply fell into line with Wall Street terminology. If a private company wished to join the Stock Exchange, this ceased to be a *flotation* and became an **IPO** (Initial Public Offering); the whole business of buying and selling companies, which became as routine as buying a cup of coffee, was bundled together as **M&A** (Mergers and Acquisitions).

Much more significantly, as the whirligig of financial activity went ever faster, the City grabbed with relish American euphemisms as a cover for what was actually going on. Nearly 200 years after the Americans had sanitised the language to remove the taint of sex, so now they verbalised the noun **leverage** (always pronounced *lev-* not *leev-*) to cover all aspects of debt, a word capable of alarming the

British bourgeoisie. In return, the government tried not to use the word *regulation*, a word that implied the City might have to operate within societal norms. Instead, the more soothing American term **oversight** would be used.

In the 1960s and 1970s, with Labour mostly in power, the term **consumerism** (around in the US since c.1915) was much in vogue in Britain, covering the rights and interests of consumers. Significant changes in the law made it harder for businesses to **rip off** their customers. But *consumerism* has another meaning, and from the 1980s onwards, this one became dominant: the obsession with acquiring consumer goods.[7]

In the 1980s the key word was *enterprise*, not an Americanism in itself but first cousin to *entrepreneur*. In 1976, shortly after Mrs Thatcher took over as Conservative leader, her mentor Sir Keith Joseph talked of Britain having an 'anti-enterprise culture'. When they gained power the new *enterprise culture* became the phrase of choice. This was not an Americanism: it was not something Americans ever needed to talk about – they were too busy pursuing it. The phrase's appearances in *The New York Times* have almost all been in stories about Thatcher and Britain.

The enterprise culture brought in its wake a whole new series of terms, mostly euphemistic, designed not to protect consumers but the better to make money out of them: '*In order to improve our service to you*' (new shorter hours with fewer staff), '*Your call is important to us*' (but not very), '*New Lower Price*' (smaller size), '*Flights from £5*' (plus a few extras). The art of capitalist exploitation/enterprise culture was refined in America, but the British form is generally cruder, partly because British industry is less innovative, and partly because the British are too docile to complain.

Inside the companies, a new series of coded terms also emerged, imported in bulk from the US. They derived initially from a school of thought about business practice, generally credited/debited to a former McKinsey consultant called Tom Peters, who co-wrote the 1982 book *In Search of Excellence*, the first modern business

---

7 Which was probably around in the US since the Pilgrim Fathers rushed off the *Mayflower* and headed to the souvenir shops to buy wampum.

blockbuster. Peters's initial thesis focused on how the best companies in America were customer-focused, though at some point in the past thirty-five years this enchanting idea seems to have disappeared under the verbiage.

It is not true that all this jargon is dreadful. Some of it has the vivacity of early American: I would love to be invited to an *open-kimono* session sometime. Nor can there be any objection to *blue-sky thinking*; in Britain we think a lot about blue skies.[8] The word *intrapreneur* – someone who thinks entrepreneurially within a large organisation – is pretty clever too. The term *elevator pitch* is inclined to make sensitive British souls wince because it has such an overwhelming American accent. Nonetheless, unlike most business jargon it is an aid to simplicity rather than complexity.

However, I must be *proactive* and *cascade* some information. The clichés create a *suboptimal mindset, impacting the idea shower*, making it *cloud-centric* and inhibiting *granularity*. Let me *reach out* to you and *get a handle* on this. If we take a *helicopter view*, *think outside the box* and *drill down* then *going forward* we can *collaboratively enhance open-source value*, *distinctively maintain extensible action items*, *fungibly iterate turnkey leadership*, *energistically predominate client-based action items*, and *uniquely re-intermediate market-driven channels*.[9]

However, hidden in the fog lie some important facts about the enterprise culture. One crucial point, pinpointed by Brummer, is the switch from companies issuing trading updates twice a year to American-style *quarterly reporting*. This seems to have been a crucial psychological change, emphasising short-term profits, with the aim of shoring up the share price and ramping up executive pay, rather than continuing the boring old business of running a quietly successful company year after year with contented staff and satisfied customers.

And the two really crucial words that emerge are †*hire* and *fire*. Hiring, in the sense of employing someone, is a very old English

---

8 This was used in the US scientific community as early as 1946.
9 The second half of that paragraph was randomly generated by the helpful webpage http://atrixnet.com/bs-generator.html.

word, pre-dating the Norman conquest. Hiring fairs were widely held to bring together farmers and itinerant labourers. But in industrial Britain, where full employment was valued more than mobility, the word was less used. One *was offered a job, employed, taken on, appointed to a position*. Hiring was for taxis; it implied impermanence.

Firing was an Americanism. 'I'll fire her this very afternoon,' a character said in J.B. Priestley's 1936 novel *They Walk in the City*. Priestley added: 'He was not an American, but when he was feeling brisk and rather brutal, he liked to use these American terms.' One might get *sacked, dismissed*, maybe even *discharged* – from the army or domestic service – but that normally involved doing something diabolical, quite likely criminal. Mild incompetence was not a good reason, especially as the strength of the trade unions was making it increasingly difficult to get shot of any employee.

The destruction of the unions was one of the most successful Thatcher projects. An effect, mostly after her own fall from power, was the rise of London as a base for overseas financial institutions, American ones included. Old industries withered. Modern production methods and communications plus freer movement and trade meant that high-wage Western economies – not just Britain – had to be much more supple to compete. That meant getting rid of staff, continually. Thus business jargon was used, most of all, as code for this purpose.

All M&As began to be judged on whether they produced *synergies*, i.e. firing opportunities to improve the **bottom line**. The new masters would **lay off, sacrifice, terminate** or **surplus** people. They would **downsize, rightsize, pare down, ramp down**, make **internal efficiencies**, become **leaner, trim fat**, just **whittle away** or maybe indulge in **conscious uncoupling**. The words were English; the phraseology was almost wholly American (although it was Britain's own HSBC that came up with *demising* jobs); the concepts were unBritish.

***

In the 1980s Ruth Slater was working in the UK office of a multinational. Suddenly she was told her department was to change its name. The Personnel Department was history; it was henceforth to be *Human Resources*. The notion that the workers might in some way be part of a company's capital had poked its head above ground before 1900; it was developed by an American social scientist E. Wight Bakke, who had studied unemployment in London in the early 1930s and developed sympathetic theories about its debilitating effects.

American companies started to have directors of human resources by 1965, a time when a British personnel manager was still very much the harassed-looking chap whose job was to tell the boss there was trouble up t' mill. By the 1980s, with the mills closing, along with the pits, factories and shipyards and all the other old staples of British employment, the role was changing, and so was the language.

By the 1990s, companies were using fine old English words to describe fine new American concepts: †*creativity*, †*empowerment*, †*engagement*, †*innovation*, †*leadership*. † *Team leaders* – a phrase that in Britain was previously applied to horses[10] – were expected to †*facilitate* a *performance culture*. 'There is nothing hard-edged about any of these words,' says Dr Slater, now a lecturer in human resources at the University of Central Lancashire. 'Or is there? These are the means by which an organisation makes things happen. The organisation now wanted every bit of you. They were appropriating the private property of the individual. They no longer just wanted your time. They wanted your brain and your heart as well.'

These terms had been popularised in books by Peters and scores of his imitators and were assumed in Britain to be brand new. But, in Slater's words: 'This totally ignored the fact that American businesses had been talking about human resources for the whole twentieth century and all these books were doing were codifying it.'

In the US, where union membership was always patchy, workers had long been used to companies taking a one-sided view of the relationship: Henry Ford wheeled food onto his assembly lines to cut the lunch break to ten minutes. In recent years it has become common for firms to ban 'bathroom breaks', and in 2002 a Jim Beam

---

10 But by 2010 an advert in the *Jewish Chronicle* demanded 'an organised and self-motivated team leader' to serve as a rabbi.

bourbon distillery in Kentucky told women to report the start of their menstrual cycles to the nice people in HR. A decade later reports of similar indignities were being visited on employees in Britain, not all of them in the most obviously dictatorial workplaces like call centres, and not all of them in American-owned companies.

With hindsight, one can see clearly how the bright modern ideas of a generation ago fit into a pattern whereby capital has yanked power back from labour. *Open-plan* offices, which were supposed to provide scope for collaboration, sociability and easy conversation between managers and staff, have turned out to be a microcosm of a Britain that, more than any other country outside North Korea, has accepted the concept of total surveillance. There is something equally coercive about *dress-down Fridays*, first recorded in the US in the 1980s. The implication is that a working dress code is not something with a job-related reason, but merely a means of control.

Some aspects of the Americanisation process caused discomfort at high levels even in the early days. In March 1986 the Cabinet Secretary Sir Robert Armstrong sent a memo to Mrs Thatcher warning of 'increasing disquiet about the things going on in the City'. However, he discounted public concern about the rapidly rising salaries of top-level executives, predicting this was 'a bubble that will be pricked in a year or two'.

Well, maybe a century or two. The average head of a FTSE company, paid more than £1,000 an hour, earned the national average wage for 2017 by midday on 4 January.

***

British politics has also been Americanised, but not with the same purposefulness or indeed any purpose whatever. In a small way, there has been some move towards the Americanisation of the political system, in that the devolution of power to Scotland, Wales and Northern Ireland has created something that looks vaguely like federalism. What is far more noticeable is that Britain has stolen the lexicon of US politics and eaten it whole. Interwar teenagers, devouring Hollywood slang, were much more discriminating.

It is hard to explain how this has happened. British politics is not the same as America's: the Queen has remained a rock-solid bulwark against 51st Stateism, and the fact that Prince Philip wore jeans once more than sixty years ago can probably now be forgiven.

Labour's return to power in 1997 was a turning point. Its ministers were Freddie Laker's children; the party's senior figures were riveted by American politics; Tony Blair, in particular, loved the veneer of relaxed-looking informality which was so useful as an aid to the accretion of power. The political journalists were equally infatuated. When the TV drama *The West Wing* started two years later, it was required viewing for the entire political class. This is what they all aspired to: walking briskly down the White House corridors having Very Important Conversations.

To some extent, the whole country can be implicated. Since the financial meltdown of a decade ago, British politics has been mainly a matter of deciding between what will be slashed overtly (local government budgets) and what will be slashed covertly (the health service). Contrast this with the magnificent and perpetual theatrics of presidential politics. And thanks to the ever-increasing extremism of the Republican candidates, the most absurd of whom actually have the habit of winning, there is a sense that American elections can make more difference to British lives than worrying about who will be cutting what in Downing Street.

There was always a convention that in Britain one *stood* for parliament while Americans *ran* for office. This was a pleasing distinction: it implied a certain British reticence. An MP was supposed to be someone with some experience of life who would reluctantly surrender life's pleasures to serve their constituents and country. Nobody stands now, they run. Like hell. Starting almost from birth.

So here is a guide to the aspirant British politician, written in modern British political jargon.

To get chosen these days, you might have to win a ***primary***.[11]

---

11 This has American roots deep in the nineteenth century. In Britain Michael Ellis was selected as Conservative candidate for Northampton North by something described as a primary in 2006.

More often in Britain the ***party machine***[12] will *fix*[13] it so its preferred candidate wins. In a safe seat the chosen one may be a ***shoo-in***.[14] But the constituency might be a †***bellwether***[15] in which the *race*[16] might be ***too close to call***.[17] Even so, it will be necessary to go out on ***the stump***,[18] during the †*campaign*.[19]

If the aspirant pays attention to the ***grassroots***[20] then, with the help of the ***spin doctors***[21] he or she might get elected. Once settled at Westminster, the new MP will be beset by ***lobbyists***.[22] Some of them may have a ***slush fund***[23] that might help the persuasion process. Meanwhile, the government will be preparing a ***raft***[24] of legislation,

---

12 A term used in the US from 1832 but startlingly borrowed as early as 1886 by the Liberal MP W.S. Caine, who referred to 'the blandishments or terrorism of the party machine' in an interview with the *Pall Mall Gazette*.

13 See pp. 63–4.

14 First used in the US to describe rigged horse races in the 1920s. The word then transferred to American politics. It was rare in Britain until the 1990s, when the media began parroting it so ignorantly that it was (and is) often misspelled *shoe-in*.

15 A *bellwether* was a castrated ram, which had a bell round its neck to help farmers track the flock. In America the term has long been used to denote a closely contested and therefore indicative constituency. In Britain it is used only by journalistic sheep, and is normally misspelled. Castration would be an appropriate punishment.

16 An election was described as a race in Kentucky in 1824. It is not clear when this transferred to Britain: presumably when MPs began to run rather than stand.

17 Traceable to 1932 in the US. A complete nonsense in Britain since British English does not use *call* in this sense. Or it didn't.

18 Dates back to 1816 in the US. Naturalised in Britain by 1879, though infrequently used at first.

19 Adapted from military use in the US by 1809; in Britain by the 1850s.

20 First recorded in the US 1912; increasingly used in Britain from 1968.

21 In *The New York Times* 1984, either from baseball slang or maybe from a play-doctor, who works on flawed scripts. By 1989 British papers were referring to Peter Mandelson as 'Labour's spin-doctor'.

22 Originally in Britain these were journalists who were members of the parliamentary Lobby and thus had (and still have) privileged access at Westminster. But the American meaning of someone seeking influence took over, as did the often grubby practice.

23 In the US by 1874; mid-1970s in Britain. Before that British politicians were less susceptible to outright bribes. But they were always fond of free trips and knighthoods.

24 First used as a synonym for 'a lot' from Canada in 1821. Rafts travel slowly and it did not reach the *Guardian* until 1983.

which *it*[25] will try to *railroad*[26] through. It may wish to cut *welfare*[27] and may appoint a *czar*[28] or two to pretend to solve intractable problems.

All being well, you might eventually get into the Cabinet and be appointed †*Secretary* of State for something.[29] Your role will then bring you into contact with the prime minister's *chief of staff*,[30] and perhaps the *Supreme Court*[31] and the *National Security Council*.[32] Your staff may need to go to the *National Archives* in Kew.[33] On a sunny day, the prime minister may invite you to sit in the Downing Street *rose garden*.

And of all the American terms imported into British politics nothing is quite as imbecilic as this one. Downing Street has no rose garden, i.e. a garden devoted to the cultivation to roses. It has a garden which, on the one occasion I was allowed into it, did indeed have a couple of rose bushes. Most British gardens do. You might as well call every garden in the country a rose garden. The name was

---

25 A government, like a sports team, traditionally takes the singular in the US. British English is confused about this.

26 In the US from at least 1850. Rare in Britain until the 1960s. *Railway* has sometimes been used as a verb in Britain but only in connection with actual trains. The image of railroading a raft is not a happy one but that does not stop the political correspondents.

27 Or, as it was called in Britain until this century, social security.

28 This is completely bonkers. The US has been appointing officials informally known as czars since 1918, when Bernard Baruch was appointed the 'industry czar'. Since the last of the real czars had fallen a year earlier, the term was not exactly well-omened. In 1997 Tony Blair appointed the ex-policeman Keith Hellawell as 'drugs czar'. The role was grandiose but useless and doomed, and so the name was really most appropriate.

29 Most cabinet members had the title *Minister* but there has been a steady drift towards *Secretary* over the past half-century, presumably to imitate Washington. During the Thatcher and Blair governments, in particular, *Secretary* was more appropriate because the cabinet was mainly required to take dictation.

30 A title 'imported from the US by Tony Blair' – *Financial Times*, 8 August 2016.

31 The Supreme Court had a purely theoretical function in England until 2009, when judicial authority was moved from the House of Lords to a new body. The name is of course American but, to be fair to the judges, they are appalled by the politicisation of their US equivalents.

32 Set up in 2010 by David Cameron, who had evidently far too much time watching *The West Wing* to think of a name that was not cribbed straight from Washington.

33 Previously the Public Record Office. Americanised 2003.

assigned to it by the press after David Cameron and Nick Clegg gave a joint press conference there in 2010. If the White House has a rose garden, British politics must have one too.[34]

It goes on and on. British political journalism is riddled with *carpetbaggers*, *backwoodsmen*, *lame ducks*, *caucuses*, *slates*, *tickets* and metaphorical *platforms*, all of them evidence of a collective failure of imagination and an ingrained culture of plagiarism from another country.[35] Indeed, on 5 May 2016, a BBC news alert flashed on to millions of screens: 'Polls open in a range of local and national elections across the UK, on what is being dubbed "Super Thursday".' It is not clear who might have done the dubbing; no normal person would have recorded the day as super. But America had just had a *Super Tuesday*, so naturally Britain had to copy it.

Sometimes this can be more than just irritating and pathetic. After the infamous christening of the Rose Garden, one of Clegg's main passions in government was an attempt to reform the unelected House of Lords by turning it into something very like the US equivalent, the *Senate*. No one doubted that it would be called the Senate. Yet no one who has observed the US Senate in operation over the past forty years could possibly regard it as a body to be emulated: it is full of self-obsessed windbags devoted only to their own continuation, almost as institutionally corrupt as the American Supreme Court. The British political classes are too transfixed by the whole Washington charade to notice.

Their confidence was jolted in 2016 before the fateful referendum on Britain's membership of the European Union, when President Obama warned that, if the British left the EU, they would be 'at the back of the *queue*' for a trade deal with the US. He had – very self-consciously, it seemed – used a word regarded by Americans as a Briticism, even THE Briticism, the word that summed up the alleged pliant and long-suffering national character. This was widely

---

34 Actually, the White House Rose Garden isn't a rose garden either. But it was once, hence the name.

35 One surprising exception: *electioneering* is not an Americanism, and dates back to the eighteenth century.

noticed.[36] Hardly anyone noticed when Nigel Farage, the leader of the UK Independence Party, replied to Obama in American. '*Butt out*,' he said.

Nor did anyone (except me) seem to think it odd two years earlier when George Osborne, then the Chancellor of the Exchequer and angling to be prime minister, opened his home and what purported to be his heart to the *Mail on Sunday*. He told them how he cooked *beer-butt chicken* and *Coca-Cola ham* at weekends; made *rainbow cakes* and *chocolate sprinkles* with his daughter; how the family hired a strawberry-coloured camper van for their holidays; and how, when he hired it, the rental agent had commented that he was *an ordinary Joe*. He also said he had been 'watching a cricket game', which no one who really watched a cricket game would ever say, because they are always *cricket matches* (or sometimes *games of cricket*). When the paper asked him a difficult question he replied that he would *take the Fifth*. Osborne did not become prime minister when a vacancy first arose but he may have a chance in some credulous corner of Kansas.

Politicians from every party are at it. '"*Hell yes*": those are the most vivid words of the campaign so far, and they came from Ed Miliband, the Labour leader,' said a *Financial Times* columnist during the 2015 election. 'No actual person in Britain talks like that. We are approaching the point where an excited politician says "*Darn tootin'!*" to some baffled crowd in Edgbaston or Harrow.'

***

One area of British life should be entirely immune from American influence. The sporting cultures of the two countries are totally different and not just in the obvious ways: American football/baseball/basketball/ice hockey as opposed to soccer/cricket/rugby.

In a completely counter-intuitive manner, American professional sport is essentially socialist. All kinds of checks and balances exist to prevent the richest teams winning everything, for instance by giving

---

36 So was research published in February 2017, suggesting that the British were increasingly unwilling to queue.

the worst club from the previous season first pick of new players from the colleges. Even at schoolboy level, there is a concept known as *mercy rules*. If one team gets too far ahead, the coach tells them to try not to score so as not to humiliate the opposition. This is something that has emphatically not crossed the Atlantic, and good luck giving that instruction to a team of British under-11s.

The first sign of sporting crossover came in 1982, when Channel 4, newly started and short of sporting rights, began showing American football and found itself with an instant hit. Indeed, for a while, with English football at a hooligan-driven low ebb, one could almost have imagined total Americanisation. The moment passed, though not necessarily forever: the possibility of a London franchise for the National Football League is again a matter of discussion.

So far, however, American football has made minimal impact on the language. Yet baseball, which has almost no following in Britain, has become a repository of instant clichés which are totally meaningless in a British context but are churned out constantly all the same.

The phrase *step up to the plate* (and variants) does not turn up at all on a search of *The Times* between 1785 and 1990. During the 1990s it cropped up about once a year. Then it began to appear about once a month, heading towards once a fortnight. The paper has applied it to sporting participants of all kinds, including yachtsmen, female pole vaulters, racehorse owners and racehorses; plus social media companies, solicitors, hedge fund managers, intellectual property consultants, the City of London in general, housewives, airlines, the Irish government, European leaders, moderate Muslims, Vladimir Putin and Prince Philip. And, just now and again, baseball players.

Quoting a West Midlands police spokesman in 2014, *The Times* used it to describe two off-duty police officers on their way to a fancy-dress party – one dressed as a monkey, the other as a zebra – who came across someone shouting abuse in a supermarket. 'PCs Griffin and Cave were faced with a very dangerous man and stepped up to the plate,' said the spokesman.

In baseball the phrase has a very specific meaning, referring to a new batter entering the batter's box on either side of home plate. It thus transfers readily to anyone accepting a challenge. If you know nothing of baseball, which will be true of almost all the British writers who employ the term so glibly, it is meaningless verbiage. Perhaps this explains why British politicians like it so much. Harassed authority figures in sports (not baseball) are also keen. 'In times of crisis players step up to the plate,' said Chris Wilder when manager of Northampton Town football club early in 2016. As a Northampton supporter myself, I would prefer them to run roughly in the direction of the goal.

Just as ludicrous are those other new favourites, *three strikes and you're out* and *left field*. Some baseball usages are self-explanatory, such as *in there pitching*, *curve ball* and *first base*, which is another one for the P.G. Wodehouse charge sheet. But it is indeed a usefully apt metaphor for where one might wish to reach on a first date.

Those estimates of the number of times *step up to the plate* has appeared in *The Times* might be described as *ballpark figures*. 'There is guidance given by the Cabinet Office year to year on ballpark figures,' said the Prime Minister's spokeswoman in 2016, talking about the number of names on the very British honours list. This implied she had no idea what the current figure was. Also, one suspects, she had no idea what a *ballpark* might be: it is, very specifically, a baseball stadium.

The one American football term that is gaining some traction is *playbook*: the manual which instructs the sport's highly paid bulked-up automata what to do before the brain damage takes over completely. Sadiq Khan, the London mayor, recently accused the Conservative Party of using 'the Donald Trump playbook'. The related Americanism *play*, as a sporting manoeuvre, has also started to enter the commentators' lexicon: 'A lovely play,' said an ITV man during the 2015 Rugby World Cup. 'That's a wild play,' said a BBC counterpart in 2016. A bedroom farce involving lots of trouser-dropping? No, it was a moment in the FA Cup final.

Though baseball has not caught on, there is a trend within British sport towards Americanisation: not a gallop, as in politics, more of a trot. Generally, US-style coaches are taking over and reducing the scope for individuality. Above them, there are now US-style owners, but unconstrained by American sporting socialism, rendering the word *club* an anachronism. The *Hall of Fame* concept has arrived.

Cricket now has **cheerleaders**. Both cricket and rugby teams have started to have nicknames tacked on to their names for promotional purposes and/or the sake of it. Rugby league has been particularly fond of giving historic teams names that appeal to the 12-year-olds employed in the marketing department: the nearest actual rhino to the Leeds Rhinos is thought to be eighty miles away in Chester Zoo.[37]

The ugly verb-turned-noun †*assist* has now made it from American soccer to English as a quasi-official term to describe the final pass that leads to a goal. It being the counterpart to *goal-scorer*, *goal-maker* would be far more elegant. Football writers talk increasingly of a †*loss* rather than a defeat, and even a **road victory** for an away win. The term **bleachers** has sneaked (or **snuck**) in, and started to lose its American meaning of an open-air seat where, on a sunny day, a spectator might get bleached. I have yet to find an instance of *bleachers* being used to describe football spectators on a wet Tuesday night in Oldham. But if it's not out there yet, it soon will be. All these are the province of sports journalists who think that using a synonym, however crass, somehow constitutes good writing.

There is also the now ubiquitous and annoying word †*rookie*. This does have some pedigree in British military slang but, as a general term, it long ago emigrated to the US, where it was safely confined in its own insular sporting argot. It returned to Britain via the American-dominated golf circuit and is now puked up mindlessly to mean a new recruit to absolutely anything.

Still, one is always safe with a cliché. Even the most fluent writers can get befuddled if they try too hard to be original. Seemingly unsure whether to use a cricket or a baseball metaphor, an *Observer* columnist once attempted both simultaneously. Writing of Prime Minister's Questions in the Commons, he said: 'You can never tell what dangerous googly might come bowling in from left field.' This is, I can assure you, physiologically as well as philologically impossible.

Although Americans rarely have a problem getting baseball and

---

37 However, the cricketer Darren 'Rhino' Gough used to play next door at Headingley. Asked by a teammate why he was called Rhino, he reputedly replied 'Cos I'm strong as an ox'.

cricket confused, they do have an issue with the convention that collective entities are singular. Take the San Francisco Giants baseball team. One has to say San Francisco *is* but, obviously, the Giants *are*, otherwise the sentence sounds ridiculous. Except that back in the 1950s when the Giants were based in New York and the arch-rivals of the Brooklyn Dodgers, the Dodgers' manager Charlie Dressen proclaimed confidently: 'The Giants is dead.'

***

British schools remain a very British shambles, a memorial to the competing egos of successive Education Secretaries. Suffering teachers are tyrannised by centrally imposed and constantly changing acronyms, not necessarily American in origin. The children, meanwhile, are tyrannised by *SATs*, a term borrowed from the US, where it represents something entirely different: a university admission test. British SATs are taken at different stages which change according to governmental whim, the ultimate aim being to force kids to do homework during those wasteful months inside the womb.

Oddly, the acronym means nothing in either country. Originally in the US SAT stood for Scholastic Aptitude Test but the full name has been abolished. When British SATs were cooked up in the late 1980s, they were meant to be Standard Assessment Tasks but the American copyright owners apparently got agitated. So the name was dropped but the British, never having met an Americanism they didn't like, continued to call the tests SATs anyway.

Eventually, British children do learn to obsess about their *grades*, even if they learn little else. *Grade* is not an Americanism as such, but it is a miniature version of *fix*, a word that has made it big in the States by multitasking, especially on roads and railways, where the British would use *gradient*, and in schools, where it means both year groups and marks. (*Make the grade* is certainly an Americanism, which made a tentative entrance into Britain in the 1930s.)

Grades certainly did exist in British schools of the mid-twentieth century, but nowhere near as ubiquitously as they do now. And there was certainly no such thing as a *straight-A student*. This constitutes a triple Americanism: firstly, *straight* in the sense of 'an unbroken sequence' was not in common British use until very recently except in the tennis sense of *straight sets*; it was then extended across sport, e.g. '*six straight wins*'. Secondly, schoolchildren were rarely called *students* in my day; they were *pupils*. Perhaps the word *student* makes them sound more like volunteers than conscripts.[38]

Funny that one never hears of *straight-B students*, never mind *straight-C, D, E* or *F*. Perhaps they just don't brag about it so much.

Anyway, *straight-A students* (unless the phrase is being used in mitigation in a courtroom) normally go on to university. There they may be based on a *campus*, which came to Britain with the green-field universities of the 1960s, and will more often measure their lives in *semesters* than *terms*. And eventually, they may go and do a *master's*, previously just known as an MA or an MSc, or simply post-grad. This involves *RE-search*, previously known as *re-SEARCH*, to be conducted with their own *RE-sources*.[39] Or they will join the ranks of the *alumni*.

Some of them may be clever enough to emerge speaking English rather than American, but perhaps not many. And some will go on to become lawyers, where they will be in the midst of the barmiest of all the battlefields in Britain's war of perceptual independence.

***

In the 1990s the lawyer-turned-journalist Marcel Berlins, then a columnist on the *Guardian*, began a campaign against the way British television depicts British courts, i.e. as American courts with wigs on.

There are several reasons for this. One is that real US trials are often televised (the O.J. Simpson trial of 1995 being particularly

---

38 On the other hand, Americans still say they are at school even when they are at university, whereas a British undergraduate feels insulted if anyone makes the suggestion.

39 The word †*sophomore*, a second-year student, which has never gained any traction in British academic life, actually originated at Cambridge University in the seventeenth century.

high-profile), whereas British trials are not.[40] Another is that the British see far more fictional American courtrooms than they see British ones. And also that US courts are also inherently more dramatic.

Berlins was inclined to blame the series *LA Law*, to which he was himself addicted, for the popular British beliefs that judges continually banged their gavels; that lawyers constantly leaped up to shout 'objection', to which the judge shouted back 'sustained' or 'overruled'; that British barristers strutted round the room *eyeballing* the jury and were called to the bench for regular whispered *conflabs*. Or, as the British used to say, *confabs*. But long before that, in black-and-white days, Raymond Burr had starred as *Perry Mason*, and went nine years without ever losing a case. There was lots of gavelling.

It was the gavel that really got to Berlins. British judges, as he kept saying, do not wield gavels or even possess them. He even spotted one in an episode of *Rumpole*, whose creator John Mortimer QC would have turned in his grave had he not still been alive at the time. Berlins found them everywhere else too: on news programmes illustrating real issues of law; on display in the windows even of London's specialist legal bookshops; and in a phone box near the Law Courts in the Strand, on a prostitute's card otherwise attractively illustrated by a busty young lady in skimpy underwear and legal gown.[41]

Then the *Guardian* itself illustrated a prominent legal article with a gavel, at which point Berlins sadly announced: 'I retire from the fray, bitter and exhausted.' But a few months later he could not resist unretiring when the government put out a leaflet publicising a course for civil servants with a gavel on the cover. The course was called 'Legal Awareness'.

Even in the real courts, where judges do not wield gavels, the power of American fiction overpowers British procedure. Witnesses are inclined to add *So help me, Gahd* to their oath as a closing flourish. And

---

40 Britain's Supreme Court is streamed live on the web but it does not conduct trials, merely hears arguments from lawyers: not the stuff of drama.
41 This was the pre-mobile era, when such professionals left cards in phone boxes and potential clients had to make calls from them.

a barrister I know was once asked by a Stratford-upon-Avon magistrate: 'Will counsel please approach the bench?' The beak had obviously been watching TV instead of the local playwright because there is no provision for this in English legal practice. 'But why not?' mused my informant. 'It was the only way we could have a conversation.'

And media reports are full of words which only have a place in the British legal system because the nation is befuddled by American TV. Fifty years ago witnesses did not normally †*testify*, they *gave evidence*. They certainly did not *take the stand* – there is no bloody stand – they *went into the box* or *the witness box*. Unexpected deaths were investigated with a *post-mortem* not an *autopsy*. †*Alimony* was long ago replaced by *maintenance* in English law until TV put it back into popular culture.

†*Parole* was an English word dating back to the seventeenth century, mainly used in *parole of honour*, whereby a wartime captive could be released if he promised not to rejoin the fray, which sounds wonderfully chivalric. *Parole* came into British law in the 1960s but one has to assume that even then it was not chosen because of its charming historical associations, but because it was already so familiar from the telly.

And then there is the use of *appeal* as a transitive verb: to *appeal* a judgment or whatever, rather than *appeal against* it, which was until this century the traditional British formula. By my calculation it takes approximately 0.23 of a second to add that extra *against*. Isn't that a small price to pay for a sliver of linguistic independence? Can't the authorities do something?

Evidently not. After a ruling against her government over whether a parliamentary vote was required on Brexit, BBC News quoted the prime minister, Theresa May, as saying 'We're appealing the High Court decision'. In the case of Prince Charles's controversial letters to ministers in 2014, Lord Dyson, the master of the rolls, ruled against the attorney-general, noting, according to the *Guardian*, 'the government departments concerned did not even seek permission to appeal it'. Was there a sound like thunder that day as generations of Dyson's bewigged predecessors read the report in the heavens? Were they banging the gavels St Peter had given them by mistake? Oh, please, please tell me the journalist misheard.

6

LET'S WAKE UP AND HAVE A CUPPA INSTEAD

On some sectors of the battlefront, through the smoke and fog, it is possible to glimpse vicious hand-to-hand fighting, as British words try to hold off the invaders. Reports received by the general staff in the situation room suggest a mixed picture.

In some cases the contest has been going on for decades, so ritualised that the combatants have reached a kind of accommodation. Britain's *films* are actually holding on quite well against America's *movies*, and we all watch them while eating ***popcorn***.[1] But that represents a less successful story of resistance.

'American popcorn' was advertised as being on sale at a bazaar in St Paul's Churchyard, London in 1874, so it is hardly new. It is made from a subspecies of maize, nurtured for its ability to produce a controlled explosion.[2] Its cousin ***corn on the cob*** was sold in Selfridges in 1927, in a special American food section of 'our Provisions Departments'.

---

1 And the Oscar still goes to the *Best Film*.

2 In 2002 *The Times* reported that popcorn, which costs almost nothing to manufacture, was not merely more profitable than the seats in the cinemas but also, with a mark-up of up to 10,000%, better than selling heroin or Kalashnikovs.

It was that and its smelly sister, tinned *sweetcorn*, which changed the language.

By the 1930s seed merchants were offering gardeners varieties that could be grown outdoors in Britain 'as easily as potatoes'. During the war these were marketed as a means of Anglo-American amity: 'There are many little ways in which we can show our gratitude and thanks to our American allies,' said an ad in *The Times* for Cuthbert's Golden Spire. 'You will certainly be able to gladden the heart of some American soldier as well as enjoying some very good meals yourself.'[3]

In the 1950s, that era of extreme British culinary conservatism, one V. Sackville-West of Sissinghurst Castle, Kent, wrote to the paper urging village shows to encourage the growing of more unusual vegetables, with corn on the cob on top of her list, followed by aubergine and 'the small Italian marrow zucchini' (now better known in Britain as a courgette).[4] 'Our attitude towards vegetables is far too insular,' she said.

It would be the 1960s before the British really took her advice, and the great corn shift took place. The OED still says that *corn* often denotes the leading crop of a district, i.e. wheat in most of England, oats 'in North Britain and Ireland', but that in the US *corn* is always maize, the plant that gives us corn popped, sweet and on the cob. Farmers round my way still say that for them corn means wheat. But generally urban England has prevailed. America has won this one.

Battleground No.3 is the complex contest between, on the one hand *chips* representing the US against the British contender *crisps*, while at the same time defending Britain's honour against American *fries*. I think this may also have reached an equilibrium; the US has gained ground without eliminating the opposition. No one would go into a McDonalds and ask for a cheeseburger and chips, except the kind of person who would refuse to go into McDonalds anyway; against that no one goes into a chippy and asks for fish and fries.

Kettle Chips (founded in Oregon, 1978) came to Britain in 1988

---

3 We have already mentioned other ways in which British women were alleged to have gladdened the hearts of American soldiers.
4 Like all squashes, including the boring old marrow, this was originally American.

to sell upmarket potato crisps and made no attempt to change its name to meet local sensibilities. But its success bred competitors like Tyrrells and Real,[5] which sold their products as crisps. And Leicester-based Walkers, who utterly dominate the lower end of the British crisp business, have made no attempt to start calling their products chips. Perhaps because they are true British patriots. Perhaps because their owners, Pepsi-Cola, who also own the US chip-leader in Lay's, know it would be a really bad idea.

On Britain's railways *freight* trains have replaced *goods* trains, which is reasonable enough, since hardly any of the consumer items that could sensibly be called goods are now transported by train. There is not much freight either, but the train operators compensate for this by treating their passengers with the same attentive customer service they would offer wagon-loads of coal.

The situation on the roads is more distressing in that *lorries* are now being driven off the motorways to be replaced by *trucks*. I only became aware how far this had gone when a delivery driver asked me to help unload something 'from the truck'. I pounced. 'So is this a truck or a lorry?' 'Oh, I'm old-fashioned,' he replied, back-tracking a little. 'I normally say lorry but the younger ones call them trucks.' Other drivers have given corroborating evidence.

Things are also going the wrong way on the *flat* v *apartment* front. Historically, the words were used somewhat interchangeably in both Britain and the US, and *apartment* does not appear in early dictionaries of Americanisms. But by the 1930s there was a clear distinction, although *apartment* retained some specialist uses in Britain, e.g. among seaside landladies. However, *apartment* has resurfaced, because its American allure appeals to estate agents (and, so they believe, potential punters), whereas *flat* sounds, well, flat.

Tuxedo v *dinner jacket* is also now a major source of alarm. There were seventy-five references to *tuxedo* in *The Times* – THE TIMES OF LONDON! – during 2016, whereas the dinner jacket had all but vanished. American **goose bumps** has gained control against *goose pimples* and old-fashioned *goose-flesh*. American **cans** v British *tins* has

---

5 Makers of Real roast ox flavour crisps – 'suitable for vegetarians'.

reached the point where both seem quite interchangeable. Sometimes one might open a can of beans; sometimes a tin. But nobody opens a tin of worms. It is always a ***can of worms***, which is a clear sign of an Americanism. It derives from fishing and seems to have been a favourite expression of President Eisenhower. It reached Britain in the 1960s.

Other skirmishes can be observed where long-standing English usages are being merely harassed rather than attacked outright by the American equivalent. *Lift* is just about holding *elevator* at bay, except when one is pitching. *Pack of cards* comes under occasional sniper fire from its old rival †***deck***. There are signs of minor infiltration by *vacation* (which has long been in use at universities) v *holiday* and *parking lot* v *car park*.

And so to the great *cookie* v *biscuit* battle that seems to lie ahead: the potential Armageddon that would spell the end times for the English language as we have known it. The background is complicated. The early American settlers took with them the idea of a biscuit, but an old English biscuit was not sweet; it was more like a ship's biscuit. In the US the word for this soon mutated into ***cracker***, which presumably accounts for the crackers now eaten with cheese in Britain.

Meanwhile, the word *cookie* has long been used in Scotland for a plain bun. But this appears to be a distraction, as the American cookie is thought to get its name from the Dutch *koekje*. In any case, the sweet biscuits/cookies now eaten on both sides of the Atlantic appear to be nineteenth-century inventions. Confused? You will be, because such things were made in the US mainly by the National Biscuit Company, later known as Nabisco.

Anyway, somewhere along the road, the Americans decided the sweet things were *cookies* and that *biscuits* were an unsweet kind of scone, tasteless on their own but rather nice drenched in gravy. And everyone got along fine in their different ways. There was virtually no overlap between cookies and biscuits, because Americans had a much sweeter tooth and ate much more sugary confections like Oreos. And the British survived happily with their favourites like custard creams and choccy digestives, etc.

Which was fine until (a) British children started using the word *cookies* because that's what the kids ate on all the American TV programmes and (b) Nabisco's new masters, an annoyingly obtrusive company called Mondelez,[6] began stuffing British supermarkets with what the wrappers loudly proclaimed were Oreo Cookies,[7] and (c) these appealed to British kids.

And that's how more than just the language crumbles. There are the teeth too.

***

But the language certainly is crumbling. Public and private conversation are both full of words that were simply not used in Britain forty, thirty, twenty, ten, even five years ago. Some of the words may be welcomed as part of the process by which Americanisms helped make the language nimbler in the nineteenth century and snazzier in the early twentieth. But the vast majority are now taken up simply out of ignorance and the constant inescapable influence of the superpower.

Americanisms that arrived in Britain in the 1980s and thereafter can be found on pp. 226–33.

***

Maybe you would like to state your feelings and have your *two cents worth*. Americans always had their two cents worth if they wanted to say something; the British had their *tuppence worth*. But that cosy little word ('*I've got tuppence to spend, and tuppence to lend / And tuppence to take home to my wife. Poor wife*') was mortally wounded, for no good reason, by the introduction of decimal currency. And now the US usage is sliding in to Britain.

---

6 Spun off from Kraft after it had taken over Britain's Cadburys and destroyed the vestiges of the company's long ethical tradition.

7 The Oreo UK website does have the standard page on its policy for the invisible kind of *cookies*, but does not take the opportunity to be humorous.

This is part of a much wider problem. Nearly half a century after the shillings-and-pence system was cast into oblivion as too complicated,[8] the British still have no affectionate familiarity with their new money. Gone are the *thrupenny bits* and *tanners* and *two-bobs* and *half-crowns*, to be replaced by what? The smallest unit of currency – the *p* – shares its name with the most popular slang term for urination. Shopkeepers often say 'Have you a *one p* or even a *one pence*' though there is no reason not to say *penny* or *tuppence*.

A letter to the *Guardian* in December 2016 included the phrase *turn on a dime*, and I started getting cross about it. Then I kept discovering more examples, some of them written by respected writers from places as American as Edinburgh and Cambridgeshire. The equivalent *turn on a sixpence* was much loved by British football writers to express the same sense of rapid manoeuvre. But no one has seen a sixpence since 1980; no idiom has risen to replace it. We no longer mint sixpences. And, so it seems, we no longer mint idioms.

Britain is a country where no one can agree on how to say or write their telephone numbers because they have been messed about so often. Creeping metrication, enforced by the education system and the law, has also created confusion and unease. Weather forecasters spent fifty years indoctrinating Britain into the centigrade system and have now finally prevailed, though for everyday purposes it is much less practical than Fahrenheit.[9] These are very rare examples of Britain becoming less like America. But it is very much all part of being a nation so ill-at-ease that it insists on speaking American.

Even the national flag is a problem. It has not – yet – had to be redesigned to encompass Scotland's resignation from the union by removing the cross of St Andrew. But far from being a force for unity, as in the US or France, it has become contentious, because it is clutched so tightly by the political right. Even its lovely, evocative name, the *union jack*, which dates back at least to 1674, has been

---

8 In 1971, at almost exactly the moment pocket calculators came on to the market.
9 The weather forecast on my iPhone offers a choice between the two systems but is otherwise Americanised, using confusing terms like *partly cloudy, partly sunny* (so what's the difference?) and, alarmingly, *smoke*, which apparently indicates, not forest fires, but mist.

snatched away, in this case by pedantic twerps at the BBC and many newspapers who insist that it must be called the *union flag*. According to the Flag Institute, which knows about such matters, this is ridiculous. And it cites a government ruling from 1908: 'the Union Jack should be regarded as the National flag'. Union flag has a much stronger connotation with the American Civil War.

Yet, like policemen, pedants are never around when you need them. Newspapers used to employ an elderly subeditor known as a *prodnose*, whose job was to act as a final line of defence against libels, errors and infelicities.[10] Increasingly, papers are so hard up that many are ceasing to employ subeditors at all. Thus do Americanisms run rampant, like bindweed in an untended shrubbery.

Some of Britain's once-national once-newspapers are increasingly international multimedia organisations, and are looking towards what may well be the mirage of internet advertising riches from across the Atlantic. The *Financial Times*, by far the most successful at making the transition, still tries to ensure it is written in jargon-free British English. But several of its most senior editors are themselves American, and the battle to stop an epidemic of *going forward*, †*tasking*, *attendees* and *drugstores* is becoming an uphill one.

In contrast to newspapers, the continued existence of the BBC is not in doubt. It is one of the pillars, along with the National Health Service and Christmas, of whatever remains of British religion. But it has increasingly become a purveyor of Americanisms as well as a shield against them. The news bulletins are mostly still unappreciated mini-masterpieces of concise and precise British English. But the reporters in the field are only human. They are creatures of the time and the foreign correspondents, ex officio, are citizens of the world. They find themselves regurgitating the American English – or US-influenced international English – that is all around them.

And the BBC's power is in many ways diminished. Its finances have been squeezed by unsympathetic governments, in thrall to Rupert Murdoch's Sky because of the perceived influence of his newspapers. British audiences are no longer glued to the major channels,

---

10 The one who sticks in my mind really did have a long, sharp nose.

and these are no longer the undisputed purveyors of quality television to the world. Creativity and daring have migrated elsewhere.

Even most of the BBC's recent popular and critical successes are souped-up rehashes of old favourites: time lords, celebrity ballroom dancers, long-lost Cornishmen emerging hunkily from the mists. 'I've got an idea,' someone must have said in a meeting. 'Imagine a detective living in, say, Baker Street …' (The OED dates the phrase *No shit, Sherlock* to 1976 – it is attributed to Charles Durden, American.)

Educated British viewers used to disdain American TV unless, like the great 1970s smash *Dallas*, it could be enjoyed as kitsch, especially after a few drinks. But in the US the changing landscape of TV has had the reverse effect. The dead-hand oligopoly of the old networks has been broken up and newer channels have commissioned programmes of startling originality, which the BBC would never have the budget or the balls to make. ('Oh no, forget Holmes and Watson. Let's have a pair of crystal-meth manufacturers as the heroes.') The BBC lives in constant fear of being monstered by press and politicians, which is why they had to conclude that in the case of Jeremy Clarkson, who turned a low-grade motoring show into a global hit, his obnoxiousness outweighed his asset value.

The relevance of this is that the export trade in English – even British English – is now in American hands, as weaponry for competing corporations in the dawning age when TV and internet start to merge. Clarkson now works for Amazon, a far more overweening behemoth than the star himself. *The Crown*, a blockbuster retrospective of Elizabeth II's reign, has been given a stratospheric budget by Netflix. Both are being streamed via the internet rather than conventional TV.

Downton Abbey, an end-of-era television costume drama, first shown on ITV in 2010, depicting end-of-era aristocratic life from the early 1920s, was ostensibly a throwback to the great days of British television costume drama, but this time with a strong flavour of cynical pastiche. Of course the Americans loved it. When shown on *Masterpiece* (heir to *Masterpiece Theatre*), the slot dominated by Britain on the BBC-ish channel PBS, it drew record audiences, a younger demographic and new corporate sponsorship.

So what if early twentieth-century nobs and their servants come up with anachronistic Americanisms like *just saying*,[11] *push comes to shove*[12] and *shafted*?[13] Only pedants care. ***Wake up and smell the coffee!***[14]

The relationship between words and power is illustrated by Britain's most successful artistic export of the past decades, the boy wizard who turned a mixture of floo powder and horcruxes into squillions of enchanted galleons for his creator, J.K. Rowling. When the opening volume, *Harry Potter and the Philosopher's Stone*, was sold to the US publishing firm Scholastic in 1997 for what seemed a very acceptable $105,000,[15] Rowling had to accept fundamental changes not only to the text but also to the intricately crafted title, *philosopher* being deemed too difficult a word to interest American children. *Sorcerer* was infamously used instead.

And out went *sherbet lemons, nutters, crumpets, matron, shan't* and even *tinned soup*. In came *lemon drops, maniacs, muffins, nurse, won't* and *canned soup*. Later of course Rowling had more power and did at least get *mom* changed back to *mum*. A few fogies protested. 'By protecting our children from an occasional misunderstanding or trip to the dictionary, we are pretending that other cultures are, or should be, the same as ours,' moaned Peter H. Gleick in *The New York Times*. 'By insisting that everything be Americanized, we dumb down our own society rather than enrich it.'

Such a change would be unthinkable in reverse. British readers might have got a *Babbitt*-style glossary, if the London publisher (or the author) had paid for it. But British children are expected to be fluent in Anglo-American, and they have no trouble meeting that expectation at least.

Language is a function of power. In America, even Scrabble players

---

11 Which probably reached Britain through teenagers post-2000.

12 c.1950s.

13 Late 1970s.

14 Popularised in thousands of US newspapers from at least the 1950s by the agony aunt Ann Landers, who was huge in the US but little known in Britain. First reference in the *Guardian*: 1990.

15 Note to American publishers: similar offers will be entertained for this volume.

are protected from the frightening knowledge that there are non-American forms of English. In the vast majority of North American Scrabble tournaments, a different, more restrictive word list is in use, based on Merriam-Webster's dictionaries, allowing around 187,000 words compared with about 276,000 in the rest of the world, where the list comes from Collins.

Many American players dislike this but can do nothing about it. Why? Follow the money. A company called Hasbro owns the game in North America, while Mattel has the rights elsewhere. Hasbro reportedly has a publishing contract with Merriam-Webster, and also sponsors the North American Scrabble Championship. Noah Webster never foresaw this when he demanded different spellings.

***

The history of modern communications is a brief guide to the history of power. Britain's status as Victorian top dog made it exempt from putting its name on its postage stamps and allowed Greenwich to become the benchmark for calculating the time. When international dialling started to come into the telephone system in the 1960s, only two countries were allowed single-digit codes: the US (with Canada coming along for the ride) is No.1; the Soviet Union, presumably not wishing to be No.2, accepted 7. Britain is 44. How the mighty had fallen.

The World Wide Web was invented by an Englishman, Sir Tim Berners-Lee, working mainly in Switzerland and France. But the centre of gravity soon moved west. And when the cyber-era took shape, the US had no need for a national suffix like everyone else. Though it is possible to use .com in other countries, .gov and .mil are specifically reserved for the US government and military.

It is arguable that to an extent the internet has been a force more for the English being globalised rather than Americanised. After all, much modern communication takes place between people who could be anyone, anywhere. However, the machines themselves, or at any rate their software, are unflinching agents of American power, pressing Noah Webster's spellings on the world like the Inquisition rooting out heresy. My photocopier keeps asking if I want to print in *color*; my phone keeps insisting I agree to some new *license,* the terms of which it banks on me not reading; I am expected to have *favorites.*

I have to ***uncheck*** boxes to avoid being ensnared into buying something I do not need or want, while email providers talk †*trash.* In an outbreak of liberalism, my version of Microsoft Word graciously allows me to write in British English but, at the slightest provocation – a simple cut-and-pasted sentence, say – it will immediately exact vengeance by reverting to American and putting bad-tempered squiggles, like an infuriated schoolteacher, under every deviation from Websterian orthodoxy. I could complain to my PC's ***action center***, but I sense there might not be much point. It is always the small indignities that are the true indicators of a hostile occupation.

And these days we all get †*mail* rather than *post.* There always was mail in Britain; it was a travelling bag, in which mail (and originally everything else) was carried. The Royal Mail dates back many centuries,[16] and there were always mailbags, mail vans and mail trains. But *mailman* fell into disuse long ago and the verb *mail* was never in common use. On the other side, the US always preferred to send mail, though it still has a Post Office run by a Postmaster-General, a title now obsolete in Britain.

And no one now gets epost; no studio is likely to produce a film called *You've Got Post.* Though *post* does have its own specialist meaning on blogs and social media, it has lost its old starring role. The internet has ensured yet another victory for American.

***

Is there now something much broader at work in the Anglo-American relationship? Is Britain changing its nature to match the behaviour of the imperial power?

Its capital has been Manhattanized, its lovingly preserved old

---

16 It was, however, practically archaic until 2002, when the Post Office rebranded after its brief New Coke-type experiment of calling itself Consignia.

buildings lost under egomaniacal †*skyscrapers*.[17] The people, especially the young, have shrugged off much of their forefathers' ancient reticence and embraced self-promotion, a certain amount of exhibitionism and an unalloyed obsession with celebrity. They are prone to confuse reality with reality TV. The country is subject to emotional spasms, from Princess Diana's death to Brexit. Political violence lurks worryingly closer to the surface and sometimes breaks cover.

Sometimes this incontinence is merely pathetic, as with the hysteria over the London Olympics and the 2014 visit to Britain of the Tour de France. Would the French have got worked up had they been graced by a visit from the Tour de Yorkshire?

The British shout on the telephone in public places; they tell you their symptoms in American-style detail, complete with technicalities (perhaps because doctors no longer have time to listen). They have nudged closer to matching the Americans' sugar consumption, which is like challenging them at baseball.[18] Overpriced and over-elaborated coffee is everywhere, and drunk as a fashion statement.

In the dwindling number of pubs, the same forces are at work. A Scottish landlord, proud of his single malts, told me that if anyone under about 40 now asks for a whisky, they want bourbon, usually Jack Daniel's, because it's heavily marketed. Or the product of those nice folks at Jim Beam (see pp. 147–8). That's if they are not demanding bubble-gum-flavoured gin, cheaply made high-margin lager or American craft beer.

Publicans long ago installed American pool tables to replace traditional pub games: they take up less space and eat up coins. And one rather suspects that, if there is a national ideal of what an English pub should feel like, it probably comes from the American TV series *Cheers*. Most pubs now of course survive by serving food. And if their

---

17 The word, I have to say, is lovely: long before it was applied to high buildings in the US, it was an old nautical term for a tall sail, and slang for someone very tall. Skyscraper (son of Highflyer) won the 1789 Epsom Derby.

18 As early as 1862 a *Times* correspondent covering the US Civil War was horrified by the soldiers' consumption of sweets 'which in England boys throw aside with their tops and marbles … the quantity of sugar sticks consumed by a single American regiment in a day is past belief'.

customers eat anything that requires cutlery then, according to a 2015 report, they will increasingly eat with their forks in their right hand, American-style.

The spread of American-style Halloween into Britain causes much irritation to the older generation, and its customs are peculiarly repellent: a celebration of avarice and sugar highs. However, it is fair to say that the home-grown alternative of Guy Fawkes Night was problematic: the number of children maimed by fireworks was terrifying and, for understandable reasons, Catholic communities never cared for it.

In 2014 it was widely reported that one in six Britons were now celebrating *Thanksgiving*: a festival to give thanks for having left benighted Britain behind. In context, i.e. in the United States, Thanksgiving, the fourth Thursday in November, is actually a delightful time, uncommercialised and family oriented. It also helps ensure that Christmas starts in December and not in July.

The one-in-six figure cannot possibly be true, though credulous journalists kept regurgitating it. But Britain really has gleefully adopted Thanksgiving's nasty neighbour, †***Black Friday***. Now this is a phrase of great resonance. Some sources say it was an old name for Good Friday; it has also been applied to dozens of other ill-starred Fridays throughout history.[19]

In the US making it a mega-shopping day has some mutual benefit because a Thursday holiday does create a problem about what to do on a quasi-holiday Friday. And it is the genuine start of the Christmas season. In Britain it is just an exploitative attempt by the major retailers to ramp up the Christmas shopping even further. And the suckers fall for it.

Mostly, an American Christmas is understated and short. It used to have one particular excess of its own: elaborate hey-look-at-us illuminations outside homes. So Britain now has those. But Christmas is all for the †***kids***, isn't it? Ah, yes, those adorable brainwashed Yankee fifth-columnists in our midst. *Kids* cannot be an Americanism in itself:

---

19 These include the Friday in 1745 when news reached London that Bonnie Prince Charlie's invading army was barely a hundred miles away, and financial collapses in 1866 (Britain) and 1869 (US). Wikipedia lists twenty others, not all of them convincing.

'Passed a few days happily with my wife and kids,' wrote Lord Shaftesbury in his diary in 1841. But its current ubiquity is undoubtedly recent and American: it was not a word used much by British parents in the 1950s. Children then were given very conservative names, for fear of ridicule. Even Matthew was considered a little *outré*. Now of course parents turn to America, especially for boys: Ethan ('Eathen? As opposed to Christian?'), Jackson, Jaxson, Mason, Hunter, Cody, Oakley, Tyler, Taylor … maybe even Poorman, Beggarman and Thief.

The Americanisation of British childhood was typified by Disney's annexation of Winnie-the-Pooh. But it was sealed by something else: a seemingly innocuous, indeed educational, and much admired TV programme that, day after day, insinuated itself into the heads of infants who are themselves now parents and even grandparents. It was called *Sesame Street*, first shown in Britain in 1971, two years after its American debut.

The BBC righteously refused to touch it. Monica Sims, its head of children's programmes, said *Sesame Street* might be needed in the US where children watched endlessly. 'We set out to discourage passive box-watching … Surely it is more valuable to watch with concentration and involvement for the twenty minutes of *Play School* and then go off and do something suggested in the programme, than to be hypnotised into gazing for an hour at a succession of fast-moving images.'

That view prevailed, within the Beeb at least. But not out there in tellyland, where two channels had already become three and would then become four before becoming infinity; where breakfast TV was on its way to being followed by twenty-four-hour TV, and where the idea of kids 'going off' was becoming unthinkable because it was statistically certain there was a paedophile lurking behind the privet.

In any case the commercial channels – first ITV and later Channel 4 – were less squeamish, which meant that a generation was able to grasp rapidly that if 'going off' was involved at all it involved going off and buying whatever the advertisers wanted them to buy. And eating cookies. And pronouncing Z as Zee.

The problem was not that *Sesame Street* was bad – the reverse. That was what made it so beguiling both to children and their harassed parents. And, though Channel 4 moved on, it is still available on at least one satellite channel with a very high number. It might have been unfortunate if a harassed mum suffered some kind of trauma which necessitated a child calling for help. Surveys at the height of *Sesame Street*'s power showed that an alarming number of British children thought the emergency number to call was not 999, but 911. Now where on earth did they get that idea from?

It did seem as though British children would always pick up the worst of America, never the best. What was hugely impressive to me, as a temporary US parent, was the way schools used symbolism and rites of passage to create a sense of pride: I was dazzled by the graduation ceremony for 11-year-olds leaving their elementary school. Instead, Britain took a shine to the teenage *prom*: a carnival devoted to the celebration of peer pressure, post-pubescent anxiety, jealousy, bitchiness, arguments and ostentation.

As Americanism and technology grow ever more dominant, so a couple of other things have been noted about the concerns of British children in those mysterious years between *Sesame Street* and the prom. When a new edition of the Oxford Junior Dictionary was published, the writer Robert MacFarlane discovered that a number of words had been deleted. These included *acorn*, *adder*, *ash*, *beech*, *bluebell*, *buttercup*, *catkin*, *conker*, *cowslip*, *cygnet*, *dandelion*, *fern*, *hazel*, *heather*, *heron*, *ivy*, *kingfisher*, *lark*, *mistletoe*, *nectar*, *newt*, *otter*, *pasture* and *willow*. Among the replacements were **blog**, **broadband**, **bullet point**, *celebrity*, **chatroom**, *committee* and **voicemail**.

Britain has been a largely urban society since the Industrial Revolution, but its city life was always accompanied by a sense of perpetual exile: the English dream was keeping a country pub or, more sensibly, having a cottage 'with roses round the door'. Many of my own generation lived that dream. That attachment between urban and rural Britain is being snapped. It seems to me highly significant that children now habitually call anything even vaguely arthropodan by the American name *bug*, even the adored *ladybird* sometimes becoming a *ladybug*. The implication is that here is something that is merely an irritant, a species whose place in the ecosystem is infinitely less useful than that of a Western child.

Meanwhile, in 2016 it was being reported that 100,000 infernally noisy garden vacs or **leaf blowers** were being sold each year, enabling the British to recreate every autumn, not merely Halloween and Thanksgiving, but the characteristic November weekend background music of the American suburb: a shriek which proclaims that primeval American urge to conquer nature wherever it rears its ugly head.

Increasingly, the British are adopting the American habit of trying to banish the natural world completely. Americans rarely have a *garden*; they call it a *yard*. The word has not yet spread but the mentality has. Sue Biggs, director-general of the Royal Horticultural Society, talked in 2016 of 'a lost generation of gardeners' – the Sesame Streeters basically – who preferred to treat their garden as 'an outdoor living room' with **decking** and a barbecue. At the younger end of the cohort, the inability to afford their own home takes young people further away from an interest in gardening.

A family might wish their deck to be painted **robin's egg blue**, a very pretty and delicate colour particularly popular for porches in the Southern states. The shade is available for wedding gifts from a company in Manchester.[20] It is not, however, available in Britain from your local robin, which lays much less distinguished speckledy eggs. The robin is supposed to be Britain's favourite bird, almost as well-loved as the ladybird; the blue-egg American version is not even a long-lost cousin – it's a thrush. In *Mary Poppins*, a robin comes through a London window to land on Julie Andrews' finger while she is singing 'A Spoonful of Sugar'. Wrong robin again.

We are back in bluebird territory, and it is very fertile. The nature writer Simon Barnes says that, of the 5,000 or so species of frog, only one makes a sound anything like **ribbit-ribbit**. But it happens to live in southern California, where, in the early talkie days, film-makers stuck a microphone outside if they wanted outdoor sound effects. Thus it is that the world now believes all frogs go *ribbit-ribbit*.

Mary Poppins was much derided in Britain for Dick Van Dyke's

---

20 The same firm also sells children's fancy dress for dozens of American characters and a handful of British ones, plus *piñatas* and items suitable for **baby showers** and **gender-reveal parties**, presumably for unborn babies but maybe also for adults.

clueless attempt at a Cockney accent. Actors trying the opposite trick used to have the same problem. In 1987 Henry Goodman, playing in a musical version of *They Shoot Horses, Don't They?*, mused self-deprecatingly to a US radio reporter about how difficult it was for a British actor of his generation (born 1950) to play Americans convincingly.

The tape and transcript no longer exist but the reporter, Michael Goldfarb, remembers the gist of it vividly. Goodman said it would be different for his kids' generation; they watched so much American TV they could already do the accents perfectly. And so it has proved: Dominic West and Idris Elba in *The Wire*; Chiwetel Ejiofor in *12 Years A Slave*; David Harewood and Damian Lewis in *Homeland*. Older actors have acquired the skills too: Goodman himself has played Americans on Broadway; Anthony Hopkins played Richard Nixon; Daniel Day-Lewis won an Oscar as Lincoln. For the black actors there is a simple calculation: for them, American productions offer a greater choice of roles; for them all it has become a test of their range, a professional rite of passage.[21]

It is certainly a new development. Pre-war Hollywood used to favour British actors who could do a not-quite-classifiable old-school American; then the British were much in demand to play villainous masterminds. The modern trend is on one level a great tribute to the skill of the actors: those who don't recognise their names would never guess they were British, yet two of them went to Eton, dammit.[22] Is even this apparent British success perhaps also a sign of the relationship between the two countries? Imitation as a form of subservience, the way Jeeves could always out-posh Wooster. Powerful Romans always liked well-educated slaves from decaying Greece to do their intellectual heavy lifting.

---

21 In March 2017 the US actor Samuel L. Jackson complained about black British actors being cast in American roles: he singled out Daniel Kaluuya in *Get Out* and David Oyelowo as Martin Luther King in *Selma*. He thought they were partly chosen because they were cheaper.

22 It is not unknown for Americans, women in particular (Meryl Streep, Renée Zellweger and Gwyneth Paltrow as well as John Lithgow), to play British roles, but it is still something of a novelty act.

There is another, much less public sign of this to be found behind the scenes in Hollywood and in the concert halls of the world. British musicians learn their own traditional note values: semi-breves, minims, crotchets, quavers, semi-quavers. Their American counterparts work on a system derived from the German: whole notes, halves, quarters, eighths and sixteenths: 'less musical, more mathematical', as one conductor put it. The British adapt easily if they work abroad; Americans often get in a tangle. So when in doubt, the US system prevails.

Is that simply because their system is easier and more logical? Or does it reflect the world order as surely as the fact that English is the default language spoken in the breakfast room of the vast majority of the world's hotels?

***

In small things and large, one senses Britain slowly lurching towards American ways. I have a suspicion more and more British people are using the euphemism and *going to the bathroom* rather than the *toilet*. Americans themselves used to go to the toilet quite happily in the nineteenth century, when the British were still on the WC. We will probably soon be talking of *restrooms*, *powder rooms* and *comfort stations*.

Euphemisms are also creeping into news reports, the BBC's included, in the matter of death – apparently a less frequent occurrence because so many people are *passing away* or, worse still, †*passing*. The playwright Mark Ravenhill complained about someone using the Americanism *passing* in the *Guardian* and was slapped about the head by the paper's language blogger Steven Poole, on the familiar but spurious grounds that *passing* is in Chaucer (see the Fowler brothers' comments, pp. 71–2). Look, if the Chaucer family from Wyoming suddenly turned up at Heathrow, they would not get automatic citizenship just because their ancestor was big in these parts in the fourteenth century.

There is a more specific argument in this case. Chaucer lived in a time when religion was not a matter of personal choice. *Passing* is now a use favoured by evangelical Christians, especially American ones, and implies an unquestioning faith in the fact that death marks a transition rather than closure (at least for those who pay their church subscriptions). One hopes this might in some way be true, but it seems unlikely the *Guardian* has firm evidence. Until that is produced, the simple verb *die* is factual and sufficient for the news media. If anyone says I have *passed* when the day comes, I shall come back and haunt them.

The use of *passing* is wholly at odds with Britain's unAmerican drift away from religion. Along with the whole realm of nature, the Oxford Junior Dictionary has also thrown out any mention of *bishop*, *archbishop*, *pope*, *crucifix*, *crucifixion* and *confession*. *Lent* has been also excluded, although there is room for *Ramadan*.

Some changes come in very fast, like the arrival of the didactic **So** as an all-purpose way of starting sentences. It is said to have originated as an in-house habit among Microsoft employees. One would therefore expect that the next edition of Microsoft Word will have a default position of starting all sentences with *So*.

Other changes arrive imperceptibly, over generations. Pronunciation works like that. The most startling change to anyone of my age group is the universal insistence of the under-40s that H should be pronounced as a phoney-posh haitch: indeed Sky TV now informs its subscribers of the wonders of Sky Haitch-D. It is certainly not American; it could have come from Ireland, but how and why? Most other pronunciation changes are all too easy to pin down. Shopping **malls** now rhyme with balls, and Pall Mall is an anomaly. There are **ske-dules** rather than *schedules*. Children who may have watched David Attenborough but not listened talk of **zee-bras** not zebras.

Perhaps one pronunciation above all stands out as a symbol of modern Britain: it is the word *lieutenant*. Traditionally it is *lef*-tenant in the British armed forces; **loo-tenant** is normal in the US military and police. In the British Army it is a laughable solecism to use the American pronunciation. Yet the vast majority of people, who spend more time watching US cop shows than talking to soldiers, now instinctively pronounce it the American way.

The recent exploits of the steeplechaser First Lieutenant exposed a frightening degree of Americanisation among racing commentators. Much more seriously, in 2011 Ed Miliband, then the leader of the Labour Party, paid tribute in the Commons to soldiers who had died in Afghanistan and exposed himself as a *loo*-tenant man. On the whole, the marginalisation of the military in any society ought to be a healthy indication of a country accustomed to peace. It seems to me far more important that children should be able to recognise catkins and conkers. But in the case of an aspirant prime minister it does help to be able to talk to army officers without sounding like a twat.

Sometimes, though, a single gesture can be worth a thousand mispronounced words. During the half-time show of the 2012 Super Bowl, the highest-profile slot in American broadcasting, the British rapper M.I.A., who had come to Indianapolis dressed as Cleopatra, decided that an audience of 114 million Americans was not quite enough for her, and in order to gain further attention slipped her middle finger towards the crowd.

She shamed her country. How crass to use the crude American gesture when the much subtler though fading British equivalent, the V-sign, was available. Using two fingers, palm inward, as a gesture of contempt is said to date back to British archers signalling 'Hop off, you frogs' at the Battles of Crécy and Agincourt. That gives it historical resonance, even though it is almost certainly untrue.

Most Americans would not have understood the gesture. And, even if they did, her PRs could have sold it as a version of the palm-outward Churchillian victory-gesture, which would have increased her credibility and possibly saved her the two years and unknown cost it took to settle the National Football League's $16m legal action. Britain's role in America is no longer even necessarily to add a touch of class.

7

NOUS SOMMES TOUS AMERICAINS, INNIT

The world, thank heaven, is not yet completely flat and homogeneous. In specialist fields there are all kinds of fascinating quirks that refuse to be ironed out. On this modern, connected and globalised hi-tech planet, one would think transport – the act of getting from one place to another – would be completely standardised. This is fascinatingly, indeed a bit worryingly, untrue.

When Britain and the US began running trains in the 1830s, the technology came from Britain, but the terminology remained stubbornly separate. Americanisms have nibbled here and there; the basics, however, have not wavered: *railway, carriage, platform, points, sleepers, driver* = *railroad, car, track, switches, ties, engineer.*

There has been a recent change whereby younger Britons have started to refer to the *train station* rather than the *railway station*. The new version has started to appear on signs, and is assumed, and condemned, by their elders as an example of creeping Americanisation. I doubt it. Fifty years ago towns had a *station*, which had trains (unless Dr Beeching had axed them), and was more formally called a *railway station*. There was also an upstart *bus station*, which was never shortened.

A new generation, using buses more than trains, felt the need to make a clearer distinction and the language gradually changed. Americans started saying *train station* first, but they also said *railroad station* ('When I went down to the railroad station, a-hunny' – Del Shannon, 1962) or, more quaintly, *depot* (*dee*-po). But mostly Americans never say anything at all on this subject, because, outside the big north-eastern cities, they hardly ever go on trains, which thus rarely play any part in their modern films or TV dramas.

The complete differentiation between motoring terms on the two sides of the Atlantic is more surprising, because cars developed just as Britain was becoming obsessed with Americanisms. Nonetheless, the vocabulary evolved differently in almost every particular: *bonnet, boot, silencer, windscreen, glove compartment, tyre, petrol* = *hood, trunk, muffler, windshield, glovebox, tire, gas*. Presumably, as with railways, since you could not travel this way from one country to the other, there was no need for any kind of standardisation. Yet the extent of the difference is puzzling, and I have yet to find a definitive explanation. Patrick Collins of the National Motor Museum theorises that early cars were built by men who had previously been in the carriage trade and that they already had their own jargon.

Yet the separation survived the takeover of much of the benighted British motor industry by American giants. And even now there have been few inroads. British driving instructors long ago took to referring to the **gas pedal** rather than the *accelerator* for fear that, by the time they had mouthed all five syllables, the learner might have crashed into a wall. And David Cameron said on TV in 2013: 'What you'll see tomorrow is a coalition government with a full tank of gas.' Speakers of business-babble sometimes fail to translate the Americanism about **looking under the hood** of a company. But by and large Britain's motoring vocabulary has survived better than its carmakers.

Sam Llewellyn, editor of *Marine Quarterly*, says: 'If you are talking about our being divided by a common language, it applies to seafaring at strength ten.' Much of this is highly technical, e.g. *lighter* = *scow*; *bottle-screws* = *turnbuckles*. But it is notable that Americans always talk *oarlocks* whereas the British talk *rowlocks*.

One would imagine that, by the time aeroplanes took wing, a

certain amount of standardisation would have been thought essential. Otherwise, planes might crash. English was long ago established as the language of international air traffic control and feet as the primary measure of altitude. However, this is far from straightforward: according to the website aerosavvy.com – run by American pilot Ken Hoke – Russia, China and North Korea (all with a history of being Bolshevik and bolshy) all insist on metres.

For atmospheric pressure, the US and Japan use inches of mercury; everyone else goes for hectopascals, aka millibars. There are further confusions over runway lengths and visibility. Different ways of measuring altitude have sometimes been blamed in the media for crashes, but Hoke is adamant that there is no problem: 'Pilots flying international routes deal with this assortment of units daily. We can juggle them in our sleep.' So that's all right then.

Less worryingly – indeed an encouraging contra-indication to the concerns of this book – Britain and the US continue to disagree regularly when a new technology breaks through. *Mobile phones* have not been displaced by *cellphones*. Thirty-five years ago the British were going crazy for *video recorders*; Americans were buying *VCRs*. Nor have the equally boring initials *ATM* taken hold in Britain for the machines that dispense cash.

The problem here is that British English has failed to agree on an alternative. *Cash point*? *Cash machine*? *Hole in the wall*? This can be a route to Americanisation by default. When it became possible to change TV channels without leaving one's armchair, the British never devised a word for the contraption that kept disappearing down the side of the sofa: 'Where's the thingy?' Americans enthusiastically grabbed hold of the *remote*. This is a little hard to judge since it is a subject most often discussed among consenting adults in private, but one senses that the Americanism may be gaining a grip.

On the subject of consenting adults, we are now getting close to the point where we need to talk about *pants*. There remain important differences between what the British and the Americans wear, even leaving aside the question of loud checks.

Americans sometimes use the word *coat* where the British would say *jacket*, but this is hardly a major problem. British kids are now less likely to wear *jumpers* ('jumpers for goalposts') or *woollies* or even an Anglo-American sweater, partly because they are disinclined to wear wool or indeed warm clothing at any time, especially when hanging around outside nightclubs in midwinter.

Nor do young people bother much with *vests*, either the sort worn under the shirt (in Britain) or over it (in the US, where it is the garment known in Britain as a *waistcoat*). American women wear *pantyhose* not *tights*. None of these poses major translation problems. However, a British male seen wearing *knickers* and *suspenders* in public would be considered rather eccentric, except at a Rocky Horror midnight matinée. An American male in *knickers* and *suspenders*, i.e. old-fashioned plus-fours and braces, might also look a little odd but would be in less imminent danger of being photographed for the more disreputable Sunday papers.

The word *pants* comes from *pantaloons* and, after many adventures – including a period when *panties* meant boys' shorts – *pants* came to mean trousers in the US and underpants in Britain. By the early 1990s there were signs that this was an aberration that would be ironed out. *Pants* was already being considered an alternative to *trousers* in Australia, where it had displaced the charming old homegrown term *strides*.

But in Britain something happened: a new expression arose whereby *pants*, usually as *pile of pants* or *load of pants*, became a synonym for anything that was rubbish – a TV programme, a job, a management decision. This seemed to me unusual on two levels: a vigorous and expressive neologism that was neither American nor a media catchphrase spreading rapidly into common parlance. How little I knew.

This new usage did a remarkable job, by curing the British of the urge to follow the American way on this one. However, it was evidently spread by BBC Radio 1, via the disc jockey Simon Mayo according to most sources, so it was a catchphrase after all. Also the Americans had eerily got there more than a century earlier. *My/your/ his etc. name is pants* was a variant on the (British-grown) *name is mud* in the US in the late nineteenth and early twentieth century. All very puzzling.

So pants as a garment have now retreated undercover again in Britain. But the word may be in retreat as well. I suspect increasing numbers of male and female Britons are now wearing *underpants*, which cannot be misunderstood. And this, in the context of maintaining the distinctiveness of British English, is a pile of pants.

***

For the reasonably clued-up modern British traveller in America there are likely to be very few insurmountable conversational difficulties. But there are some. Any visitor over about 6 would know *sidewalk* means *pavement*; they would not necessarily know that *pavement* means the *roadway*. So an instruction to 'drive on the pavement' could cause mayhem.

There are certainly known cases of visitors staying in private houses and causing alarm by offering to *lay the table* and *wash up*. *Washing up* involves a minor distinction between washing the dishes (UK) and washing one's hands (US). *Laying the table* has been known to set the American mind racing in all kinds of strange directions.

There is more scope for embarrassment the other way. The word *shag* has been used in Britain since at least 1937 as a term which has nothing directly to do with long hair, carpets, a 1930s dance or the crested cormorant, although some or all of the above might in some way be involved. In America this usage is at best patchily understood, though the slang-ologist Jonathon Green does cite US teenage sexual uses and it did become briefly familiar in the US during the heyday of the Austin Powers films, particularly *The Spy Who Shagged Me* (1999). However, the US seems to have regained its innocence on this point. In 2015 a St Louis Cardinals pitcher, Randy Choate, had T-shirts printed for his teammates saying ALL-STAR SHAGGING RELIEF CORPS. This (I think) referred to the pitchers' role during batting practice: to track down, or shag, baseballs.

Americans in Britain might also cause raised eyebrows by using the noun *fanny* as innocuous slang for the bottom. This has been current in the US since the 1920s, at least half a century after the British, less innocuously, began using it as slang for the front bottom.

There is also the noun *spunk*, used primarily in the US to denote a display of pluck and spirit; in Australia to mean a sexually attractive person; and in Britain ('coarse slang' – OED) to mean seminal fluid. There appears to be some interchange, and it is probably best to avoid the word altogether except among very good friends or when granted a private audience with President Trump.

To move on swiftly … the *middle class* in the US is the working class, much lauded at election time but a stratum from which the ambitious young are anxious to escape. In Britain it is, if anything, well above the middle. This may be an example of the Americans using language to glorify the humdrum, the process whereby *undertakers* became **funeral directors** or *morticians*; *estate agents* made themselves into *realtors*; and *rat-catchers* into *exterminating engineers*.

Perhaps this also explains the American use of *rock* to indicate a *stone*, especially when it is chucked at the police. This inflationary use was first noted as a Western peculiarity by the traveller Samuel Parker in 1838. Now smallish projectiles are often solemnly reported as *rocks*, often to justify the armed response, even if these were kids throwing what might not be much more than a pebble. From the evidence of having played I-Spy recently with a bright English 9-year-old on a country walk, I sense this habit is spreading. Why else would he have flummoxed me with R for rocks, when only small bits of grit were visible?

Yet there are American words and phrases I would be happy if Britain had imported. What about the wonderful Texanism *all hat and no cattle* (cf. *fur coat and no knickers*)? What about all the magnificent Yiddishisms that Americans have adopted: hardly any non-Jewish people in Britain, and a decreasing number of Jewish ones, can explain the exact nuances that separate a *schmuck* and a *schlemiel* or precisely define *chutzpah*.[1]

And why not just a few of the words we cast off and have not

---

[1] Pronounced hoot [rhymes with foot]-sper, but the start is guttural. The writer Israel Zangwill defined this in 1894, long before Thatcherism, as 'enterprise, audacity, brazen impudence and cheek'. It is much needed to describe the politics and finances of the early twenty-first century.

yet taken back? Like that charming euphemism *homely* to describe a person unlikely to make it in Australia as a spunk. Or the graphic *come out at the little end of the horn*. Or such long-forgotten playthings as *womblecropped* and *obfliscated*. There is nothing wrong with taking in refugee words if they can make a contribution to society.

I think Ben Yagoda would agree with me on that. And it is now time to introduce him into the script: Yagoda is an affable and hospitable man who is professor of English and journalism at the University of Delaware. He also runs a blog called *Not One-Off Britishisms*: '"*Ginger*," "*Bits*," "*Whinge*," and other UK expressions that have got popular in the US.'

In a sense we are adversaries: Holmes and Moriarty locked in struggle as we tumble toward the turbulent waters far below. But then again, we are sort of on the same side: 'The premise of this blog is that the gap between the two brands of English — American and British —is diminishing and will one day recede to nothing,' he said in one post. And that is precisely the premise of this book, except that I would add the rider at the end: 'unless something is done'; I refuse to give way to despair. We also clearly share the view that homogenisation would be a disaster.

The difference is that Yagoda seems to think the languages will meet somewhere in the mid-Atlantic. I reckon the meeting point will be within sight of the American coast. He lists about 250 Britishisms[2] that have made sometimes fleeting appearances in the US, mostly in the elite media, even if they are not exactly one-off: most of the Americanisms listed in these chapters are now so well camouflaged that their ancestry is largely forgotten. I reckon many words on Yagoda's list constitute passing fads.

Don't get me wrong. Yagoda's blog is erudite and enjoyable. I am just not impressed by his grievances. 'In the *New Yorker* alone, *inverted commas* [rather than the normal Americanism, *quotation marks*] have been mentioned several times in the past decade,' he wrote. Well, la-di-dah. When comparing the indignities with those

---

2 William Safire, the much-missed words columnist in *The New York Times*, preferred to call them Briticisms.

heaped on British English, he can sound a bit like a White House spokesman threatening nuclear retaliation for an outrageous and provocative attack launched by the armed forces of Rutland.

It does occasionally do the heart good when visiting the US to discover British spellings used to give establishments a certain cachet. One of Washington's fanciest shopping malls calls itself the Pentagon *Centre*; one of its most prestigious apartment complexes is spelt *Harbour* Square. Sometimes apartments are marketed as *flats*, the reverse of British thinking. But none of this is remotely typical of life out there in Trumpland.

It is also slightly encouraging to know that the spirit of Dick van Dyke is still alive and well in what's left of American journalism. In June 2016, four days after British voters had decided it would be fun to leave the European Union, the England football team suffered a spectacular humiliation even by their own standards and were knocked out of the European Championship by Iceland. The New York tabloid the *Daily News* devoted the front page to a picture of a small boy in England kit, face down and in tears, and the words:

MIGHTY MY ARSE, MUMMY!
As reeling Brits call bollocks on Brexit, England humiliated in historic footy flop

There are probably more Britishisms in those few words than on any front page published in New York since before independence. Shame the words don't actually make sense. It is, however, a reminder of how much we need to cherish that versatile and expressive word *arse* as opposed to *ass*. Yes, I know Shakespeare must have said *ass* – why else would Bottom have been transformed into one? Why is *arse* worth having? Well, I can't be arsed to explain; and, as Louis Armstrong said when asked to define jazz: 'Man, if you gotta ask, you'll never know.'

***

One oddity of Yagoda's website is his subtitle: one of his three words is not really a Britishism at all. † *Whinge* came from solid British stock all right, perhaps dating back to the twelfth century. And it is indeed the perfect onomatopoeic word to describe the sound made by a 4-year-old not getting their own way. But it emigrated to Australia and was used only sporadically in Britain until the 1980s. That evidently changed for two reasons: the continual Australian taunting of 'whingeing Poms' whenever their team beat England at cricket, which was more often than not; and the popularity of the Australian soap *Neighbours*, which started on British TV in 1986.

I suspect *Neighbours* may also have played a role in the spread of uptalk, the practice, now common in British people under 40, of uttering each statement with a rising tone. So it sounds like a *question*? Like *this*? As though the speaker has no confidence in what they're actually *saying*? This is often thought to have originated with the Californian Valley Girls of the early 1980s. But it was an older and more general phenomenon among Australian women, and was often taken to be an indicator of their subordinate position in society and their lack of confidence in their own opinions. There is a new academic theory that this is not the case, and that uptalk, in Henry Hitchings's words, 'is a means of asserting control; the speaker is requiring me to confirm that I am paying attention – and perhaps even that I agree with what is being said'.

Frankly, this is not convincing. In December 2016, after a spate of disturbances at British jails, the Justice Minister, Liz Truss (just over 40), went into full uptalk mode against a hostile House of Commons. Believe me, she was not asserting control. It was a clear sign she hadn't got the foggiest what she was talking about, and knew it.[3]

Australia makes a fascinating comparison with the British experience of Americanisation. It is a substantial, rich, monoglot English country, in some respects a halfway house between Britain and the US. The climate, the informality, the lifestyle and the materialism are very Californian. The language is much closer to British English: even more ironic, if anything, but with less prevarication.

---

3 Valley Girls probably do get the credit, if that's the word, for exporting the declaratory forms of *as if*, *whatever!*, *totally*, *OMG* and *seriously*. And of course the all-purpose *like*.

The spelling is almost wholly British: there was a mild infatuation with Websterian endings, which has now disappeared except for the Australian Labor Party and a few small Harbors, not including Sydney Harbour. Aussie variations on the language are inventive, poetic and sometimes daring, like *budgie smugglers* for pairs of tight Speedos for men.

But having a much smaller population than Britain, Australia is even more prone to outside influences, and the irritation caused by Americanisms can be even greater. There has long been concern that the rich Aussie vernacular was being submerged. A news report in 2005 said mournfully that 'Many younger Australians are now more likely to say *hi* than *g'day*, and *vacation* rather than *holiday*. *Bloke* and *mate*, long regarded as quintessentially Aussie, are giving way to *dude* and even *bro*.' 'It reflects the fact that we are still somewhat insecure about ourselves,' said Professor Roly Sussex of Queensland University.

On the great battleground words, Australia is somewhat further along the Americanisation path than Britain. According to Bruce Moore, chief editor of the Australian National Dictionary, *trousers* and *pants* are now interchangeable; *chips* would normally be sold in packets, though *fish 'n' chips* and *hot chips* are clearly understood; and the highways are full of *trucks*, 'though we would know *lorry* as being Pommish'.

In the housing market, Moore says, a clear class distinction has emerged: 'If I was buying, it would be an *apartment*. If I was out of money, I'd rent a *flat*. We do talk of sharing as *flatting* with someone.' And *biscuits* remain standard Australian, although *cookies* are widespread. But even in a country where not much is sacred, this is the point where Australia dug in its heels.

What is sacred is Anzac Day, the commemoration of the Australian and New Zealand Army Corps' sacrifice at Gallipoli in 1915 and by extension the sacrifice of all the country's fallen. And there is also the sacramental wafer, the Anzac biscuit, a variant on the special supplies that the troops' loved ones sent them, because they kept well: 'made of bricks, mortar and a little dash of flour,' as one old soldier put it. The use of the word Anzac is tightly controlled; it requires permission, with potential imprisonment for offenders. One year a company started making Anzac cookies ...

The Australian government website has a section referring to the regulations governing use of the word Anzac. The relevant paragraph now reads: 'Applications for Anzac biscuits are normally approved provided the product generally conforms to the traditional recipe and shape, and are referred to as "Anzac Biscuits" or "Anzac Slice". Referring to these products as "Anzac Cookies" is generally not approved, due to the non-Australian overtones.'

Bruce Moore sees this as a sign that there is a consciousness of the country owning a specifically Australian version of English, which is an important part of their national identity. This is not as obvious as it might sound. Until about the late 1960s, Australianisms were considered slang by definition. Later, there was a terror that Americanisms were taking over. He thinks that is abating.

'Until 1976 we didn't even have a dictionary edited in Australia. There's a confidence now that the language is accepted. And I think we're a country confident in our language. It's something the Australians are pleased with. I think that's led to a relaxed acceptance that it can take words from outside our culture and no longer feel threatened by them.'

It would be nice to feel as relaxed about British English. Perhaps sunshine helps. But at least one country, also with better weather than Britain's, feels Americanisation not just as an irritation but as an existential threat.

***

The poet and scholar Sir Michael Edwards is a unique figure. In 2013, nearly four centuries after the foundation of the Académie française, he became the first Briton to become a member, one of *les immortels* who guard the French language against the barbarians howling at the gates. He has long been effectively Anglo-French, and despite his loyalty to, knowledge of and affection for France, he still brings a certain British scepticism to the vexed issue of patrolling and controlling the language. He thinks it is right to make the effort; that does not mean he expects success. Much the same applies to the way we all have a hankering after immortality, whether one is elected to the Académie or not.

France's everlastingly tortured relationship with the United States has continued unabated, periods of calm alternating with skirmishes. In the 1960s President de Gaulle tried to triangulate the world by setting France up as an independent nuclear power – opposed to the Soviet bloc but sceptical about the US, unlike those craven British lapdogs. And he shook his head sagely as the Americans marched, bright-eyed, into Vietnam.

In 1967 the journalist and politician Jean-Jacques Servan-Schreiber published a book called *Le Défi Américain* (The American Challenge), which became France's fastest-selling book since the war. His thesis was that the world was indeed on its way to having three great powers, but that the third would be composed of pan-European American industry. His message was that Europe had to match it and compete.

The next few decades were quieter, partly because post-de Gaulle presidents had a more realistic view of France's place in the world and partly because the US lost its enthusiasm for open-ended entanglements. Indeed, France was even chosen as the home of Euro Disney in 1992 ('Paris will be one of the attractions,' said a Disney spokesman generously) and, after some early skirmishes, embraced it nervously. Everything changed one fine September morning in 2001. The French newspaper *Le Monde* headlined its front-page comment: *Nous Sommes Tous Américains*.

The mood did not last. The following spring a French journalist and activist Thierry Meyssan had a book out called *L'Effroyable imposture* (The Appalling Deception); the English translation was entitled *9/11: The Big Lie*. It was another huge bestseller, at least in France. Meyssan revealed that the attacks were arranged by elements within George W. Bush's administration in *cahoots* with the British, and the well-known CIA asset Osama bin Laden. And probably the 'lizards, snakes, serpents and reptiles' that French readers believed infested America in the eighteenth century. You knew this? C'mon, everyone knows this. All reputable criticism of Meyssan's book concluded his theory was not just incredible but impossible. It was an appropriate start to a century in which truth would be buried in a sealed coffin, and nonsense would orbit compellingly through cyberspace.

Before 2002 was out Bush had indeed mastered the big lie technique himself in order to justify invading Iraq. France was adamantly opposed, and was subject to toytown vilification by US politicians, who insisted that *French fries* should be replaced on Congressional menus by *freedom fries*.[4]

The distrust did not go away even in the next decade, when France had itself become a particularly vulnerable target of Muslim attacks. On the fifteenth anniversary of the attacks, 11 September 2016, the polling firm Odoxa asked a thousand French respondents who was responsible for 9/11: 45 per cent said the answer was not clear and 28 per cent said the Bush administration was in some way complicit. The young took the anti-American line more strongly than their elders.

Obviously, their generation righteously refuses to have anything to do with these infernal Yanks and their insidious language. Or maybe not. 'Our grandchildren are French,' said Michael Edwards philosophically. 'They say *cool*; *it's mega*; *super*; *hyper* [EE-per]. Our grandson is into body-building, *la musculation*. But he's more likely to say body-building.'

I walked the streets from the Académie with him to get a coffee. We passed countless English signs, including those on the swanky-looking offices of Wall Street English, one of forty-eight branches all over France: 'TESTEZ VOTRE ANGLAIS NOW!'

In central Paris, this was hardly a surprise. But a few months earlier, I had been wandering round a furniture chain store on an industrial estate on the edge of a railway town in Aquitaine: a modern version of that mysterious Erewhon, *La France Profonde*. Then I glimpsed the children's bedroom department. On offer were duvets covered with stars and stripes, and cushions shaped as packets of Lay's very American potato chips. The choice of bedroom decorations had legends like LOONEY TUNES, ROUTE 66, TRUST MUSIC, KEEP MOVING, FIRE CHIEF and I'M JUST A GIRL. Or a stylised list of New York City district names.

---

4 In 1918 there had been an equally mad attempt to change *sauerkraut* to *liberty cabbage*.

Around town, there were the usual signs for My Cornetto, Ben & Jerry's Cookie Dough, 'Wings, Burgers and Fries' and Easy-on Durex. A shop selling 'Surplus Americains' offered an 'Official US marshall [sic] fleece'.

In France there are plenty of stories around about novel Anglicisms. The Paris-based journalist Simon Kuper told me that a clapped-out footballer or politician is now dismissed with *il est hasbeen*, and that someone obsessed with celebrities is described as *très people*. Edwards relates, with some relish, how Scotch tape has turned into a one-word generic verb. Someone anxious to stop working or watching TV but unable to quite manage it will use the verb *descotcher*: to unstick oneself.

Part of the problem, it seems to me, is that the French authorities give off conflicting messages. On the one hand, they want their young people, the most monoglot in Western Europe (anglophones excepted), to learn English to make France competitive. On the other hand they want French itself to be kept pure. In this world, conscientiously learning English is doing what you're told; slipping English words into French sentences is a form of youthful rebellion.

The French find the second option more attractive. In the 1960s came *le weekend*, *le parking* and *le pressing*. The government responded with new laws, especially in the 1990s, when the culture minister Jacques Toubon imposed stringent rules enforcing the use of French in official documents, advertising and TV programmes.

Toubon (or, as some rechristened him, Jack Goodall) was much mocked. And indeed part of the law was struck out by the courts as contrary to free speech. But what should the French have done? Offered a Gallic shrug – which at least is their very own body language. As the philosopher Michel Serres put it, there were fewer signs in German on the streets in Paris during the Occupation than there were in English fifty years later. And there have been reports of young offenders addressing the judge as 'Your Honor' rather than 'Monsieur le Juge'. There is little doubt that the enemy here was not Britain, which merely functioned as a kind of unofficial American ambassador to Europe, but the all-devouring giant across the ocean.

The French have had a few partial successes: the picturesque *courriel* competes with email; *l'ordinateur* is fighting off the computer. 'It is rather a good word,' says Edwards. 'It means to put in order, which is more accurate than computer.' But, as the Americans say (and thus probably the French), it is a game of *whack-a-mole*: hit one and another immediately pops up, taunting.

The Académie website has a linguistic agony-aunt column called *Dire, ne pas dire*, which answers questions about what is and is not permissible in French. In 2016 it ruled against *label*:

On dit *Une nouvelle marque de vêtements*
On ne dit pas *Un nouveau label de vêtements*

The website has also pronounced against *relooker*, i.e. given a new look (*'fruit des amours monstrueuses d'un verbe anglais et d'un préfixe français'*), *délivrer*, *stalker* and even its faux-French cousin *stalqueur*, *fan zone*, *listing*, *versus*, *punch line*, *guest*, *past président*, *come back*, *wine maker* and *after shave*. It is rather sweet that the French, even when smuggling in words, insert an accent as a disguise, like a little beret.

The website column is said to be very popular; how effective it might be is a separate question. 'I think in the past the Academy has been a kind of brake,' Edwards told me. 'There's no way we can tell whether it's having an effect. The French language has become more loose, and maybe that's not a bad thing. One of the features of French is linking words to each other, and it can be a little bit fussy.'

'Do ordinary people worry about all the English words coming in?'

'Probably not. What the French are more aroused about is what they take to be the official Anglo-Saxon policy of forcing people to speak English.'

'But there is a sense of things getting more acute and running out of control?'

'Yes,' said Edwards. Then he paused before asking:

Have you ever been to Beirut? Lebanon used to be a French colony. Now everything is in English and you look around to find anything in French. Even Arabic would be quite nice. In apparently French-speaking countries in Africa, over large swathes of the continent, French is unpopular. They aren't interested in learning French, and they want English.

France has imported vocabulary before. In the Renaissance a lot of Italian words came in. English words came in during the eighteenth century. The word *vote* came from Britain. All these were assimilated. Now there are new words every day. How do you deal with that?

***

Other Western European countries, which might also feel a little aggrieved about the impact of English, have their own historic reasons for being cautious. 'In Germany the English language was seen as cool in the 1950s, 1960s and 1970s,' Dr Ulrike Bavendiek, senior lecturer in German at the University of Liverpool, told me. 'We wanted to rebuild the language in an outward-facing way. Not so much in everyday use but among the young. So now English is everywhere in advertising and business: *downloaden, uploaden, keyboard, files* and *laptops.*

'Germans don't make much difference between American English and British English,' she said. 'But I have noticed the pronunciation of English words in German has become more American. Especially the Rs. When I was young the teachers spoke British English.'

A couple of pressure groups try to keep out examples of what are called *Denglish* but even now in Germany the shadow of the last war is such that any kind of nationalistic expression has to be hedged about with politeness and diffidence, making it hard to defend the language with any degree of forcefulness.

'We don't want to be language purists,' said Cornelius Sommer of the German Language Foundation, 'but we want people to be aware of how they speak and that certain linguistic imports just don't fit into German.' Sommer almost criticised the increasing academic practice of teaching in English: 'University courses taught by professors with poor English to students with poor English. That can't be good.'

Similar forces are at work in Italy. As *The Oldie* reported in 2015: 'A route that takes you past the Green Life Bio Concept Store, Lele's Barber's Shop, the Farmer's Market, the Tech It Easy gift emporium, a bank offering Personal Finance, and a Sexy Shop offering Sexy Toys brings you not to Willesden High Street, as you might expect, but to the Colosseum.'

The report added that even the young women have changed. Those who used to be *formose*, meaning shapely, are now described by the Italians as *curvy*. The Renault Clio is advertised with the slogan 'Seduction is an Attitude', and the Toyota AYGO with 'Go Fun Himself'. But in Italy protecting the language is associated with fascism: Mussolini tried to purify Italian and banned babies from being given foreign Christian names. So complaints have to be muted. And smaller European countries – especially those too small to get Hollywood blockbusters dubbed into their own language – have long ago had to reach their own kind of accommodation with the linguistic reality of the world.

Indeed, there is one small European country where they might think the fate of British English rather salutary, given the brutal way Britain tried to eradicate – and successfully marginalised – that country's own language in the not too distant past. So can I make my apologies to the Republic of Ireland and ask them to recognise this is now a joint problem?

Every language in the world now exists in apposition to English, and every form of English exists in apposition to American English. With just one possible exception ...

***

In the autumn of 2013 a secondary school in south-east London put up notices banning the use of a series of words and phrases from its classrooms and corridors: '*coz, aint* [sic], *like, bare, extra, innit, you woz, we woz* ... beginning sentences with *basically*; ending sentences with *yeah*'. The edict came from the head of the Harris Academy, Upper Norwood, one of those new and frankly rather sinister academy-chain schools that have somehow grabbed control of much of Britain's education system.

To a non-Londoner the list might have seemed strange and random. ('Please, sir, can I do some *extra* maths?' 'How dare you say that word!') But it was evidently intended as an attack on the new form of English now mainly known as MLE, Multicultural London English.

MLE's primitive form was perhaps first informally identified for public consumption by the comedian Ali G in the late 1990s. It became a subject of academic study in the early 2000s. Its most public voice was that of the engaging if somewhat post-musical musician Dizzee Rascal. And it first hit middle England in the face when the right-wing controversialist David Starkey blamed MLE for the London riots of 2011. I probably first heard it in the early days of the London Overground, and started to think of it in my own mind by merging its most characteristic words: *Fuckovinnit*.

Starkey blamed the riots on a 'violent, destructive and nihilistic' black culture. Then he added: 'A substantial section of the chavs have become black. The whites have become black. Black and white, boy and girl, operate in this language together ... which is wholly false, which is a Jamaican patois that's been intruded in England, and this is why so many of us have this sense of literally a foreign country.'[5]

According to Tony Thorne of King's College. London, the major component is not Jamaican patois but more a black British vernacular. But it also has elements of traditional London working class, British South Asian (*innit?*) and the occasional soupçon of Polish and Somali and heaven knows what else. But there is an unusual absentee: it is the most American-free zone in modern British language.

While standard British English has practically ceased innovating, MLE has emerged from the bottom up as a wholly home-grown, functioning, practical but not uncrackable code, as rhyming slang did in early Victorian times.[6] Far from being divisive, it is a force for unity

---

5 *Literally* was not one of the words banned by the Harris Academy, though perhaps it should have been. The youthful habit of using the word hyperbolically, reversing its traditional meaning, has now been recognised by the OED. It is, however, banned in the Engel household, where *literallies* are charged at the standard swearing-rate because the youngest family member was saying *literally* literally a million times a day.
6 There are some very minor borrowings from US hip-hop culture, says Thorne, notably *feds* for police and *whip* for car.

among the young members of the different ethnic groups in London that have previously found almost nothing to bring them together. 'It isn't just about communicating,' says Thorne. 'It's also a badge. It's a statement about oneself.'

Starkey's attack is wholly in the tradition whereby the chief constables, headmasters and judges attacked the faux-American gangster slang of the 1930s. Now Americanisation is far more pervasive, if less strikingly obvious, than it was eighty years ago. And MLE is the only sign of a sustained fightback.

It has now rippled outwards, in modified form, to other British cities, other suburbs and even to the more genteel corners of the Home Counties, where teachers can be a little more relaxed and amused at middle-class white teenagers' attempts to redefine *bare* (plenty of) and *extra* (excessive, inappropriate, out-of-order).

Thorne does not think MLE is ever likely to grow up and be more than a youthful slang because its vocabulary is so dominated by the concerns of youth, notably sex, drugs and rock 'n' roll. Its intonation – its very unAmerican rhythms and pronunciations – may, however, be harder to shrug off. And one can sympathise with the Academy's intentions.

As a spokesman told the *Croydon Guardian*, the school wanted students 'to develop the soft skills they will need to compete for jobs and university places ... and the skills they need to express themselves confidently and appropriately for a variety of audiences'. In other words, in order to thrive in modern Britain, they need to speak American like everyone else.

8

FROM ABRASIVE TO ZING

But we have barely started. In addition to those singled out in the text, hundreds more American words and phrases have come to Britain, with ever increasing rapidity, since *guaiacum* first failed to cure syphilis.

The lists in this chapter include all those other terms I have so far collected in regular use in British English that (a) I believe to be American in origin or (b) were originally used in Britain only as regional words or became extinct, and then returned as Americanisms.

As I said from what some would call the get-go, these lists are not comprehensive. And I may have included some words in error – but these will be far outweighed by those omitted, because their origin seemed uncertain or because I simply failed to spot them. Lexicography in itself is not an exact science, and this novel branch of it is very inexact indeed.

It is nearly always impossible to say precisely when something moved into common usage (except in the case of a catchphrase). Until recent times the written language was generally much more formal than the spoken language. And for the first three and a half post-*guaiacum* centuries there was no means of recording the human voice. It may be, just as St John Ervine theorised that Ethelred the Unready habitually said 'Hello, big boy', that Queen Victoria was constantly responding to Gladstone's complaints with *I could care less*. Still, the listings are given sort-of chronologically, from the best information available, in separate groupings.

What has been possible for me is to use digitised newspaper files to track down early references. In many cases this completely changes the previously accepted history of words. But the scanning process that precedes digitisation is not an exact science either, especially when it involves tiny print in fragile old newspapers.

And furthermore there are known unknowns and all that stuff: a single itinerant American reporter or subeditor doing a few shifts in Fleet Street without quite mastering the nuances can wreak havoc on one's judgment. We have already seen how the youthful Americophile Samuel Taylor Coleridge (who was possibly stoned at the time) may have bamboozled generations of philologists with a single rogue Americanism: *reliable*.

What follows is the first effort, which I hope may be the basis of a future, more definitive, database. It will, I believe, astound those British readers who imagine they rarely use Americanisms. The title of this chapter reflects the alphabetic extremes. But in the import-export business of words, Britain has gone from *ahead of the game* to *zilch*.

So here then is a set of exhausting if not exhaustive lists of words that have not previously been chewed over in the text, mostly arranged according to the approximate era that they entered British usage. This does not include Americanisms that we know are Americanisms even as we use them. (*Aw, shucks!* That would be an impossible job. *Do the math!*)

As elsewhere in the book, words that were born in Britain and died there before returning home as imports from the US are denoted by a †.

THE PICKERING LIST
The following words and phrases in John Pickering's 1816 dictionary of Americanisms arrived before 1900:

back and forth It was apparently more common in Britain to say *back and fore* or *back and forward*. A letter-writer to *The Times* used the modern (though quainter-sounding) version in 1896.

balance (as noun, meaning the remainder) '*Balance*, long familiar to American ears, is becoming so to ours' – *Blackwood's Edinburgh Magazine*, 1875.

gouge (as verb) In the physical violence sense; Pickering says that in Virginia it was considered fair fighting, as in an old rugby scrum. By 1839 it had reached the ruffians of Cheshire: 'another monster … was endeavouring to work his right eye out,' said a not wholly objective *Times* report, 'exclaiming "You b****, I'll *gouge* you."' Other uses come much later.

†*hub* (of a wheel) Probably Midland dialect originally. Re-imported from the US when cycling became popular.

immigrant *The Times* started to use the word in the 1840s, but at first almost always in an American context; there was no talk of immigrants coming to Britain, because it was not an issue: people, Irish people in particular, were more interested in getting out.

jeopardize American usage seems to have quickly overwhelmed the once more common verb *jeopard* (which would be a useful rhyme for leopard). The *Manchester Guardian* picked it up in 1828.

†*loan* (as a verb) The OED has no British uses between 1664 and 1880.

†*lay* (as in lie) *Lay* was used in the eighteenth century as a 'vulgarism' in Britain and the US and left John Witherspoon the revolutionary pedagogue, Lowth the grammarian and Pickering all infuriated. It seems to have been more general in the US. It still infuriates some of my correspondents as a shocking Americanism; one suggests lay-bys should be changed to lie-bys. Bob Dylan's 'Lay Lady Lay' may have been decisive in its ultimate British success. It is indeed preferable, when in bed, to get laid than to tell lies.[1]

---

1 Witherspoon said *lay* was an original Americanism, unconvincingly. To *lay* sexually and to *get laid* are almost certainly Americanisms, picked up by Graham Greene and

presidential Understandably rare in Britain before the US acquired a president. *The Times*'s first non-US usage was in 1816.

sleigh Obviously a more urgent means of transport in pre-motor car New England than in old England, with its less energetic snowfalls. The term evidently began to seep into English usage in reports from the Crimean War, rather than the US. But 'Jingle Bells' (written 1857 by the Bostonian James Pierpont) would have helped it stick.

spell (as a period of particular weather)

test (as to try and put to the proof) Specifically cited as an Americanism by Robert Southey when he uses it in 1838.

†*tidy* (as in neat) Certainly used colloquially in parts of Britain from olden times. General acceptance of the word seems to have followed its popularity in the US.[2]

tote (as in *gun-totin'*, *tote-that-barge* and, rather later, *tote bags*) First OED British reference cites the war correspondent Archibald Forbes, 1883.

MORE VICTORIANS

The following words also appear to have been imported before the end of the nineteenth century:

almighty (as an adjective describing anything – an *almighty mess*, an *almighty row*, *almighty nonsense* – rather than just God)

antagonise

axe to grind In the *Daily Telegraph* as 'grind the axe' in 1881.

back down Reached *The Times* in an American report in 1856 and domestically 1874: 'The umpire [in a rowing match] ... would not back down for fully five minutes.'

bark up the wrong tree 'You are barking up the wrong tree, Johnson,' said a character in *Legends of the West* (1832). It took

others in the 1930s. Americans normally say *lay of the land*, the British still say *lie of the land*, though there is a garden centre called Lay of the Land, owned by the Lay family, in Settle, Yorkshire.

2 On the Welsh border 'a tidy farmer' is the customary form of approbation to convey not just tidiness, but competence and efficiency.

another seventy years before *The Times* said the same of Sir
William Harcourt MP.

bee-line

bite off more than one can chew

blizzard One of a group of expressive extreme-weather words that the
British borrowed from the US for anything that remotely approaches
American-style meteorological excess. *Blizzard* went into general US
use during the harsh winter of 1880–81. British papers began to follow
later in the decade for cases of the wrong kind of snow.

bogus Believed to have applied to a machine for making fake coins
in Ohio in the 1820s. In general British use by the 1880s.

boss (as a master, not a decorative feature)

burgle Contrary to the belief that *burglarize* is a modern American
example of complicating a simple verb, *burglarize* apparently
came first and was regarded by *The New York Times* (and the
American pedant Richard Grant White) as the respectable word,
while the British were apparently managing without a verb at
all. In London the *Standard* reported in 1874: 'New words with
which the American vocabulary has lately been enriched: "to
burgle", meaning to injure a person by breaking into his or
her house.' The word was popularised by W.S. Gilbert when
The Pirates of Penzance made its debut in 1880: 'When the
enterprising burglar's not a-burgling / Not a-burgling'. How did
anyone commit burglary without it?

cloudburst Cloudbursts began to happen in the English papers in
the 1890s, though usually in the US or somewhere else far away.
The Times finally reported one in Yorkshire in 1908.

cold snap Yet another vivid Americanism to describe vivid weather.
The *Observer* finally allowed it to fly out of quotation marks to
describe the English winter of 1897.

corner (verb, both as in *cornering the market* and putting someone
under pressure) Americans were trying to corner various markets
for decades before *The Times* finally used it in a British context
in 1899.

cowboy Originally in English as just that: a boy who tended cows.
In the US it came to be a contemptuous phrase applied to

loyalists in the Revolution. As the mythical hero of the West, it reached *The Times* in 1883. **Cowboy builders** came nearly a century later – probably also an Americanism to the extent that cowboy meaning a reckless driver was recorded in the US in 1942.

crank (noun) The verb *cranky* was found in various British dialects from Cumberland to Leicestershire. The noun was an Americanism, evidently picked up by the British in 1881 as the standard description of Charles Guiteau, assassin of President Garfield.

crook (meaning criminal) Dates back to at least 1879 in the US. Reached the *Westminster Gazette* in 1896.

dead wood (in the figurative sense)

dry up (as in stop speaking)

dump (as a verb)

electrocute In the US by 1889. In a classified ad in *The Times* 1899: 'Continuation of the Monster Holiday Show. Marvellous performances … See to-day, at 3 and 8, Dr. Walford Bodie electrocute a man.' The first use of *electrocution* as capital punishment was in New York state in 1890.

engineer (as a verb)

enthuse The British, not being a very enthusiastic race, never felt much need for such a verb. An unknown American said in 1827: 'My humble exertions will I trust convey and enthuse, and draw attention to the beautifully varied verdure of North-West America.' The word got into the *Pall Mall Gazette* in 1887 as a characteristic British negative: 'I don't get enthused at all, sir, over all this Greek business.'

face the music Origin unclear, though it may well refer to a soldier being drummed out of his regiment. The *New Hampshire Statesman* was demanding in 1834: 'We want no equivocation—"face the music" this time.' The OED's first British use has Cecil Rhodes saying it by refusing to say it. 'I will not refer to the vulgar colloquialism that I was afraid to face the music' – *Westminster Gazette* 1897.

feel free

fix As Dickens noted (see pp. 63–4), this is the all-purpose American

word, like *wee* in Scotland or *bloody* in Australia. In addition
to the uses he encountered, it is also the dose of a drug, not
normally one available on prescription, and two separate ways
of dealing with an uncooperative politician. 'It is expected of us
that we should *fix* the Governor of Pennsylvania,' was recorded in
1790, and no doubt something similar has been said many times
since. *Fixing* in this case could mean a bribe, or it could mean the
governor's body ending up in the Susquehanna River. All these
uses have come to Britain. *Fixer-upper*, which is realtor-speak for
a house in need of repair, has not crossed the Atlantic. Yet.

fizzle In Tudor times it meant a silent fart. Its current verbal use
crept back to Britain in the late nineteenth century.

freeze out

full blast

get along Picked up as an Americanism by both Dickens and
Harriet Martineau. Became naturalised by the 1880s.

go ahead! (as instruction)

go-ahead (as adjective)

goatee

go the whole hog

graveyard The early-nineteenth-century traveller Basil Hall
was baffled by the word. Presumably the British, with their
established religion, were used to everyone being buried in the
same churchyard. The idea of the non-denominational cemetery
came to Britain later.

greased lightning Bill Bryson dates this back to 1826. In 1888 the
Paddington Times reported a speech by Lord Randolph Churchill
saying that a measure 'passed through parliament, to use an
American expression, like greased lightning [Laughter].' Four
years later Mr J. Lowther was using it in the Commons without
comment or laughter. It had passed into the language like
greased lightning.

Great Scott! In US c.1850 after US General Winfield Scott. First
British reference 1885.

half-cock Speaking metaphorically rather than ballistically.

hang (as in *get the hang of it*)

hang around

†*hide nor hair* Old Scottish dialect phrase that went to America.
Its return to Britain may be due to John Hay, later US Secretary
of State, and author of 'Little Breeches', one of a set of demotic
Illinois country poems *The Pike County Ballads*, a big hit in 1871:

> At last we struck horses and waggon,
> Snowed under a soft white mound,
> Upsot, dead beat – but of little Gabe,
> No hide nor hair was found.[3]

highfalutin'

Indian summer First recorded in Ohio 1790. The Americans had
more need than the British for a phrase denoting sunny and
warm autumnal days. There was a more specific European
phrase, *St Martin's summer*, denoting the warm spell traditionally
associated with St Martin's Day, 11 November, a meteorological
phenomenon not obvious in Britain. When needed, *Indian
summer* had certainly arrived in Britain by 1877. 'Everybody
should come to Brighton just now,' said a correspondent in the
Illustrated London News. 'We are having the most delightful
"Indian summer".'

in short order

in the soup

interview Originally a meeting between princes, e.g. Henry VIII
and Francis I at the Field of the Cloth of Gold. In 1897 the
Westminster Gazette suggested Joseph M'Cullagh of St Louis was
the inventor of the modern newspaper interview.

jackpot

junk (as in *junk shop*)

keep a stiff upper lip Not listed as an Americanism by the OED but
its first three references are all from the US, including both *The
Clockmaker* and *Uncle Tom's Cabin*. It appears in *Punch* in a Tom
Thumb parody in 1846 then goes missing again except when *The
Times* quotes a US Civil War colonel in 1862: 'Keep a stiff upper

---

3 *Dead beat* in that sense is probably not an Americanism, but a ***dead-beat*** is. Little
Gabe, I am happy to say, was found safe and well before the end of the poem.

lip, boys, the day will soon be ours.' In 1896 the Marquis of
Lorne, a former governor-general of Canada, prefaces the phrase
with 'what was called on the other side of the water'. QED, I
think.

kill (in the political sense of defeating a bill)

knock into a cocked hat (and probably *into the middle of next week*
as well. And *spots off*)

landslide The old British term *landslip* was gradually pushed
aside through the nineteenth century by the more dramatic
Americanism. Landslip is still preferred by organisations like
Network Rail who, unlike the media, have an interest in playing
down such occurrences.

larrup and *lather* (for walloping) Possible ancestry in British dialect
in both cases.

law-abiding

let up

loafer (a person not a shoe)

make one's pile

mammoth (as adjective)

manicurist

mass meeting

mean (adjective, as shabby or cruel, not just ungenerous)

mileage Bartlett's 1859 *Dictionary of Americanisms* describes this as
'a very large and even extravagant allowance made to members
of Congress, and some others of the favoured, for travelling
expenses: $8 for every 20 miles'. The term had reached the
Manchester Guardian by 1873. The official Treasury-approved UK
rate in 2016 was 45p per mile – fractionally higher.

non-committal Recorded in the US 1829. Mr Campbell gave a 'most
judicious non-committal reply,' reported the *Sunday Times* in
1886.

once in a while In the US from at least 1765; naturalised in Britain
circa 1877.

on the fence In the political sense made a classic transatlantic
journey that can be traced through the *Manchester Guardian*.
Used in a report from a US correspondent in 1866, it was quoted

with the rider 'as the Americans say' in 1872, without comment but in quotes 1876, then unfettered 1886.

operate To control the working of a machine or, corporately, as to operate, e.g. a railway. 'A linguistic outrage' – Sir Herbert Spencer, 1902.

own up

pile it on

pile on the agony

†*placate*

precious few

pull up stakes

read like a book

†*recuperate*

†*resurrect* Both transitive and intransitive uses. The Americans generally remain more confident about the idea of resurrection.

rough and tumble Originally US boxing slang.

rowdy

scallywag Clearly American originally: perhaps Liverpool's maritime connection with the US helped 'scally' become localised. Lord Charles Beresford told the House of Commons in 1898 'I was a scallywag myself.' It would be nice if more MPs admitted it.

self-made man

†*setback*

shake a stick at

slave-driver

slump (in the financial sense)

†*snarl* (as in traffic) Has East Anglian roots but it took the long way round to reach general British use.

sour To start to dislike someone or something.

square meal

squat (on unoccupied land)

stampede From Mexican Spanish.

steep Extravagant.

strike To discover, as with gold or oil.

strike it rich

stump To confront with an insuperable difficulty. I always assumed it came from cricket. In fact, pioneers were the first to be stumped: when faced with the very American problem of their ploughs being obstructed by tree stumps when the forest had been imperfectly felled.

†*sundown*

take a back seat

take the cake *Take the biscuit* appears to be twentieth century and British.

telegram Credited to a reader of the *Albany Evening Journal*, who suggested in 1852 it might be a catchy description of the new telegraphic communication. A classic example of the American gift for finding the right neologism. Edward Bulwer-Lytton wrote this couplet in 1860:

> Ere a cable went under the hoary Atlantic,
> Or the word *telegram* drove grammarians frantic.

time and again

transpire (in the sense of to happen)

under the weather

vim

†*wallet* Formerly a bag. In the late Victorian era Britain gradually adopted the American term to convey a much smaller object, mainly for carrying paper money. This replaced the misleading word *pocketbook*.

wild and woolly

†*wilt* To wither.

†*yank* May have Scottish origins as a sudden blow but acquired its present verbal meaning – 'to jerk powerfully' – in New England, which is appropriate when you come to think about it.

There is a whole variety of other words that came into British use before 1900 whose progress back and forth (or back and fore, whichever) cannot be recorded with any certainty. ***Died with his boots on*** sounds obviously Wild West, but there was a startling claim in 1895 that it was actually East Anglian dialect, suggesting widespread Victorian gunslinging in rural Norfolk.

I think it can count as a probable Americanism, along with

accountability, *bitter end*, *endorse* (except as a legal term), *nerve* (meaning courage) and *nip* (as a small, surreptitious gulp of spirits rather than a measure of beer).

Receptionist certainly smacks of an Americanism. But unexpectedly *The Times* has a classified ad mentioning receptionist in 1878, whereas nothing turns up on a *New York Times* search until 1924, when it is presented as a neologism for *reception clerk*. Mencken claims *kick the bucket* for the US, but British references pre-date American ones. (Kicking the bucket is presumably less painful if you die with your boots on.)

Obnoxious has also been claimed as an Americanism; it had an earlier, neutral meaning: to be open or subject to something ('We are obnoxious to accidents' – 1712). But *The Times* was regularly saying measures it disliked were obnoxious in the 1790s.

Teetotal is regarded as a lexicographical puzzle. The Lancashire temperance campaigner Richard Turner is described on his gravestone as the author of the word, in an 1833 speech. But in the same year Davy Crockett mentioned the word *teetotalaciously*. It appeared in his ghost-written memoir simply to say he never said it, which does suggest that *teetotal* itself had been round for a while. So it looks like an Americanism after all.

EDWARDIAN WORDS, WARTIME WORDS

Words and phrases that came to Britain in the first two decades of the twentieth century included:

ahead of the game
a-plenty
audition (in the entertainment-industry sense, not a scientific term for hearing)
brainy
bully for you The favourite phrase of Teddy Roosevelt.
cakewalk 'A black Americans' contest in graceful walking, with a cake as the prize.' Later used to mean any easy task: 'West Bromwich Albion appear to have a cakewalk against Gainsborough Trinity at The Hawthorns.' – *Daily Mirror*, 1908.

cavort

count me out

dope (as in inside dope)

dough Money.

ear to the ground

fan (as in football)

fill the bill

flurry Another of those American weather-words. The *Manchester Guardian* recorded its first snow flurry in 1908.

for my health What I'm not doing this for.

gee-whiz

get a move on

give the game away

go for it

hard case

hell's bells

hold-up

horse sense

How's tricks?

husky (adjective) Rugged and manly.

itemise

keep me posted

Let her rip! Reached the *Illustrated London News* in a Michelin advert, 1912.

low-down trick This first appeared in the *Manchester Guardian* in 1906, then reached *The Times* in 1912 when fifty-three crew members of the *Titanic*'s sister ship, the *Olympic*, refused to sail in the wake of the disaster and were charged with mutiny. The commander of the *Olympic*, Captain Haddock (sic), told the court their behaviour was 'a low-down trick'.

multimillionaire

nip and tuck

Ouch! Now this is surprising. But it looks as though it went to the US from the German *autsch* and thus to Britain. No one appears to say it in any of the novels of George Eliot, the Brontë Sisters or Thomas Hardy, even though a great deal of pain is inflicted one way or another. What on earth did the Victorians say if someone pinched them? 'Ow!' I suppose.

peter out

†*pile* (of money) It's in Shakespeare's *Henry VIII*, written when he had made his pile, but it emigrated thereafter.

poppycock

previous (meaning presumptuous)

pull the wool over one's eyes

Put it there!

railroad (as a verb) The British had long since decided that trains ran on railways and the modern use of railroading through legislation comes later. But in a London court case of 1901 a barrister talked of a man being railroaded.

raise hell

†*riled* Annoyed. Old dialect word regarded as an Americanism for much of the Victorian era and after. Evidently in First World War British military slang, though it is not wholly clear whether this came from the US or from within.

rope in

scrawny

sex appeal Its debut in the *Daily Mirror* was a 1919 attack by the drama critic Herbert Farjeon on suggestive songs in pantomimes, 'these essentially adult ditties with their frequent sex appeal'. The phrase's next appearance, eight years later, quoted G.B. Shaw as saying 'The public want to see pictures without sex appeal'. Did they now? The *Mirror* became less fastidious later.

sidestep (as a metaphor)

sissy

size up 'We cannot quite size up the match,' said C.B. Fry in a *Daily Express* cricket report in 1903.

†*sleuth*

slim chance

spellbinding

square deal

stub one's toe One can only assume the British never did such a thing before they learned to say 'Ouch!'

take a back seat
talk through one's hat
underdog This is a little tricky in that American usage usually meant
the loser in a contest rather than the combatant expected to lose.
It is hard to know exactly how, where, when or why it shifted.
whoopee

THE WODEHOUSE COLLECTION

So, as discussed on p. 79, will the defendant please rise. Sir Pelham
Grenville Wodehouse, you are hereby charged, that on dates between
1912 and 1952, you smuggled into Britain the following words and
phrases rightfully belonging to the United States of America:

AWOL	1949	in the non-military sense
bender	1951	a piss-up
breeze in	1923	
buckle down	1934	
call it a day	1919	
crackerjack	1925	
curtains	1918	the end
easy money	1923	
eat up (the ground)	1919	
feel like a million dollars	1925	
fifty-fifty	1913	
going some	1915	
have a stab at	1915	
hit the ceiling	1930	
hookey	1923	truant
hook, line and sinker	1924	
†*hopping mad*	1915	Used by the poet Charles Cotton 1675, then went west
josh	1921	
kick in	1936	
lowdown	1924	
on hand	1923	
on the blink	1912	

on the level	1914	
on the map	1919	
pack them in	1917	
pass up	1932	
put the bite on	1934	
rolling in the aisles	1940	
say it with flowers	1932	The slogan of the Society of American Florists from 1918
sitting pretty	1932	
start something	1917	
stomp	1929	
strapped	1952	
whoop it up	1939	
wise guy	1922	
zing	1919	

THE *BABBITT* GLOSSARY

bawl out

beat it

bonehead

bootleg

darn

doodads Thingummies, but usually called *doodahs* in English (if we remember the word *doodah*).

fall for To be taken in by. (The more optimistic and romantic meaning is probably also an Americanism.)

fly-by-night

gabby

gee

gogetter

golly

gosh

grouch

guff

guy Fellow (it says here). Did the British really not know what a guy was, Bonfire night aside? Maybe not: the first British reference in the OED is from D.H. Lawrence in 1928.

heck

†*hicks* Used in Britain to describe *bumpkins* up to the eighteenth century.

hit the hay

hooch

hunch

jeans Trousers (it says).

knock Disparage.

lounge lizards 'Men hanging about in hotels for dancing and flirting.'[4]

nut Madman.

pan Strongly disparage.

peach of a

pep

pull Perpetrate.

root for Cheer for.[5]

slick (adjective) Defined here as 'smart'.

spiel

sting Overcharge.

tightwad

totty

whale of a

THE 1920s

The following Americanisms appear to have made the journey to Britain before the end of the decade:

cafeteria

chunky

---

4 Maybe no one does say *lounge lizard* any more but it's such a great phrase I shall try to bring it back.

5 This phrase should be used with caution in Australia, where *rooting* is a mildly vulgar synonym for having sex.

down and out

frazzled

make the fur (or *feathers*) *fly*

gangster

gentlemen's agreement This arose from the unenforceable deal
between US and Japan in 1907 whereby the US promised not to
ban Japanese immigration if the Japanese did not allow anyone
to emigrate.

gets my goat

give a hoot (or *two hoots*)

going Dutch

hefty

hell-bent In American use since at least 1731. An American
comedy called *Hell-bent fer Heaven* reached the West End in
1926. Within twenty years the term had reached the Welsh
coastal resort of Pwllheli, where a local councillor tried and
failed to stop the building of a Butlins holiday camp, saying
the Welsh should be protected from 'a foreign body *hell-bent*
on pleasure'.

No kidding!

offset

rattled

rip-roaring

snoop According to Bartlett's 1859 Dictionary of Americanisms
this is a peculiar New York term (from Dutch) meaning 'to
clandestinely eat dainties or other victuals that have been put
aside'. Wonderful!

spill the beans

sucker

top-notch

try out

white collar

HORWILL'S LISTS

Herbert Horwill's *Dictionary of Modern American Usage*, published in

1935, has three separate categories. The main group comprises Americanisms that had not then crossed the Atlantic which he felt needed translating. But he had two other groups as well, which recorded: (a) words he considered had become naturalised in England since 1900, when he first went to New York and became interested in the subject, and (b) words that were in 1935 on their way to becoming naturalised. Horwill is a trustworthy source, perhaps even reliable, and his own first-hand memory is immensely helpful in tracking the movement of words in this era.

This is the first list, the 1900–35 arrivals. It has been edited to exclude words previously discussed in this text and a few that, even if they were naturalised, never quite settled.

anyway Horwill says *anyhow* was previously more common as a synonym for 'at any rate'.
back number
blow in 'Look who the wind's blown in.'
boom (noun) What Chancellors of the Exchequer always promise.
comeback
cuts (noun) What Chancellors of the Exchequer actually impose.
feature (verb)
filled to capacity
†*fleet* (in the non-nautical sense, e.g. lorries or planes)
fudge (the sweet)
park (verb) The car. Origin of parking children, etc. less clear.
put across
register (verb – at a hotel)
rush hour
turn down (verb) Reject.
up against it

This is the second, much longer, list of those words that Horwill considered were on the cusp of being Anglicised in 1935, again slightly edited, mainly to exclude those that never quite made it.

all of As much as.
all there is to it
bank on Count on.
baron Magnate or tycoon.
beat up
brass tacks
cereal (at breakfast rather than in a field) Kellogg's first
    manufactured Corn Flakes in 1902, brought them to Britain in
    1925 and opened a factory in Manchester in 1938.
close-up As in pictures
contact (noun) Journalists need good contacts …
cover (verb) … so they can cover a story.
cuts no ice
date (noun) Social/romantic engagement.
ditch (verb) Discard.
dolled up
dyed-in-the-wool
fall down (on the job, for example)
for keeps
get a move on
get busy If this wasn't already in the country, children watching
    Sooty in the 1950s learned to say 'izzy-wizzy, let's get busy' before
    almost anything else.
get wise to
good and (as intensifier, e.g. *good and hard*)
good for (e.g. a week's travel)
hard-boiled Unsentimental.
hold down (a job)
hold up (a bank – and the traffic)
†*hustle*
joy-ride
kick (as in 'I get a kick out of you' – Cole Porter, 1934)
mixer (in the sociable sense)
money to burn
on the side
rally Mass-meeting.

release (noun – e.g. press release)
round-up
see the light
shape (noun – e.g. in good shape)
showdown
shut-down
sit up and take notice
snap (as in judgment)
†*snap* Pep (Scottish roots).
snowed under
soapbox (for making speeches not storing soap)
soft-pedal
spotlight
stag (as in dinner or party)
stage (verb – in a non-theatrical sense)
stay put
strike (verb) To meet or reach: *strike a hill*, *the path*, *town*, etc.
take a chance Take a risk. Probably spread by the craze for
    Monopoly in the 1930s, though Community Chest never caught
    on.
take one's medicine (figuratively)
up against
usher (at weddings and funerals)
win out And, Horwill might have added, *lose out*
wisecrack
yes-man

THE NON-HORWILLS

There is another category of pre-war words: those that Horwill did not include which, nonetheless, appear to have settled Britain by 1939, four years after his dictionary was published. The size of the list is a sign of the sheer pace of Americanisation in the 1930s.

Act your age!
And how!
bat an eye

beautician
bellyache
bum (a person, not part of a person)
bunk
check up (verb)
chip on one's shoulder
classy
curvaceous
cute Pretty.
dish it out
dumb blonde
flat broke
fly off the handle 'Keep calm. You … tend to fly off the handle at inopportune moments,' the *Daily Express* stargazer warned Virgos in 1934.
goner
he-man
high, wide and handsome
hiking Walking.
hitch-hiking
hoodoo 'Australia is now wondering whether Larwood has a "hoodoo" over Bradman,' said a cricket report from the Reuters agency in Australia in November 1932, launching the word into the sports writers' lexicon.
hot spot (a nightclub rather than a war zone)
hunky-dory
keeping up with the Joneses A US cartoon strip from 1913. Britain failed to keep up on this one until Gracie Fields recorded a comic number in 1935:

> We've got to keep up with the Joneses.
> Our manners improve every day.
> Even Granny says 'Pardon!' and runs up the garden
> When her food has gone down the wrong way.

keep tabs
life of Riley
like crazy

livewire

†*mayhem* A legal term for wounding since at least the fifteenth century. In the US it became a generic word for violence. Its modern British incarnation usually implies a gentler kind of chaos.

milk shake

mobster

monkey business

moron Coined in US psychological circles in 1910 to mean a child with 'mild mental retardation'. It quickly became a general insult, first in the US and then the UK, rendering it useless to the psychologists.

put the skids under

ritzy 'The Hotel and Catering branch of the Employment Exchange in Denmark Street is the ritziest place run by the Ministry of Labour' – *Daily Express* 1938.

†*say-so*

slick (noun) As in oil.

slope off

smart alec

sweat shop

take the rap

talk turkey

thanks a million Dick Powell film, 1935.

trunks As in swimming.

None of us would *bat an eye* at hearing a single one of those words and phrases anywhere in Britain today.

THE 1940s

baby-sitter Possibly popularised by the 1948 film *Sitting Pretty*.

backlog

for the hell of it

Get lost!

gunning for

horse trading In the non-equine sense. The phrase became

entrenched during the protracted post-war international negotiations.

I'll say

logjam

readership References to *readership* in the sedate papers before the 1940s always refer to the academic (occasionally ecclesiastical) position of reader. Americans were using the word in its modern meaning by 1901, and there is evidence that the British newspaper industry was using it as jargon in the 1930s. But its general use comes surprisingly late.

snap judgment

splurge An Americanism dating back at least to the 1820s, meaning an ostentatious display before it meant extravagant spending. 'We do not want a frantic splurge of building,' said Churchill in 1944.

teenage and *teenager* There is a reference to 'teen age' girls in a 1921 Canadian newspaper, but there is no sign of Britain picking up either the noun or the adjective when it was lapping up Americanisms in the 1930s. The *Daily Mirror* had an earnest report in 1947 about 'a teenage charter for boys and girls entering the boot and shoe industry'.

what I say goes

There was one unusual development in the 1940s in which a long-established English word rapidly and completely lost its old meaning and assumed another. The word was the noun *natural*, which was previously a relative polite word for the village idiot. Then suddenly it took on the American meaning, something almost wholly opposite: a person with a particular innate talent, perhaps amounting to genius. Truly America is a place of magic.

THE 1950s

backtrack

beatnik

bulldoze Originally *bull-dose*: a severe whipping, mainly for slaves. The verb predated the *bulldozer*. In 1953 the MP for Ilford

South begged the government not to bulldoze proposals for ITV through the Commons.

cagey

cahoots

check out (verb)

chief executive The first British companies were starting to rebrand their managing directors in the American fashion.

chip in (conversationally, rather than on the golf course)

crying all the way to the bank The response to his critics of the much-derided entertainer Liberace.

Don't call us, we'll call you Perhaps popularised by the 1959 film *Some Like It Hot.*

double talk

emoting

gravy train

jack-knifed

jet set

kick around (an idea rather than a football)

living it up

maverick From Sam Maverick, nineteenth-century Texan rancher and politician who left his calves unbranded. The word started gaining traction in Britain as a synonym for individualist, even before the arrival of the TV western of the same name.

muscle in

neck of the woods

parking meter

†*rare* (as in meat)

shoot one's mouth off

soap opera

square

thrown Disconcerted.

workforce

You can say that again!

You said it!

THE 1960s

abrasive (the figurative use, as in an abrasive comment)

back off

Black Power

blue collar

burp In Britain the burp-gun came before the burp. If my
generation was never burped as babies, does that explain why we
were so much trouble?

butt out

count me in

hard sell and indeed *soft sell*

long hot summer

making out The sexual aspect of this phase appears to have been
through two meanings in the US before it became well known
in Britain. In the 1930s it meant intercourse but was then
downgraded and more often referred to teenage canoodling. It
retains a certain ambiguity.

motorcade This word was used occasionally in Britain in the 1930s,
but the whole concept is more American than British, and it
passed into common use only when President Kennedy was
assassinated while taking part in one.

panic button

raise The American transitive use of raising children now became
more common.

spin-off

take a shine to

the whole shebang

THE 1970s

asap

author (as a verb)

belly-up

check it out

dugout (in sport)

high roller

iffy

on track

paramedic Previously used in the US (notably during the Vietnam War) to describe someone actually parachuted into a battle zone or remote area to offer medical help, before growing into its current meaning.

rip off (verb) And indeed *rip-off* (noun).

†*scrimp* Rare until 1975, though the Beatles did sing 'We shall scrimp and save' in 'When I'm Sixty-Four'.

stopover

think-tank

tough it out President Nixon's failed strategy during Watergate.

trade-off

whistle-blower

THE 1980s

cherry-pick

fax

Have a nice day!

hit the spot

ID

†*No way!*

PDQ

post-traumatic stress syndrome

veteran (as a term for an ex-serviceman, however young)

THE 1990s AND AFTER

awesome In the reverential sense, this dates back to at least 1598. It had become a diagnostic word for the Californian Valley Girl dialect Valspeak by 1982, when a *Guardian* parody ('I'm sure totally. It's so awesome, I mean fer shurrr, toadly, toe-dally! ... Ohhhhmigawwwd!') explained the argot to incredulous readers. But this was no passing fad, and by the early twenty-first century, *awesome* had escaped from the teenage female ghetto on its way to becoming something like a trans-global term of approbation.[6]

---

6 California may also be responsible for the strange growling habit known as vocal fry.

†*baggage* In ordinary British use, meaning the cases an individual takes on a journey; this was displaced by *luggage* in the late nineteenth century. International air travel has given it a second coming.

buy (meaning believe)

call out One used to call out a plumber. Lately people are being called out all over the place, usually because they have uttered an opinion with which the caller-out disagrees. In the US since circa 1981. A sinister little phrase.

chill (out)

downplay Previously *play down*.

dude Has lost its old US meaning as a dandy, and has come to Britain – US vowel sound intact – perhaps after being used throughout the 1998 Coen Brothers cult film *The Big Lebowski*. It can now (a) mean anyone at all, probably but not necessarily male ('There was this *dood*') or (b) be used as an intensifier, like *man* ('Aw, *dood*, c'mon') or (c) act as a compliment akin to the great Yiddishism *mensch*. 'I love him. I can't stop thinking about him. He's a *dood*!' said Irish jockey Paddy Brennan on Channel 4 after winning a big race. He was talking about his horse Cue Card. If every Americanism but one were to be expelled, I would let this dood survive.

dumb Meaning stupid. It probably rippled out from the 1930s Hollywood stereotype of the *dumb blonde* and has now, along with *dummy*, become an all-purpose playground insult. In these PC times, can't we ban it as insulting to dumb animals?

faze A miserable synonym for *disturb* or *perturb*, which roared into Britain like a disease in the 1990s, almost certainly through the media. It is not even useful for Scrabble to most of the journalists who insist on writing it, because they keep misspelling it *phase*.

feisty A word that subtly changed meanings long before it reached the British media in the 1990s. It originally meant loud, uppity and irritatingly aggressive (your neighbour's terrier) but later implied a brave and spirited form of aggression (your own terrier). It is derived from *fist*, US dialect for a small dog, or just maybe from the medieval *fist*, yet another word for a fart. All in all, it helps prove the rule never to put anything into your mouth – including words – unless you know where it's been (cf. *spunk*).

fun (adjective)

glass ceiling

Groundhog Day Became a dull, repetitive cliché for a dull, repetitive life after the 1993 Bill Murray film.

hash (as in #) Also known as the pound sign in the US or, technically, an *octothorp*. Almost unknown in Britain pre-smartphones and Twitter.

head up (to somewhere) Tautologous verb form.

heads-up Noun meaning warning or tip off, origin unclear (though perhaps in a roundabout way from baseball). Popularised in Washington-speak during the first Bush administration and taxonomised by *The New York Times* language columnist William Safire in 1991. I have not yet worked out who brought this Oreo Cookie of a word to Britain, but when I do, I will strangle the person responsible and proudly phone the police to give them the heads-up.

heist

hike (verb and noun) A remarkable case of one Americanism displacing another. *Hike*, meaning a long, healthy walk, traipsed from the US to Britain as part of the interwar fresh air craze. No one talks about going hiking any more, even if they still walk. The modern usage, as in *price hike*, travelled east in the 1970s, seemingly through the business pages of the newspapers, and was seized on for its pithiness by the headline writers. (TAX HIKE THREAT TO DIESEL DRIVERS – *Evening Standard* front page, 7 June 2016.) Some rather sad people may now actually say such things in conversation.

hospitalise/-ize Listed by Mencken among dozens of other American -ize formations including *backwardize*, *scenarioize* and *moronize*. Very few of these survived at all, let alone crossed the Atlantic. This one attempted to make landfall in 1935 and was denounced in a *Times* leader as an example of bad English. In 1940 it popped up again when it was widely reported that a wartime committee had threatened compulsory powers to 'hospitalize' TB sufferers. This drew a magnificent letter to the paper from the Conservative MP for Norwich, Henry Strauss:

> Sir – I thank you for putting 'hospitalize' in inverted commas and the BBC for putting it into English. The word does not mean, it seems, to convert into a hospital but to 'send to hospital' and its use can hardly be explained by a passion for pointless illiteracy. What happens to a 'hospitalized' man when he is cured? Is he 'dehospitalized' or 'homeized'? He cannot be merely 'sent home'.

Strauss must have secured another deportation order because I swear this verb was never used in my childhood. I first came across it in *Time* magazine, which was also fond of such words as *infanticipating* instead of giving birth. In Britain you always went either *to* hospital or *into* hospital. I would prefer not to do either, but – message to paramedics – I absolutely refuse to be hospitalized.

I'm good The pet hate of many members of the National Union of Pedants and Fogies. As one of them likes to say in response, 'You can tell me if you're well. I'll tell you if you're any good.'

it sucks US student slang now used by British children aged 3 to about 30 to describe anything they dislike from broccoli to Brexit. Origin unclear but I dread to think. It does suck, really it does.

lobby In addition to its political uses, this has now displaced *foyer* as the entrance hall of a hotel. Presumably lobbyists hang around there too.

†*meet with* In the sense of having a meeting with someone. Used by Sir Walter Scott in 1828, though it later became wholly American. Not any more.

no-brainer

outage An ugly Americanism for a cut in supply (power, water, etc.), increasingly used by journalists and semi-literate functionaries. Easy to misread as *outrage*.

park up

party (verb) 'Come on Barbie, let's go party.'

per diem A rare American Latinism.

pesky 'Annoying, disagreeable, abominable, hateful' (OED). Just like the word itself.

pickle Used in the US to mean a pickled cucumber. Normally this would be said in full in British use to avoid confusion with pickled onions, eggs, etc. But not by children weaned on *The Very Hungry Caterpillar* (1969) by Eric Carle, in which a pickle gets a prominent mention. Since worldwide sales are way over 20 million, pickle's future, like Carle's, seems secure.

†*pinkie* A pinkie is both Scottish and American for little finger. In Doncaster, which is in neither Scotland nor America, there is a shop called Perfect Pinkies. Does it only look after little fingers? Are there are other shops that look after ring, middle and index fingers? And what about thumbs?

†*poop* Originally in Britain a soft fart, like a fizzle, *poop* also meant a short toot on a horn. In some places (Cornwall and parts of Scotland, for sure), the poop actually produced something. This meaning took hold in America. Other British babies pooed in their nappies until very recently.

price gouging

†*recuse* Used in Britain since the 1990s as a quasi-legal term meaning to disqualify oneself from taking part in a decision, 'I *recuse* myself from this case,' an honest judge might say. 'The defendant is my mistress.'

†*rendition* Euphemism for illegal extradition by kidnap, as practised by Britain or its allies.

ridership The number of passengers using a form of transport, in the US since 1951. Very rarely used in Britain before 2000 except as professional jargon; when John Prescott, deputy prime minister and chief language-mangler, used the term in 1999 he was mocked in the *Guardian.* But by analogy with *readership,* it's quite elegant. And *readership,* as those who have been paying attention so far will know, is also an Americanism.

rolling (as in strikes, blackouts, etc.)

†*sick* The OED tracks this back to the ninth century AD, so it is certainly not an Americanism. But for most of the twentieth century the English use of both verb and noun specifically

referred to vomiting (a euphemism, thought Sir Ernest Gowers). That distinction has now vanished again, maybe through US influence, maybe because of the very British football joke-phrase *sick as a parrot*, maybe because of the spread of the Australasianism *sickie*.[7]

†*specialty* Was driven to lurk in corners in Britain long ago by the much more elegant *speciality*, with its delicious rolling syllables. On a menu a *speciality* always tastes better than a *specialty*. Amid the current anarchy it has emerged from hiding, helped by the medical profession's US-driven preference for it. ('My pinkie hurts, doctor.' 'I'm sorry but my specialty is middle fingers.')

tad Meaning a little. First recorded by the OED in the US in 1940, and a known Americanism thereafter. Did not appear at all in the *Guardian* or the *Observer* throughout the 1980s but popped up 133 times in the 1990s. In 1992 the *Observer* words columnist, John Silverlight, tried to explain its sudden spread, but couldn't. Nor can I.

tote (as in bag)

water cooler A place for in-office conversation. Could we have the tea trolley back please?

way above my pay grade

The following words are making their way stealthily towards acceptance:

closet Making some headway in the sense of being a storage space or wardrobe, as well as something from which to emerge metaphorically.

†*garbage* Not an Americanism per se but the application to rubbish collection certainly is American.

go postal Go into a murderous rage. This came into the American language in the early 1990s as a black-humoured response to a spate of mass shootings by disgruntled postal workers against their colleagues. This has no equivalent in Britain, where postmen just get bitten by dogs and do not fire on them. So it

---

7 Eric Partridge unearthed a seventeenth-century reference to *melancholy as a parrot*.

is meaningless in a British context. The phrase may have been popularised by fans of the (British) writer Terry Pratchett. No.33 of his Discworld series was entitled *Going Postal.*

†*life vest* (rather than *life jacket*) Made it on to the BBC News in 2015. Since a *vest* in Britain is an undergarment, this might be dangerously confusing; people might strip off to try to put it on, and drown in the process.

†*medal* (verb) Team GB medalled a lot at the last two Olympics, due to the government chucking money at elite athletes rather than anyone else. Team GB is itself a North American formulation, which (I think) dates back to Team Canada at the 1978 Commonwealth Games. It is also inaccurate, since the initials GB inherently exclude Northern Ireland.

†*mom* Increasingly appearing on birthday cards to British mothers from their US-indoctrinated offspring. It was also traditionally used in Birmingham though not, according to a correspondent, in nearby Coventry, where she was always *mam.*

ornery A corruption of *ordinary*, a blameless word which somehow mutated under western skies to mean cantankerous. The Australians do things better, using *ordinary* as a euphemism for *dreadful.* Much favoured by Australian cricket captains, who will often describe their team's performance after a bad defeat as 'pretty ordinary'. British writers who just copy the Americanism fit that description.

†*roil* (verb) Annoy. Twin brother to *rile*, which returned from the US a century ago. This one stayed away – until lately.

misstep *Mistake*'s uglier sister.

†*monkey wrench* This is a far cleverer and wittier term than *adjustable spanner*, and if anyone were saying it for that reason, that would be great. But I bet they aren't.

†*pocketbook* Abandoned 150 years ago in Britain because the US usage *wallet* was much clearer. Now this silly word's begging to come back again.

rambunctious American for *rumbustious.*

retiree Crawling into the media, though not yet, I think, into conversation.

scuttlebutt Gossip. Since a *scuttlebutt* was the water-cask on board
　　ship, this does have a nice history: it is the water cooler's
　　great-great-grandfather.

†*schoolyard* A joyless alternative to playground.

†*snicker* Rather than *snigger*.

the smarts Natural intelligence or acumen. In US since at least 1940;
　　very rare in Britain until the 1990s. Its use conveys a sense that
　　the speaker or writer believes they also possess this mysterious
　　quality. *Smart* meaning clever has long been understood in
　　Britain, though more common in the US. It is much used in
　　the *Economist* magazine, where it has the additional meaning of
　　'someone who agrees with us'.

9

WHAT IS TO BE DONE?

In 2016 Britain's voters made the fateful decision to leave the European Union after forty-three years. They were not required to make any decision about an alternative strategy.

Given that the Americans decided shortly afterwards, though not by a majority, to fall under the sway of Donald Trump, it seemed improbable that the British would voluntarily choose to follow Peter Preston's prediction (see p. 6) and accept a formal role as the 51st State. But who knows how desperate the times might become?

Indeed, at times during the research for this book, it has seemed to me as though statehood might be promotion.[1] 'This isn't a country,' the writer Gore Vidal once said on a visit to Britain, 'it's an American aircraft carrier.'

And yet there is a paradoxical connection between support for Brexit and opposition to the influence of the American language. The forces who are most active in spreading Americanisms into every cranny are precisely those who were most enthusiastic about

---

1 In a number of respects, individual US states have considerably more autonomy than members of the European Union.

remaining European: big business; most politicians; most of the elite media; the young; the well-travelled; the urban; the south-east; the footloose …

Whenever I have written about the loss of the British language, I find those most receptive to my message are those who are also quite likely to have voted for Brexit: the over-40s, the provincial; the small-town and rural; the well-rooted and quite possibly well set-up but at the same time vaguely pissed-off. People who know a hollyhock when they see one and appreciate a decent cup of tea.

There is not necessarily a contradiction here. Colonel John Low, who held the post of British resident at Lucknow in the 1830s, wrote to his bosses in Calcutta: 'There is a common feeling which exists all over the known world, viz., a dislike of foreign masters and new usages.' A generation later those twin grievances exploded into the Indian Mutiny, with Lucknow at its heart. In Britain in 2016 they somehow gave us Brexit.

Whether that was a sensible response to the issues at hand will be the subject of thousands of other books. Might it just possibly help the problem outlined in this book – the unthinking outsourcing of a national language to another nation? Well, it is remotely possible that one outcome might be the emergence of a constructive nationalism, a collective acceptance of an inclusive Britishness. This could include a genuine pride in the language, of the sort that Bruce Moore talked about in Australia: a language that can be absorbent yet still resilient.

More likely Britain will revert to its default position, drifting aimlessly in mid-ocean, buffeted by each Atlantic storm, at the mercy of passing icebergs. Meanwhile, in linguistic terms, it would continue to devour regular airdrops of freshly packed Americanisms while manufacturing a diminishing number of words and exporting few of them. It is time for a new phase.

***

In the title sequence of the early episodes of the TV blockbuster *Homeland*, the permanently overwrought CIA agent Carrie always says the same thing: 'I missed something once before,' referring to the events of 9/11. 'I *won't*, I *can't*, let it happen again.' Her calm boss and mentor Saul replies soothingly: 'Everyone missed something that day.'

What British journalists missed that day, and I was one of them, was the significance of the word *boxcutters*. These were supposedly the weapons used by the hijackers to threaten, and possibly kill, the pilots to enable them to take control of the four planes. We all solemnly repeated it as though it meant anything to the readers back home, thus failing in our duty to enable people to understand what the hell had happened.

Well, ours was not the worst crime that day, and there was a mood of frenzy that did not even start to subside for months. But hardly anyone charged with interpreting the day's events even seemed to ask the question: 'What's a boxcutter?' The answer, in most of the non-American Anglosphere, is what we call a *Stanley knife*. Yet a database search, not necessarily exhaustive but a useful guide, suggests that only six newspaper reports – four in British papers, two in Australian[2] – actually mentioned the term *Stanley knife* in the first five days of the crisis against hundreds who wittered on about *boxcutters*.[3]

It was symptomatic of a state of mind that has if anything got worse since then: that America speaks English and Britain speaks English, and no translation or interpretation is necessary. The US media does not have this problem: if anything it is inclined to make its informants be heard in American, whether they talk that way or not.[4]

✳✳✳

---

2 Most of these reports carried multiple bylines, but one can give credit to Ben Macintyre of *The Times* and Duncan Campbell of the *Guardian*.

3 And it was 2004 before a Congressional commission was told there was no evidence that boxcutters were used at all. The weapons may have been larger utility knives. There being no survivors from the four planes, we shall never know.

4 The chief constable of Northamptonshire was quoted as using the phrase 'the almost normalcy' by *The New York Times* in 2013. I refused to believe anyone had ever used such a phrase in Northamptonshire. However, when the county's police force advertised for a successor in 2015 candidates were told it needed an 'agent of change' who can get 'client-side' and 'is a pioneer in blue-light collaboration'. So anything's possible.

All this does lend itself to a feeling of despair which is difficult to shrug off. The trend, after all, seems inexorable. But it is not inevitable. Consider the stories of three people: two men – one Welsh, one American – and one seemingly ordinary English housewife.

The Welshman was Gwynfor Evans, the first ever Welsh Nationalist MP and president of his party, Plaid Cymru, for twenty-six years. In 1979 Welsh voters voted down the chance to have their own devolved Assembly and Evans lost his seat in parliament.

The nationalist movement was moribund, and the newly elected Thatcher government in London decided it was perfectly safe to renege on a promise to set up a dedicated Welsh-language TV channel. Whereupon Evans announced that he would starve himself to death.

He gave the government five months' notice of his plans and through the summer of 1980 his demoralised party was galvanised into action. Hundreds of activists refused to pay their TV licence fees; the Welsh Secretary's car was besieged when he tried to attend the Eisteddfod; and Evans quietly kept reiterating that he was prepared to die. And since everyone agreed that he was an inflexible man of principle/difficult old sod – 'a Welsh Gandhi' was one regular description – no one doubted he was serious. Three weeks before his fast was due to start, the government gave in.

Evans lived until 2005, when he was 92. By that time Wales not only had its TV channel but also an Assembly; the centuries-long decline in the Welsh language had been halted and Welsh culture had acquired an unprecedented dynamism and energy. Had Margaret Thatcher let him die, it is reasonable to theorise that Wales would not have its own Assembly, but its own independent parliament, having left the United Kingdom in disgust. Evans couldn't lose.

The second figure is Mary Whitehouse, gone but not quite forgotten: a name which was for decades instantly recognisable as the voice – and perhaps, for all most of us knew, sole member – of the National Viewers' and Listeners' Association, which campaigned against sex, bad language, blasphemy, sometimes violence, but above all sex, on Britain's TV screens.

Flat Midlands voice, silly hats, beliefs most churchmen had left behind years ago – no one took her seriously at first. But she fought her corner like a raging lioness. And from the 1960s to the 1980s any TV executive planning a programme that remotely nudged the tightly drawn boundaries of Mrs Whitehouse's perception of accept-able taste had to consider the consequences of coping with her wrath. It was a powerful incentive towards erring on the side of safety, and it undoubtedly had an influence.

The third person is Noah Webster. He gave the American lan-guage its own spelling not because anyone else particularly wanted it but because he was a force of nature and because he cornered the market in spelling books and dictionaries. The Declaration of Inde-pendence ends beautifully: 'we mutually pledge to each other our Lives, our Fortunes, and our sacred *Honor*'. As originally drafted by Thomas Jefferson, it read *Honour*, according to H.L. Mencken, and the change was probably just a mistake, not a matter of principle – Webster would not even begin his campaign for another seven years.[5] From then on, it was a matter of his drive and the young nation's polite acquiescence.

It is not true that language is some unstoppable tsunami. It can be transformed in all kinds of ways. It is certainly true that a distant French-style Academy, sitting in solemn conclave, swords and all, is no match for peer-group pressure in a school playground. But given a mixture of Evans's quiet single-mindedness, Whitehouse's rhino hide and Webster's puppy-dog energy, the British language could be saved too. It is a matter of willpower.

I am not sure I can offer any of these qualities single-handed. But I can tell you that if there were enough emailed complaints and Twitter-shamings every time a BBC correspondent said *specialty stores* or *life vests* or *appealing the decision*, the number of incidents would decline dramatically. It needs a pressure group to orchestrate this.

Ridicule can work wonders too. The late, great comic Victoria Wood had a sketch in her 2009 Christmas special featuring a spoof language disc: 'Always wanted to talk rubbish and never had the con-fidence to try? With "Let's Talk Rubbish" you'll be talking rubbish

---

5 And *neighbouring* is spelt the British way.

in no time ... ***Tell me about it!*** ... ***Don't even go there!*** ... *Whatever!* ... "***How yer doin, guys?***" "***Yeah!***"'. It should be on the national curriculum and played by English teachers repeatedly.

Some changes are now happening so fast they almost certainly are unstoppable. According to one major research project, the Spoken British National Corpus 2014, the word *awesome* is now used in conversation seventy-two times per million words, whereas *marvellous*, used 155 times per million words twenty years earlier, is down to twice per million.[6] *Cheerio* and *fortnight* have also declined precipitately.

The fate of *fortnight* is particularly poignant: America's scourge of the Britishism, Ben Yagoda, had complained about it creeping over there only two years earlier. It is also telling: the word's decline in Britain, after a millennium when it appears to have been used interchangeably with *two weeks*, suggests that its (almost) total absence from American media is more influential than its presence in British conversation.

If the use of the word *guys* were logged, it might now come in at about 100,000 times per million. It has lost its association with maleness; indeed if anything it is now used more among groups of young women. It also smacks of the schoolteacher striving too hard for informality.

The writer Philip Norman has plausibly pinned the 'verbal eczema' of *guys* to a single source, the TV series *Friends*, first shown in 1993, which may also have been crucial in Britain's switch from tea to coffee. What a suggestible nation we have become. *Friends* may also be responsible for the other phrases in the Victoria Wood riff and more besides: ***hanging out***, for instance. This phrase dates back to 1846 in the US but Britain managed to steer clear of it for about a century and a half. Theresa May was of course pathetically desperate to hang out with Donald Trump after his election, even if she did not say the words.

Still, we are not remotely alone. It has been shown that the songs

6 One assumes these figures are extrapolated from a sample survey, though it is of course possible that all British conversations are overheard and logged by the security services.

of humpback whales from the South Pacific have now superseded the songs of the humpbacks on the other side of Australia, in the Indian Ocean: a quite extraordinary development. Perhaps the humpbacks' mournful plaint could be adopted as Britain's new national anthem: a lament for a dying language.

Let me say this one last time. I am not anti-American. I am not against the American language. It has over the years performed a great service for the British language. But we need to regard these languages as distinct and independent – as Jefferson, Webster and Mencken all wanted – and not have one as a craven subject of the other.

In an 1892 book, the American essayist Brander Matthews cut through a lot of the Victorian nonsense that bedevilled the subject and announced: 'The existence of Briticisms and of Americanisms and of Australianisms is a sign of healthy vitality.' He then quoted a Professor Freeman,[7] who had contrasted a few words from each side of the Atlantic and concluded 'Neither usage can be said to be in itself better or worse than the other. Each usage is the better in the land in which it has grown up.'

That sounds like a pretty sound rule. It is time for Britain itself to grow up again and take charge of its own language, and not let it decline into a feeble echo of anyone else's. Let the get-go be gone.

7 Possibly the Oxford historian E.A. Freeman.

ENDNOTES

INTRODUCTION

p. 1 The expert on war songs is Murdoch (1990) p186.

p. 2 The BBC's controller of programmes: quoted in Lewis (1986) p185.

p. 2 The absence of bluebirds is confirmed by the British Ornithologists' Union official list of bird species recorded in Britain at bou.org.uk.

p. 2 John McEwen: *The Oldie*, September 2014.

p. 2 RAF uniforms: *Guardian*, 21 October 1991.

p. 2 Vera Lynn quotes: *The Times*, 9 May 2007.

p. 4 Adverbial particles: Fowler/Gowers (1965) p451.

p. 5–6 For information about dead languages see linguisticsociety.org and ethnologue.com.

p. 7 Churchill on the 49th state: *The Times*, 9 March 1946.

p. 10 Research on Scotland: *Mail on Sunday*, 29 September 2013.

p. 10 Vera Lynn again: Lewis (1986) p185.

CHAPTER 1

p. 14 guaiacum: Read (2002) p6.

p. 16 a great shaggy continent: Nevins and Commager (1942) p2.

p. 17 Mary Rowlandson: The versions vary and the original was lost. It can be found online as *Narrative of the Captivity and Restoration of Mrs. Mary Rowlandson* at http://www.gutenberg.org/files/851/851-h/851-h.htm.

p. 17 Harvard Library: Mencken (1936) p125.

p. 19 Josselyn on pubs, hurricanes and snakes: Josselyn (1672/1865) pp23 and 36.

p. 19 Marshes, swamps etc: Bryson (1994) pp23–4.

p. 20 Barbarous bluffs: Moore (1744) p24.

p. 20 Chesterfield on Porters: Letter cxlii.

p. 21 Johnson on Americans: Nicolson (1960) p320.

p. 21 David Crystal quote: Crystal (2004) p419.

p. 21 Hitchings quote: Hitchings (2011) p104.

p. 21 Comte de Buffon quote: Dugatkin (2009) http://www.press.uchicago.edu/ucp/books/book/chicago/M/bo5387723.html.

p. 22 Hume to Franklin: Read (2002) p41.

p. 22 Stamp tax: Nicolson (1960) p207.

p. 22 Johnson on Stamp Tax: Taxation No Tyranny (1775) http://www.samueljohnson.com.

p. 22 Chesterfield on Americans: http://www.gutenberg.org/files/3361/3361-h/3361-h.htm.

p. 23 Washington's tea-drinking: Mair and Hoh (2009) p206.

p. 23 Speaking Greek: Algeo ed (2001) p59.

p. 26 -ize vs. -ise: http://blog.oxforddictionaries.com/2011/03/ize-or-ise/.

p. 27 For Shame: Read (2002) p50.

p. 27 Jefferson on Raynal: Jefferson (1787 edition) p190 http://web.archive.org/web/.

p. 29 Lambert (1810) vol. 2, pp505–7.

p. 30 Webster quote: Andresen (1990) p79.

p. 31 Quotes from reviewers: Cairns (1918 and 1922) *passim*.

p. 31 'The famous sneer …': Mencken (1936) p13.

p. 31 'In the four quarters of the globe …': Smith (1859) vol. 1 p292.

p. 32 'It was the question …' Cairns (1922) p11.

p. 33 'Until about 1820 …' Burchfield (1985) p163.

p. 35 The story of OK: *Los Angeles Times*, 20 October 2002, *Economist*, 24 October 2002 (obituaries of A.W. Read), Algeo ed. (2001) p196, Partridge (1958/1966) p450, Mencken (1936) p206.

p. 36 *The New Monthly* (1820) vol. 14 p629 [the original has *clush* not *slush* but that is surely an error].

p. 37 Constitutionality: *The Times,* 6 March 1810.

p. 37 Christianization: *The Times*, 8 May 1838.

p. 37 Deputize: *The Times*, 8 November 1895.

p. 37 Squirm: *The Times*, 10 April 1890.

p. 37 Slush: *Observer,* 23 January 1842.

p. 38 Webster's fading nationalism: Gustafson (1992) p304.

CHAPTER 2

p. 39 Cobbett on America: Ingrams (2005) pp20 and 143.

p. 42 'They eat with the greatest possible rapidity': Trollope (1832/1969) p38.

p. 42 'I never saw any people …': ibid. p57.

p. 42 'The most striking circumstance…': Hall (1829) p108.

p. 42 Dickens (1842): chapter 2.

p. 43 Commander Hall and the scholmarm: Hall (1829) pp27–9.

p. 44 'Youngsters filled with a vast impatience': Mencken (1936) p133.

p. 45 Joseph Shorthose: Barnett (1962) p595.

p. 45 'Words like *bitch*': ibid. p190.

p. 46 'Modest little trousers': Marryat (1839) vol. 3 chapter 1.

p. 46 'Too frankly sexual': Mencken (1936) p302.

p. 46 Cock-roaches: B.D. Walsh quoted in OED under *roach*.

p. 46 The American Academy: Gustafson (1992) p41.

p. 47 385 editions: ibid. p309.

p. 47 'Americans incline to give every syllable …': Marsh (1862) p475.

p. 48 Lengthy: *The Times* 1 July 1785; 6 April 1842.

p. 50 Conditions in parliament: Sparrow (2003) p25.

p. 50 Coleridge's American obsession: Holmes (1989) p65.

p. 51 Alford on *reliable*: quoted Fowler/Burchfield (1996) p665.

p. 51 Fitzedward Hall on *reliable*: Hall (1877) pvii.

p. 52 Coleridge on *talented*; Baugh and Cable (1978) p384.

p. 52 Cooke on *scientist*: *The Listener*, 3 April 1935.

p. 52 Huxley on *scientist*: *Annals of Science*, June 1962.

p. 52–3 Coxe on *reliable*: *Forum*, 1886.

p. 53 *The New York Times* on *reliable*: 15 October 1899.

p. 54 Ashley Cooper (undated) p14.

p. 54fn Stratton on his creator: *New York Review of Books*, 23 March 1978.

p. 54 *Observer* on Sam Slick: 21 May 1837.

p. 56 For the full story of the Astor Place riots see Cliff (2007) *passim*.

p. 57 Uncle Tom Mania: Meer (2005) pp1–2 and 134.

p. 57 Great Exhibition: Rydell and Kroes (2005) p98.

p. 59 Hawthorne on *The Lamplighter*: American National Biography Online.

p. 59 *The Lamplighter* in Lancashire: *The English Common Reader* (Richard D. Altick, 1957) p246.

p. 59 Twain's words: The Background of Mark Twain's Vocabulary, Charles J. Lovell *American Speech* April 1947 pp88–98.

p. 60 Matthew Arnold on the funny man: *The Nineteenth Century*, vol. XXIII 1888.

p. 60 'He knows he's telling a whopper': *Observer*, 26 January 1834.

p. 61 Cast list on the *State of Nebraska*: Rydell and Kroes (2005) p105.

p. 62 The press grovels to Cody: 7 May 1887.

p. 62 The American System of Manufactures: Rydell and Kroes (2005) pp113–14.

p. 63 Heiresses and chorus girls: Thompson (1988) p107.

p. 63 A Victim: 19 April 1873.

p. 64 Coxe on Dickens: *Forum* 1886.

p. 66 Ahoy!: Lerer (2007) p210.

CHAPTER 3

p. 67 The Kaiser's early warning: *The New York Times*, 2 January 1900.

p. 68 The Delaware–Lackawanna station: Quoted in Stead (1901) p443.

p. 68 Gladstone's prediction: ibid. p343.

p. 68 Stead's own prediction: ibid. p23.

p. 69–70 Americanization of the tube: Martin (2012) p142.

p. 70 *Manchester Guardian* on *made good*: 8 September 1909.

p. 71 Obscene translation: *The New York Times*, 29 June 1913.

p. 71 The American ambassador's views: *Manchester Guardian*, 20 May 1906.

p. 71 On Americanisms: Fowler (1906) pp23–4.

p. 72 Fowler on Kipling, ibid. p25.

p. 73 Dent's words of the year: Dent (2004) pp158–9.

p. 74–5 Wilson's speech: de Grazia (2005) p1, Friedman (2004) p1.

p. 75 imperium, emporium: de Grazia (2005) p3.

p. 76 Pells on *Fordismus*: (1997) pp9–10.

p. 76 Negro orgies: *Daily Mail*, 26 April 1926.

p. 77 Alcock and Brown's landing: *The Times*, 16 June 1919.

p. 77 Cooke on Lindbergh: Cooke (1973) p322.

p. 78 The restless inventiveness of American English: de Sélincourt (p28) pp61–3.

p. 79 Wodehouse in New York: McCrum (2004) pp68–9.

p. 82 Lejeune on *came-the-dawners*: *Observer*, 4 October 1942.

p. 82 Nix and a bib-full: Graves and Hodge (1940) p138.

p. 83 On quota quickies: *Daily Mirror*, 15 June 1934.

p. 83 *Manchester Guardian* competition: 23 January 1929.

p. 83–4 Bats in the belfry: *Daily Express,* 15 June 1917.

p. 85 Freedland on Jolson: *The Independent*, 27 September 2007.

p. 85 Critics on *The Jazz Singer*: 30 September, 30 September and 28 September 1928.

p. 85 Critics on *The Terror*: 26 October, 26 October and 28 October 1928.

p. 86fn *The New York Times* on *The Terror*: quoted by Glancy (2014) p84.

p. 86 'Oh that American twang!' etc. Letters in *Picturegoer* 1929: Quoted ibid. pp91–2.

p. 86 Editorial comment in *Picturegoer*: ibid. p90.

p. 87 Glancy on *Blackmail*: ibid., pp92–4.

p. 87 Headmaster from Diss: *The Times,* 23 December 1933.

p. 87 Headmaster from Finchley: *The Times*, 27 July 1936.

p. 88 Headmistress from Bridlington: *Sunday Times*, 13 June 1933

p. 88 Chief Constable of Wallasey: *Manchester Guardian* 11 February 1933, though this outburst made it as far as the *Washington Post*.

p. 88 The Southwark coroner: quoted Read (2002) p81.

p. 88 Stanley Baldwin: *Manchester Guardian*, 22 October 1931.

p. 89 Edward VIII: *Manchester Guardian*, 2 March 1936, *The Listener*, 4 March 1936.

p. 89 Cooke on Baldwin: *The Listener*, 30 June 1937.

p. 90 Mencken and the war: Teachout (2002) pp130–32.

p. 91 Mencken in the *Daily Express*: 15 January 1930.

p. 92 Pansy cast: Mencken (1936), p264.

p. 92 Ervine on Ethelred the Unready: *Observer*, 6 August 1933.

p. 92 Paston Letters: *Manchester Guardian*, 10 October 1933.

p. 93 Frame-up in Australia: *Sydney Morning Herald*, 25 September 1929.

p. 93 Father Murphy: Baker (1945) p287.

p. 94 Two boys, of Cardiff: *Daily Mirror,* 11 December 1935.

p. 94 The new language of dating: Tebbutt (2012) pp127–8.

p. 94 Mauss on deportment: quoted ibid. p145.

p. 95 A race of jitterbugs: *Daily* Mirror, 3 December 1938.

p. 95 Lambeth Walk in Germany: *The Times,* 18 October 1938.

p. 95 Restraint on the dance floor: Tebbutt (2012) p268.

p. 95 The English style: Nott (2015) p254.

p. 95 Charlie Kunz: ibid. pp201–2.

p. 96 Odious singing: Scannell and Cardiff (1991) pp189 and 293.

p. 97 The Postmaster-General: *The Times,* 1 July 1937.

p. 98 *Punch* cartoon: Reproduced in Scannell and Cardiff (1991) p186.

CHAPTER 4

p. 100 Phoney war: *Observer,* 7 April 1940.

p. 100 Cash-and-carry war: *Manchester Guardian,* 6 March 1940.

p. 102 American wealth: Reynolds (1995) p437.

p. 102 Uninhibited routines: Nott (2015) p254.

p. 102 Norman Collins: Morley (2001) p4.

p. 103 Advice to GIs: Short Guide to Great Britain (1942) pp2–3.

p. 104 Longstop and Banana Ridge: *Washington Post,* 24 May 1943.

p. 104 'As has sometimes been suggested': e.g. by Hugo Williams, *Times Literary Supplement*, 8 May 1987.

p. 104 The story of gobbledygook: Mencken (1945) p414; *The New York Times*, 21 May 1944.

p. 104–5 Horwill's PS: *Manchester Guardian,* 5 October 1945.

p. 106 Mr Justice Birkett: *Manchester Guardian,* 27 February 1945.

p. 106 H.W. Seaman's list of words: Mencken (1945) pp452–3.

p. 106 Chamberlain: ibid. p509.

p. 106 *Church Times* on Life of Christ, 30 January 1942.

p. 107 The BBC and English: McKibbin (1998) p509.

p. 107 Democratic appeal of US: Cockburn (1973) p103.

p. 107 Mackenzie on BBC: Scannell and Cardiff (1991) p298.

p. 107 'Second-class citizens': Pugh (2008) pp298–9.

p. 108 Orwell on American slang: Davison ed. (1998) vol. XVI p220.

p. 109 Danny Kaye's triumph: Hopkins (1964) p108.

p. 109 Japanese baseball: Conrad (2014) p196.

p. 109 France and Coca-Cola: Kuisel (1993) p52.

p. 110 The real Rip van Winkle: Baldwin (1949) p122.

p. 110 Mahmoud on Cinerama: Conrad (2014) pp13–14.

p. 111 Hire purchase and TV sales: Moran (2013) p81.

p. 112 ITV and bubonic plague: *Daily Express,* 23 May 1952.

p. 112 General fog: quoted Hopkins (1964) p405.

p. 112 Cars to a deodorant: 9 June 1953.

p. 113 Bullmore: quoted Fletcher (2008) p34.

p. 114 Get busy with the DDT: O'Sullivan (1989) pp108–9.

p. 114 Bucknell's postbag: Moran (2013) p317.

p. 115 Knitting wool sales: ibid. pp116–17.

p. 115 Power station tourism: Ogilvy (1963) pp135–6.

p. 115 £2,000 a year: ibid. p42.

p. 115–16 Productivity, *Titfield* and *The Maggie* : Kynaston (2007) pp467–9.

p. 116 50s teenagers: Hoggart (1957) pp248–9.

p. 117 *Gun Fury* and *Rock Round the Clock*: *The Times*, 6 September 1956.

p. 117 'My man rocks me': Green (1998) p1,004.

p. 117–18 Cool at Buxton: *Manchester Guardian*, 19 May 1959.

p. 118 Cab Calloway: McCrum (2010) p129.

p. 118 Balding and gangling: Foster (1968) p40.

p. 118 Gimmick: *The Times*, 9, 17 and 23 September 1952.

p. 119 'Earls in blue jeans': *Daily Express*, 9 June 1919.

p. 120 Washington's all-night party: Washington's Diaries, quoted OED under *barbecue.*

p. 120 Buchwald on Wimpy Bars: *Washington Post*, 5 June 1955.

p. 121fn *Gay* in the press: *Manchester Guardian*, 28 November 1954, 4 December 1957 and 5 April 1959.

p. 121 The Ox in Flames: *Observer*, 18 September 1960.

p. 122 Brain drain: *Guardian*, 28 February 1963.

p. 122 'from the outlying provinces': Conrad (2014) p251.

p. 123 'STOP!': Mackenzie Stuart (2013) p198.

p. 123 Fringed, frisky and friendly: *Daily Mirror*, 7 February 1964.

p. 123 Cronkite: Conrad (2014) p252.

p. 123 Ed Sullivan Show: http://www.edsullivan.com/artists/the-beatles.

p. 125 Tommy Vance: Obituary in *The Independent*, 7 March 2005.

p. 126 The W3 controversy: The main source for this story is 'Ain't That the Truth' by David Skinner, *Humanities,* vol.30 no. 4 (2009).

p. 127 'Inundated': *Observer*, 29 April 1962.

CHAPTER 5

p. 129 The Burchfield–O'Brien dispute: *Guardian*, 28 June and 1 July 1978; *Observer*, 2 and 30 July 1978; Reuters, 27 June 1978; *Encounter*, October 1978; private information.

p. 133 Kahane on the No.1 languages: Kachru ed. (1992) p211.

p. 134 The virtues of English: Barzun (1986) pp130–32.

p. 135fn The masculinity of Brexit: *Guardian*, 22 October 2016.

p. 136 Rushdie on Indian English: Abley (2008) p55.

p. 137 'GO OUT MUBARAK': Rowse (2011) p81.

p. 137 Indonesian romance: ibid. p97.

p. 137 Globish to endanger English-speakers: McCrum (2010) p9.

p. 140 Cooke on Americanisms: *The Listener*, 3 April 1935.

p. 144 Joseph on anti-enterprise culture: *Observer*, 31 October 1976.

p. 144 Peters's initial thesis: See Peters and Waterman (1982) *passim*.

p. 148 Reporting menstrual cycles: *Boston Globe*, 29 September 2002.

p. 148 Toilet breaks in Britain: hazards.org/toiletbreaks/.

p. 148 Armstrong memo: *Morning Star*, 30 December 2014.

p. 148 Chief executives' pay: theguardian.com, 4 January 2017.

p. 150fn 'blandishments of the party machine': *Manchester Guardian*, 4 June 1886.

p. 153fn Unwillingness to queue: bbc.co.uk, 16 February 2017.

p. 153 Osborne the faux-American: *Mail on Sunday* 28 September 2014.

p. 153 Darn tootin': *Financial Times*, 4 April 2015.

p. 154 Police in fancy-dress: *The Times*, 31 July 2014.

p. 154 Northampton Town manager: *Guardian*, 12 February 2016.

p. 155 PM's spokeswoman: *Guardian*, 23 August 2016.

p. 155 'The Donald Trump playbook': *Observer*, 7 May 2016.

p. 156 'Googly from left field': *Observer*, 8 April 2001.

p. 156 'The Giants is dead': Barnett (1962) p172.

p. 157 SATs copyright: *London Review of Books*, 21 May 2015.

p. 158 Berlins's war: *Guardian*, 15 December 1992, 26 April 1994, 10 January 1995, 20 July 1999, 23 October 2000, 11 December 2000, 15 January 2001, 27 March 2001, 29 October 2001.

p. 160 Master of the Rolls: theguardian.com, 12 Mar 2014.

CHAPTER 6

p. 161 American popcorn: *The Times*, 20 November 1874.

p. 161fn More profitable than heroin: 1 May 2002.

p. 162 'As easily as potatoes': *The Times*, 12 March 1938.

p. 162 'gladden the heart of some American soldier ...': 29 May 1943.

p. 162 Sackville-West on *corn*: 13 September 1955.

p. 166 The union jack: http://www.flaginstitute.org/wp/british-flags/the-union-jack-or-the-union-flag/.

p. 168 Downton Abbey on PBS: *Guardian*, 2 March 1915.

p. 169 Changes to US Harry Potter: http://www. fanpop.com/clubs/harry-potter/articles/4309/title/ difference-between-american-british-versions-harry-potter-series.

p. 169 Complaint about US Harry Potter: *The New York Times,* 10 July 2000.

p. 169–70 American Scrabble: *New Yorker,* 4 August 2015.

p. 172fn US soldiers sugar habit: *The Times,* 29 January 1862.

p. 173 Eating with forks: *Guardian,* 19 October 2015.

p. 173 One in six celebrate Thanksgiving: *Daily Telegraph* and *Guardian,* 27 November 2014.

p. 174 Lord Shaftesbury and his kids: Quoted OED under *kid*.

p. 174 Monica Sims on *Sesame Street:* Letter to *Guardian* 22 December 1970.

p. 175 Acorn to voicemail: the guardian.com 27 February 2015; *London Review of Books,* 18 September 2015.

p. 176 Leaf blowers: *The Oldie,* January 2016.

p. 176 'Lost generation of gardeners': *Daily Telegraph, The Times,* 23 May 2016.

p. 176 Ribbit-Ribbit: Barnes (2014) p565.

p. 178 toilet: Marckwardt (1958) p125.

p. 178 passing: *Guardian.com* 13 May 2013.

p. 178 'I gesse': Fowler (1906) p24.

p. 179 Bishop out, Ramadan in: *The Oldie,* January 2015.

p. 180 Miliband and 'loo-tenant': *dailymail.com*, 28 November 2011.

p. 180 deadline.com, 2 February 2015.

CHAPTER 7

p. 182 Cameron and a tank of gas: Andrew Marr, BBC1, 6 January 2013.

p. 183 Flight safety: http://aerosavvy.com/metric-imperial/.

p. 184 My name is pants: See OED on *pants*.

p. 184 Simon Mayo: *Guardian,* 22 September 1994; http://www. worldwidewords.org/topicalwords/tw-pan4.htm.

p. 185 shag in the US: Green (1998) p1,052.

p. 185 shagging in St Louis: StLToday.com, 25 June 2015.

p. 187 Yagoda's premise: https://britishisms.wordpress.com/2015/05/27/ cheeky-nandos/.

p. 187 Yagoda on inverted commas: https://britishisms.wordpress. com/2015/11/06/inverted-commas/.

p. 188 'Mighty my arse': *Daily News,* New York, 28 June 2016.

p. 189 Uptalk longstanding in Australia: *Canberra Times,* 20 December 1992.

p. 189 'A means of asserting control': Hitchings (2011) p279.

p. 190 Australians saying hi not g'day: *Daily Telegraph* (London), 13 July 2005.

p. 190 'Made of bricks': Australian National Dictionary.

p. 191 'Applications for Anzac biscuits': http://www.dva.gov.au/ commemorations-memorials-and-war-graves/protecting-word-anzac.

p. 192 'Paris will be one of the attractions': Kuisel (2012) p162.

p. 193 French poll on 9/11: http://www.france24.com/en/20160911-fifteen-years-september-11-conspiracy-theories-linger-among-french.

p. 194 Street signs and Your honor: Kuisel (2012) pp309–11.

p. 196 Cornelius Sommer: Reuters, 27 July 2010.

p. 197 'A route that takes you past …': *The Oldie*, Summer 2015.

p. 197 'coz, aint, like …': *Guardian*, 15 October 2013.

p. 198 David Starkey: *Daily Mail,* 15 August 2011.

p. 199 'to develop the soft skills': *Croydon Guardian*, 15 October 2013.

CHAPTER 9

p. 234 Gore Vidal: quoted in obituary, *Evening Standard*, 2 August 2012.

p. 235 Colonel Low: quoted by Ferdinand Mount, *New York Review of Books*, 20 June 2013.

p. 236fn Northamptonshire police: *The New York Times*, 23 December 2013/ BBC News, 7 May 2015.

p. 238 honor: Mencken (1921 edition) Chapter 8.

p. 239 awesome, etc.: *Guardian*, 26 August 2014.

p. 239 fortnight and Yagoda: https://britishisms.wordpress.com/2012/05/12/fortnight/.

p. 239 verbal eczema: *New Statesman*, 8 December 2015.

p. 240 humpback whales: Barnes (2014) p210.

p. 240 Professor Freeman: Matthews (1892) pp29–30.

BIBLIOGRAPHY

DICTIONARIES, etc.

Australian National Dictionary, 2nd edition, edited by Bruce Moore (2016)

Bartlett, J.R., *Dictionary of Americanisms* (1860)

Chapman, Robert L., *American Slang* (1994)

Craigie, Sir William and Hulbert, James R. (ed.), *A Dictionary of American English on Historical Principles*, 4 volumes (1938–44)

Elwyn, Alfred L., *A Glossary of Supposed Americanisms* (1859)

Farmer, John S., *Americanisms Old and New* (1889)

Fowler, H.W., *A Dictionary of Modern English Usage* (1926)

Fowler, H.W., *A Dictionary of Modern English Usage*, 2nd edition, revised by Sir Ernest Gowers (1965)

Fowler, H.W., *The New Fowler's Modern English Usage*, 3rd edition, edited by R.W. Burchfield (1996)

Görlach, Manfred (ed.), *A Dictionary of European Anglicisms: A Usage Dictionary of Anglicisms in sixteen European Languages* (2001)

Green, Jonathon, *Cassell's Dictionary of Slang* (1998)

Green, Jonathon, *Green's Dictionary of Slang*, 3 volumes (1992)

Horwill, H.W., *A Dictionary of Modern American Usage* (1935)

Horwill, H.W., *An Anglo-American Interpreter* (1939)

Lighter, J.E., *Random House Historical Dictionary of American Slang* (1994)

Mathews, M.M. (ed.), *A Dictionary of Americanisms on Historical Principles* (1951)

Oxford English Dictionary (online edition)

Partridge, Eric, *A Dictionary of Slang and Unconventional English* (1937)

Partridge, Eric, *Origins: A Short Etymological Dictionary of Modern English* (1958/1966)

Pickering, John, *A Vocabulary or Collection of Words and Phrases which have been Supposed to Be Peculiar to the United States of America* (1816)

Thornton, R.H., *An American Glossary*, 2 volumes (1912)

PHILOLOGY, etc.

Abley, Mark, *The Prodigal Tongue* (2008)

Alford, Henry, *The Queen's English* (1864)

Algeo, John (ed.), *The Cambridge History of the English Language: Volume 6, English in North America* (2001)

American National Biography (online)

Andresen, Julie Tetel, *Linguistics in America 1769–1924: A critical history* (1990)

Ayto, John, *Euphemisms* (1993)

Bailey, Richard W., *Images of English: A Cultural History of the Language* (1991)

Bailey, Richard W., *Speaking American* (2012)

Baker, Sidney J., *The Australian Language* (1945)

Barnett, Lincoln, *The Treasure of our Tongue* (1962)

Barzun, Jacques, *A Word or Two Before You Go …* (1986)

Baugh, Albert C. and Cable, Thomas, *A History of the English Language*, 3rd edition (1980)

Beal, Joan C., *English Pronunciation in the Eighteenth Century* (1999)

Bolton W.F. and Crystal, David (ed.), *The English Language* (1987)

Boyd, Charles, *Linguistic Change in Present-Day English* (1964)

Bragg, Melvyn, *The Adventure of English* (2003)

Bryson, Bill, *Made in America* (1994)

Burchfield, Robert, *The English Language* (1985)

Burchfield, Robert, *Unlocking the English Language* (1989)

Chapman, Robert L., *American Slang* (1986)

Chirico, Rob, *Damn!: A Cultural History of Swearing in Modern America* (2014)

Coleman, Julie, *The Life of Slang* (2012)

Collinson, W.E., *Contemporary English: A Personal Speech Record* (1927)

Crystal, David, *English as a Global Language* (1997)

Crystal, David, *Making Sense* (2017)

Crystal, David, *The Stories of English* (2004)

Crystal, David, *The Story of English in 100 Words* (2011)

Crystal, David, *Words* (2014)

Dent, Susie, *Larpers and Shroomers: The Language Report* (2004)

De Sélincourt, Basil, *Pomona: Or the Future of English* (1928)

Dillard, J.L., *Toward a Social History of American English* (1985)

Fennell, Barbara A., *A History of English: A Sociolinguistic Approach* (2001)

Fisher, John H., *The Emergence of Standard English* (1996)

Flavell, Linda and Roger, *The Chronology of Words and Phrases: A Thousand Years in the History of English* (1999)

Foster, Brian, *The Changing English Language* (1968)

Fowler, H.W. and F., *The King's English* (1906)

Görlach, Manfred (ed.), *English in Europe* (2002)

Grote, David, *British English for American Readers* (1992)

Hall, Fitzedward, *On English Adjectives in -Able with Special Reference to Reliable* (1877)

Heffer, Simon, *Strictly English: The correct way to write ... and why it matters* (2010)

Hickey, Raymond (ed.), *Eighteenth-Century English: Ideology and Change* (2010)

Hitchings, Henry, *Dr Johnson's Dictionary* (2016)

Hitchings, Henry, *The Language Wars: A History of Proper English* (2011)

Horvath, Barbara M., *Variation in Australian English: The Sociolects of Sydney* (1985)

Howard, Philip, *New Words for Old* (1977)

Jespersen, Otto, *Growth of the English Language* (1948)

Kachru, Braj (ed.), *The Other Tongue: English across Cultures* (1992)

Kövecses, Zoltán, *American English: An Introduction* (2000)

Krapp G.P., *The English Language in America*, volume 1 (1925)

Lerer, Seth, *Inventing English* (2007)

Macintyre, Ben, *The Last Word: Tales from the tip of the mother tongue* (2009)

MacNeil, Robert and Cran, William, *Do You Speak American?* (2005)

Marckwardt, Alfred H., *American English* (1958)

Marsh, George P., *Lectures on the English Language* (1862)

Mathews, M.M. (ed.), *The Beginnings of American English: Essays and Comments* (1931)

Matthews, Brander, *Americanisms and Briticisms* (1892)

Matthews, Brander, *Essays on English* (1921)

McKnight, George H., *Modern English in the Making* (1928)

McCrum, Robert, *Globish: How the English Language Became the World's Language* (2010)

McCrum, Robert, Cran, William and MacNeil, Robert, *The Story of English* (1987)

McDavid, Virginia, *American English* (1974)

McWhorter, John, *The Power of Babel: A Natural History of Language* (2001)

Mencken, H.L., *The American Language: An Inquiry into the Development of English in the United States*, 4th edition (1936)

Mencken, H.L., *The American Language: An Inquiry into the Development of English in the United States*, Supplement 1 (1945)

Moon, G. Washington, *The Dean's English* (1865)

Moore, Erin, *That's Not English* (2015)

Newman, Edwin, *Strictly Speaking* (1974)

Norris, Mary, *Between You & Me: Confessions of a Comma Queen* (2015)

Ostler, Rosemarie, *Let's Talk Turkey: The Stories behind America's Favorite Expressions* (2008)

Partridge, Eric, *A Covey of Partridge: An anthology* (1937)

Partridge, Eric and Clark, John W., *British and American English since 1900* (1951)

Potter, Simeon, *Our Language* (1950)

Pyles, Thomas, *Words and Ways of American English* (1954)

Random, W.S. (ed.), *English Transported: Essays on Australian English* (1970)

Read, Allen Walker (ed. Bailey, R.W.), *Milestones in the History of English in America* (2002)

Rowse, Arthur E., *Amglish in, like, Ten Easy Lessons: A Celebration of the New World Lingo* (2011)

Schele De Vere, M., *Americanisms: The English of the New World* (1872)

Simpson, David, *The Politics of American English 1776–1850* (1987)

Spencer, Herbert, *Facts and Comments* (1902)

Strevens, Peter, *British and American English* (1972)

Trask, R.L., *Why Do Languages Change?* (2010)

Tucker, Gilbert M., *American English* (1921)

Wilson, Richard, *How Not to Talk Like an Arse* (2011)

GENERAL

Altick, Richard D., *The English Common Reader* (1957)

Ashley Cooper, Anthony (Earl of Shaftesbury), *Speeches on the Condition of the Working Classes* (undated)

Baldwin, Monica, *I Leap Over the Wall: A Return to the World after Twenty-eight years in a Convent* (1949)

Barnes, Simon, *Ten Million Aliens* (2014)

Bigsby, C.W.E. (ed.), *Superculture: American Popular Culture and Europe* (1975)

Brogan, Hugh, *The Penguin History of the USA* (1985/2001)

Cairns, William B., *British Criticisms of American Writing 1783–1815* (1918)

Cairns, William B., *British Criticisms of American Writing 1815–1833* (1922)

Chandler, James, *England in 1819: The Politics of Literary Culture and the Case of Romantic Historicism* (1998)

Chesterfield, Earl of, *Letters of Lord Chesterfield to his Son* (1929)

Clark, Jennifer, *The American Idea of England 1776–1840* (2013)

Cliff, Nigel, *The Shakespeare Riots: Revenge, drama and death in nineteenth-century America* (2007)

Cockburn, Claud, *The Devil's Decade* (1973)

Conrad, Peter, *How the World Was Won: The Americanization of Everywhere* (2014)

Cooke, Alistair, *Alistair Cooke's America* (1973)

Davison, Peter (ed.), *The Complete Works of George Orwell*, volume XVI (1998)

De Grazia, Victoria, *Irresistible Empire: America's Advance through Twentieth-Century Europe* (2005)

Dugatkin, Lee Alan, *Mr Jefferson and the Giant Moose: Natural History in Early America* (2009)

Fearon, Henry B., *Sketches of America* (1819)

Fletcher, Winston, *Powers of Persuasion: The Story of British Advertising* (2008)

Fowler, David, *The First Teenagers: The Lifestyle of Young Wage-earners in Interwar Britain* (1995)

Fowler, David, *Youth Culture in Modern Britain c.1920–c.1970* (2008)

Friedman, Walter A., *Birth of a Salesman: The Transformation of Selling in America* (2004)

Gallop, Alan, *Buffalo Bill's Wild West* (2001)

Gambaccini, Paul, Rice, Tim and Rice, Jonathan, *British Hit Singles*, 9th edition (1993)

Glancy, Mark, *Hollywood and the Americanization of Britain: From the 1920s to the Present* (2014)

Graves, Robert and Hodge, Alan, *The Long Week-End: A Social History of Great Britain Between the Wars* (1940)

Hall, Captain Basil, *Travels in North America in the Years 1827 and 1828* (1829)

Hebdige, Dick, *Hiding in the Light: On Images and Things* (1988)

Hoggart, Richard, *The Uses of Literacy* (1957)

Holmes, Richard, *Coleridge: Early Visions* (1989)

Hopkins, Harry , *The New Look: A Social History of the Forties and Fifties in Britain* (1964)

Horn, Adrian, *Juke Box Britain: Americanisation and youth culture 1945–60* (2009)

Horrall, Andrew, *Popular Culture in London c.1890–1918* (2001)

Ingrams, Richard, *The Life and Adventures of William Cobbett* (2005)

Jarvis, Robin, *Romantic Readers and Transatlantic Travel: Expeditions and Tours in North America 1760–1840* (2012)

Jefferson, Thomas, *Notes on the State of Virginia* (1782)

Johnson, Samuel, *Taxation No Tyranny* (1775)

Josselyn, John, *Account of Two Voyages to New-England: Made during the years 1638, 1663* (1672/1865)

Kuisel, Richard F., *Seducing the French: The Dilemma of Americanization* (1993)

Kuisel, Richard F., *The French Way: How France Embraced and Rejected American Values and Power* (2012)

Kynaston, David, *Austerity Britain 1945–51* (2007)

Lambert, John, *Travels Through Lower Canada & The United States of North America* (1810)

Lynn, Dame Vera, *Some Sunny Day* (2009)

Mackay, James A., *Sounds Out of Silence: A Life of Alexander Graham Bell* (1997)

Mackenzie Stuart, Amanda, *Diana Vreeland: Empress of Fashion* (2013)

Mair, Victor H. and Hoh, Erling, *The True History of Tea* (2009)

Major, John, *My Old Man: A Personal History of Music Hall* (2012)

Marryat, Captain Frederick, *Diary in America: Series One* (1839)

Martin, Andrew, *Underground, Overground: A Passenger's History of the Tube* (2012)

Marwick, Arthur, *Culture in Britain Since 1945* (1991)

McCrum, Robert, *Wodehouse: A Life* (2004)

McKibbin, Ross, *Classes and Cultures: England 1918–1951* (1998)

Meer, Sarah, *Uncle Tom Mania: Slavery, Minstrelsy and Transatlantic Culture in the 1850s* (2005)

Mesick, Jane Louise, *The English Traveller in America* (1922)

Moore, Francis, *A Voyage to Georgia* (1744)

Moran, Joe, *Armchair Nation: An intimate history of Britain in front of the TV* (2013)

Morley, Patrick, *This is the American Forces Network: The Anglo-American Battle of the Airwaves in World War II* (2001)

Murdoch, Brian, *Fighting Songs and Warring Words* (1990)

Nevins, Allan and Commager, Henry S., *A Pocket History of the United States* (1942)

Nicolson, Harold, *The Age of Reason* (1963)

Nott, James, *Going to the Palais: A Social and Cultural History of Dancing and Dance Halls in Britain 1918–1960* (2015)

Nott, James, *Music for the People: Popular Music and Dance in Interwar Britain* (2002)

Ogilvy, David, *Confessions of an Advertising Man* (1963)

Osgerby, Bill, *Youth in Britain Since 1945* (1998)

O'Sullivan Timothy, *Percy Thrower: A Biography* (1989)

Oxford Dictionary of National Biography (online)

Pells, Richard, *Not Like Us: How Europeans Have Loved, Hated and Transformed American Culture Since World War II* (1997)

Peters, Thomas J. and Waterman, Robert H. Jr, *In Search of Excellence* (1982)

Pugh, Martin, *We Danced All Night: A Social History of Britain Between the Wars* (2008)

Reynolds, David, *Rich Relations: The American Occupation of Britain 1942–1945* (1995)

Rixon, Paul, *American Television on British Screens: A Story of Cultural Interaction* (2006)

Roger, Philippe (trans. Sharon Bowman), *The American Enemy* (2005)

Rowlandson, Mary, *Narrative of the Captivity and Restoration of Mrs Mary Rowlandson* (also under other titles) (1682)

Rubin, Barry and Rubin, Judith Colp, *Hating America: A History* (2004)

Russell, Bertrand, et al., *The Impact of America on European Culture, etc.* (1951)

Rydell, Robert and Kroes, Rob, *Buffalo Bill in Bologna: The Americanization of the World 1869–1922* (2005)

Scannell, Paddy and Cardiff, David, *Social History of British Broadcasting: Volume 1, 1922–1939* (1991)

Servan-Schreiber, Jean-Jacques, *The American Challenge* (1968)

Smith, Rev. Sydney, *The Works of Rev. Sydney Smith*, 2 volumes (1859)

Sparrow, Andrew, *Obscure Scribblers: A History of Parliamentary Journalism* (2003)

Stead, W.T., *The Americanization of the World: The Trend of the Twentieth Century* (1901)

Stevenson, John, *British Society 1914–45* (1984)

Tamarkin, Elisa, *Anglophilia: Deference, Devotion and Antebellum America* (2008)

Teachout, Terry, *The Skeptic: A Life of H.L. Mencken* (2002)

Tebbutt, Melanie, *Being Boys: Gender, Youth and Identity in the Inter-War Years* (2012)

Thompson, F.M.L., *The Rise of Respectable Society* (1988)

Tocqueville, Alexis de, *Democracy in America* (1835/1840)

Trollope, Frances, *Domestic Manners of the Americans* (1832)

Walsh, Robert, *An Appeal from the Judgments of Great Britain Respecting the United States Of America* (1819)

War and Navy Departments, Washington, *A Short Guide to Great Britain* (1943)

ACKNOWLEDGEMENTS

In July 2010 my wife said there was a phone message saying that Andrew Franklin from Profile was interested in my book. My reply was 'What book?'

It is very flattering to a writer if a publisher one does not know suggests a book one did not know one was going to write. But in this case, I had already decided that I did not want to write a book about Americanisms: although I had begun writing and broadcasting about the subject, I found it impossible to envisage how to turn it into something more lasting and worthwhile. Seven years on, readers will have to decide whether I was right the first time. I hope not.

Seven years is nothing in the great scheme of things. Dora Russell, wife of Bertrand, signed a contract to write *The Religion of the Machine Age* in 1923, and duly presented it to her publishers, Routledge, in 1983, when she was 88. The chairman of Routledge at the time was Andrew's father, Norman.[1] The son was patient, but not that patient; he was, however, very supportive, and I am hugely grateful to him for making me make it happen.

My thanks also to Andrew's colleagues at Profile for their professionalism

---

[1] Norman Franklin forbore to remind Lady Russell of the £50 advance she had been given sixty years earlier. When he later told the story to colleagues at Oxford University Press, they claimed that the chemist Sir Harold Hartley had kept them waiting even longer for a book, and that the Coptic Dictionary had taken 150 years.

and high tolerance threshold, especially Penny Daniel, Louisa Dunnigan, Hannah Ross and Patrick Taylor, and to Neil Burkey, a calm, empathetic and ultra-efficient copy editor.

Of those seven years, I spent five trying to steel myself for the task, while engaging in various displacement activities (including my previous book for Profile, *Engel's England*). I spent much of the remaining two years doing research that often resembled hacking through virgin jungle, especially in the largely unmined lodes of gold that are the newly digitised newspaper files, and in the London Library's philology section. This took some finding the first time in itself; and I discovered several important books that may have been untouched by human hand since before Dora Russell signed her contract.

My thanks to the staff at the London Library for being ready to offer help when needed (especially, for assistance beyond the call of duty, to Guy Penman and Gosia Lawik); also to the staff of the British Library, the Wellcome Library and the Library of Congress in Washington. I am grateful as well for the kindness and patience of senior editors and staff of the Oxford English Dictionary, who treated my ignorant questions with great tolerance.

And I would like to express my appreciation to my colleagues on the *Financial Times* and the *Guardian* for uncomplainingly producing the newspapers without contributions from me for weeks on end as my book deadline approached. Heaven knows how they managed.

And thanks also to Neil Barnes, Professor Steven Barnett, Professor Charles Barr, Dr Ulrike Bavendiek, Andy Bernhardt, David Bishop, Suzanne Blumsom, Simon Bradley, Alex Brummer, Patrick Collins (National Motor Museum), Polly Coupar-Hennessy, Steve Cox, James Croll, Professor David Crystal, Tim de Lisle, Christopher Douglas, Frances Edmonds, Sir Michael Edwards, Anthony Engel, Rachel Engel, Tom Engel, Norman Franklin, Paul Gambaccini, Michael Goldfarb, Mark Gwynn, Murray Hedgcock, Murdo Jamieson, Professor Robin Jarvis, Rob Jenkinson, Andrew Karney, Captain Paddy Keating, Simon Kuper, Christopher Lane, Christine Leslie, Lord Lisvane, Sam Llewellyn, Professor Josephine Maltby, Andrew Martin, Dr Bruce Moore, Andrew Nickolds, Sir Roger Norrington, Sue Norrington, Mick O'Dea, Nicola Sanderson, Harriet Sherwood, Dr Ruth Slater, Dr Andrew Smith, Dr Thomas Smith, Professor Laura Spira, Stefan Stern, Tony Thorne, Katharina Turner, Ken Watkins, Richard Whitehead, Douglas Wright, Ben Yagoda and (last as usual in such lists, but emphatically not least) Donald Zec.

I mentioned one of the joint dedicatees, Marilyn Warnick, in the Introduction; without her this book would certainly never have happened. Even more profound is my gratitude to the other dedicatee, my wife Hilary, who as ever brought her editorial skills to reading the text and made many helpful suggestions, particularly in curbing my wilder flights of fancy. And to my daughter Vika who, apart from cheering me up, was a constant source of new and ever more outrageous Americanisms. The undimmed memory of my late son Laurie was throughout both a pervasive sadness and an inspiration.

Matthew Engel, Herefordshire, 2017

INDEX OF NAMES

INDEX OF AMERICANISMS

The following words and phrases, which have become naturalised in Britain, are believed to constitute Americanisms. Where words have more than one definition (e.g. *abrasive*), the meaning involved will be found in the text. As elsewhere in the book, † denotes a word that originated in Britain but was later re-imported from America.